After Utopia

T0339399

After Utopia

The Rise of Critical Space
in Twentieth-Century
American Fiction

Nicholas Spencer

University of Nebraska Press   Lincoln & London

Sections of chapter 3 were previously published
in "Social Utopia: Hannah Arendt and Mary
McCarthy's *The Oasis*" in *Lit: Literature
Interpretation Theory* 15.1 (2004): 45–60. Copyright
2004 from "Social Utopia: Hannah Arendt and
Mary McCarthy's *The Oasis*" by Nicholas Spencer.
Reproduced by permission of
Taylor & Francis, Inc.,
http://www.taylorandfrancis.com.

Sections of chapter 5 were previously published
in "Beyond the Mutations of Media and Military
Technologies in Don DeLillo's *Underworld*" in
Arizona Quarterly 58.2 (Summer 2002): 89–112.
Reprinted by permission.

Library of Congress Cataloging-
in-Publication Data
Spencer, Nicholas, 1966–
After utopia : the rise of critical space in
twentieth-century American fiction / Nicholas Spencer.
p. cm.
Includes bibliographical references and index.
ISBN-13: 978-0-8032-4301-9 (cl. : alk. paper)
ISBN-10: 0-8032-4301-4 (cl. : alk. paper)
ISBN-13: 978-0-8032-2076-8 (pa. : alk. paper)
1. American fiction—20th century—History
and criticism.   2. Utopias in literature.
3. Setting (Literature).   I. Title.
PS374.U8S66 2006
813'.509372–dc22
2005030532

for Edith Spencer

Contents

Acknowledgments

I would have been unable to arrive at the point of completing this book if it were not for the help and support of many people. I am grateful to the marvelous persons at the University of Nebraska Press for their sustained encouragement and belief. My institutional home in the Department of English at the University of Nebraska–Lincoln has provided me with many benefits, opportunities, and kindnesses. Without such a warm and stimulating educational environment, the pursuit of literary and theoretical scholarship would not be as meaningful to me as it is. As the former chair of the department and my personal mentor, Linda Pratt has been an especially beneficial influence on my professional development. I offer my most heartfelt thanks to all my departmental colleagues. Thanks also to the Research Council at the University of Nebraska–Lincoln for a grant-in-aid that was of great benefit to my work.

Since this is my first book, it is impossible for me to resist the temptation to acknowledge those people who have had a lasting impact on my ideas. I am one of those fortunate people who have been assisted by the care, interest, and intellectual skill of numerous great educators. My teachers at Wigan College of Technology—Bernadette George and Caroline Weston—persuaded me to apply to an institution of higher education and encouraged me to take the entrance exam for the University of Oxford. The tutors I learned from at St. John's College, Oxford—John Kelly, Catherine LaFarge, Caroline Larrington, and John Pitcher—gave me vast and exciting landscapes of literary knowledge and analysis. My mentors at Emory University— the late Jerry Beaty, John Johnston, Walter Kalaidjian, and Ronald

Schuchard—allowed me to pursue varied interests in graduate school and facilitated my understanding of the profession of academia.

I also think of the friendships I have enjoyed over the years as powerful and enduring educational experiences. The inspiration and intellectual influence provided to me by the following friends inform many of the ideas in this book: David Benson, Julian Berriman, Paul Cobley, David Curley, Stephen Fairclough, Paul Grady, Michael Gregory, Neil McCartney, John Slam, Brian Stephen, and, especially, Stephen McGarty. I am also grateful to Andy, Barb, Gill, Dad, Fred, and Helen for acts of generosity and moments of togetherness that only family relations can bring. I owe the biggest debt of gratitude to my mum, Edith Spencer, to whom this book is dedicated. Her lifetime of labor inside and outside the home is, to me, a monumental example of human strength and courage. All of my work is guided by the influence of Mum's insight, compassion, and skill with language. Finally, my deepest and warmest thanks are to Suzanne Spencer, my wife, for her intelligence, integrity, and love.

After Utopia

Introduction

Over the past decade the study of textualizations of space has become one of the most widespread and influential trends in many areas of cultural criticism. For some observers, the popularity of spatial critique is an unwelcome sign of faddishness.[1] However, it is, I think, more appropriate to regard the extent of contemporary spatial analyses as the sign of a legitimate sharing of concerns. Critical assessments that simply repeat existent conclusions or fail to develop their outlook in any depth should, of course, be accorded limited acclaim. But rather than striving to curtail spatial analyses in the belief that such endeavors are now passé, critical culture is best served by building upon existing spatial critique and creating new frameworks and contexts for investigations into cultural space. In this book I seek to accomplish both these goals. *After Utopia* mobilizes the concept of "critical space" to reorient scholarly perspectives on twentieth-century American fiction. The critical paradigm that is articulated in the following chapters is rooted in one of the most influential theses of contemporary spatial critique. Speaking of early-twentieth-century culture, Michel Foucault argues, "Space was treated as the dead, the fixed, the undialectical, the immobile. Time, on the contrary, was richness, fecundity, life, dialectic" ("Questions" 70). In a related argument Foucault claims "that the anxiety of our era has to do fundamentally with space, no doubt a great deal more than with time" ("Of" 23). In other words, Foucault perceives in late-twentieth-century culture a reversal of the dominance of temporality over spatiality that he attributes to the earlier part of the century. Taking Foucault's theorization as its starting point, *After Utopia* examines the function of spatiality at several points in the course of twentieth-century American fiction. Unlike the work of spatial theorists such as Edward Soja and Fredric Jameson, which reconceptualizes Foucault's pronouncement as a distinction between modernism's obsession with history and postmodernism's preoccupation with spatiality, this book identifies a continual process of transformation in fictional spatiality.[2] In turning away from the monolithic terminology of modernism and postmodernism, I hope to provide a nuanced account of the rise of critical space in twentieth-century American fiction. *After Utopia* does argue that late-twentieth-century American fiction is dominated by spatial concerns. However, such dominant spatiality takes heterogeneous forms and must be viewed as a transformation of the spatial thematics of radical American fiction of the early decades of the twentieth century. Moreover, I argue that in such early-twentieth-century American fiction, models of history are coarticulated with notions of critical space. In the later American fiction assessed in the following chapters, textualizations of critical space reinscribe and then supersede principles that are central to the dominant historicity of the earlier fiction that I discuss.

The argument of this book encompasses five distinct moments in the rise of critical space in twentieth-century American fiction: the naturalist fiction of Jack London and Upton Sinclair; the 1930s trilogies of John Dos Passos and Josephine Herbst; the midcentury novels of Mary McCarthy and Paul Goodman; the 1970s fiction of Thomas Pynchon and William Gaddis; and novels by Joan Didion and Don DeLillo from the final decades of the twentieth century. In each chapter I discuss perspectives in critical theory that illuminate, problematize, or mirror the concerns of the fictional texts that I discuss. In so doing, I highlight conceptions in twentieth-century critical theory that correspond at key places with examples of American fiction. In these theoretical analyses, I posit that struggles among ideas of history and spatiality inform the developments involving Marxism and post-Marxism that we see in the fiction and theory discussed in this book. By arguing that similar transformations regarding the rise of critical space take place in twentieth-century American fiction and continental theory, I hope to demonstrate that these cultural forms constitute a transnational and transgeneric textual field. As part of this project, I point out the insistent presence of critical space at many points in trajectories of Marxist and post-Marxist theory. In *Postmodern Geographies*, Soja argues that the collapse of the Paris Commune in 1871 signaled the victory of historical over spatial critique in the radical tradition. The newly dominant historicity was, according to Soja, "stripped of its more geographically sensitive variants (such as the utopian and anarchistic socialisms of Fourier, Proudhon, Kropotkin, and Bakunin [. . .])" (31). Soja concludes that spatial critique remained largely dormant during the modern period, but his account underestimates both the role of utopian spatiality in Marx's social theory and the legacy of such utopianism in the spatial concerns that play a prominent role in much Western Marxist theory of the early twentieth century.[3] In pursuing readings that are informed by the spatial concerns of Marxist and post-Marxist theory, I do not undertake an "application" of theory to fiction. Brian Massumi criticizes the application of scientific theories in the humanities because, he argues, such an approach either turns theoretical authority into "a form of imperialist disciplinary aggression" or reduces theoretical concepts to the status of "metaphor" and "exotic pet" (19). As an alternative to application, Massumi advocates "treating the scientific concept the way any other concept is treated" (20). Similarly, I seek to bypass the uncritical and ad hoc qualities that are endemic to theoretical application, and I strive to analyze the critical space of both theory and fiction through their interrelation.

In the first chapter I argue that the fiction of London and Sinclair inverts key aspects of the American utopian fiction that flourished and quickly subsided in the late nineteenth century.[4] Utopian novels such as Edward Bellamy's *Looking Backward* are dominated by depictions of idealized social space. Representations of historical process play a crucial role in these texts, but they are secondary in importance to spatial descriptions. For example, in *Looking Backward* there are two arcs of naturalist evolutionary process that support the laying out of utopian space—the transition from Bellamy's own time to the imagined world of 2000, and the movement beyond the year 2000 into the utopian future. Unlike the idealized space of the novel, these historical arcs are both portrayed in uncertain and inconsistent terms. In contrast to Bellamy, London and Sinclair prioritize the representation of naturalist process in their fiction. The naturalism of these authors is governed by versions of socialist theories of dialectical struggle and deterministic history. The totalized and monolithic utopian space that we see in novels such as *Looking Backward* is transformed into a set of spatial representations that express a utopian impulse. Subordinate to the naturalistic history that London and Sinclair prioritize, these utopianistic spaces are localized models of social practices and relationships that serve to inspire the dialectical struggles of history. Like the arcs of history in *Looking Backward*, the social spaces represented by London and Sinclair are usually flawed and incomplete. The details of London's and Sinclair's narrative conjunctions of utopianism and naturalism differ greatly, but for both authors the relation between models of history and representations of spatiality is filled with tension, conflict, and instability. In order to unpack these varying elements, I analyze conflicts within and between London and Sinclair in relation to models of history and spatiality articulated by the Marxist theories of Georg Lukács and Ernst Bloch. The novels of London and Sinclair are *not* examples of utopian fiction, because they do not privilege the depiction of fully realized ideal societies. Nevertheless, the critical spatiality that is articulated in these novels exhibits tendencies that exemplify the influence of late-nineteenth-century utopian fiction.

With reference to Gramsci's writings on hegemonic processes of transformation and the complex landscape of social space, the second chapter demarcates key issues in the trilogies of Dos Passos and Herbst. In the fiction of Dos Passos and Herbst, the general characteristics of London's and Sinclair's textualizations of history and spatiality are reiterated. All these writers prioritize the representation of historical process and assign social space a related but lesser role. However, the certainties of deterministic history that are at times expressed by London and Sinclair have, in these later writers, given way to diffidence. The problematic of history remains central in these trilogies of the 1930s, but London's and Sinclair's promotion of singular visions of history is replaced by Dos Passos's and Herbst's exploration of various possible ways in which social transformation can be imagined. Also, the role of critical space is more prominent in the work of Dos Passos and Herbst than in that of London and Sinclair.

As strong teleological convictions give way to variegated and open-ended conceptions of societal change, spatial representations become an increasingly important source of social analysis and critique. The forms of social space that interest Dos Passos and Herbst are distinct in nature, but they share the characteristic of being less utopian and more critical than the spatial aspects of the work of London and Sinclair. In Dos Passos and Herbst we witness a key moment in the rise of critical space in twentieth-century American fiction because these authors narrate the point at which the analytical significance of spatiality often appears to be greater than that of historicity.

Two varying theoretical analyses are discussed in chapter 3. After reading Mary McCarthy's *The Oasis* in light of Hannah Arendt's conceptualization of social and political space, I assess Henri Lefebvre's reflections on the social space of everyday life as part of a reading of Paul Goodman's *The Empire City*. In the section on McCarthy, I argue that *The Oasis* represents the abandonment of the general critical model that London, Sinclair, Dos Passos, and Herbst fictionalize. That *The Oasis* takes the form of a satire on utopia indicates the dominance of spatiality in this text. In other words, *The Oasis* represents a further advance in the rise of critical space beyond the position that spatiality occupies in the fiction of Dos Passos and Herbst. Yet McCarthy's satirical intent means that spatiality in this novel is used to critique bourgeois capitalism, utopianism, and theories of history associated with Marxism. In challenging the opposition between capitalism and radicalism, McCarthy's enfolding of historicity into critical spatiality strives to discredit the spatial and historical critiques that are featured in the work of London, Sinclair, Dos Passos, and Herbst. As an analysis of the divergence of social space in midcentury American fiction, the third chapter contrasts the spatiality of *The Oasis* with that of Paul Goodman's *The Empire City*. Like *The Oasis*, *The Empire City* negates models of history and thus further suggests the departure from Marxist models of temporality in midcentury fiction. Goodman's novel also shares McCarthy's dual articulation of a preoccupation with spatiality and a critique of utopianism. Such similarities demonstrate the validity of locating these two novels at a distinct moment in twentieth-century American fiction. But whereas McCarthy's novel liquidates the spatial and historical tendencies that animate radical fiction of the early twentieth century, *The Empire City* revivifies the critique of social struggle through fictionalized spatiality. Goodman achieves this end by assigning to his representation of social space the principles of dialectical struggle that, in the fiction of London, Sinclair, Dos Passos, and Herbst, are foundational to representations of historical process. In its replacement of utopian space with spatial dialectics, Goodman's novel establishes critical space as a primary means of articulating social struggle in fiction.

In my discussion of Thomas Pynchon and William Gaddis in chapter 4, I assess the ways in which these authors enlarge the spatial dialectics of Goodman's novel. Lefebvre's theorization of the production of space and the urban revolution provides a framework for the discussion of these authors. Whereas *The Empire City* focuses on localized struggles on the social terrain of New York City, the novels of Pynchon and Gaddis depict larger patterns of transformation within urban and social space. Both Pynchon and Gaddis fictionalize the coming of what Lefebvre describes as "abstract space" (*Production* 49). For Lefebvre, abstract space refers to the homogenization and fragmentation of social space that is associated with the practices of neocapitalism in the post-1945 era. In Pynchon's *Gravity's Rainbow*, the events at the conclusion of World War II facilitate the emergence of abstract social space. For much of this novel, the formation of abstract space struggles against "lived space," which Lefebvre defines in terms of autonomous social spaces that oppose abstract space (*Production* 39). Along with its negation of models of history, the novel's treatment of spatial dialectics exemplifies its reworking of principles that are central to the pre-1939 fiction studied in this book. The dialectic of abstract and lived space in *Gravity's Rainbow* culminates in the representation of the urban space of Los Angeles. In these final scenes of the novel, Pynchon's descriptions of the urban infrastructure of southern California in the 1970s evoke the seemingly decisive confrontation between abstract and lived space. The threat of the colonization of lived by abstract space with which *Gravity's Rainbow* concludes is realized in Gaddis's *JR*. In this novel, abstract space takes dominion in the urban environments of New York, and the possibility of oppositional lived space is eradicated. As the narrative of a failed dialectic, *JR* represents the terminal point of textualizations of dialectics that play a vital role in the rise of critical space in American fiction.

The fifth chapter analyzes the novels of Joan Didion and Don DeLillo as fictionalizations of dominant critical space that depart from dialectical models. The first section of this chapter considers the novels of Joan Didion in relation to Gilles Deleuze and Félix Guattari's theorization of spatiality and territoriality. Didion's extraordinarily reiterative novels depict fluctuations of social space in the context of opportunistic networks of economic and political power. Conceptions of history and utopianism are absent in these novels. The struggles of social space, which are of major concern to Didion, take the form of various flows and blockages of movement and communication that circumscribe behavior and agency. Through the conflicts of social space, Didion conducts a critique of American capitalism that is as integral to her writing as a similar critique is in the novels of Sinclair and Dos Passos. However, the critical spatiality of these novels is devoid of the binary oppositions and mediated syntheses that characterize representations of dialectical conflict. In the second section of this chapter, I analyze Don DeLillo's *Underworld* as an engagement with technological concerns that are central to the writings of Paul Virilio. DeLillo's novel describes how media and military technologies serve to eradicate social space. The speed of these technologies means that spatiality enters a critical condition, a condition characterized by the possibility of the disappearance of critical space. As a result, *Underworld* involves both a critique of transformations of social space and a commentary on the technological erosion of the significance of distance. By concluding with an analysis of the crisis of critical space, *After Utopia* emphasizes the heterogeneity and precariousness of forms of spatiality in late-twentieth-century American fiction.

While the chapters of *After Utopia* analyze chronological transformations within American fiction, they do not constitute what Stuart Elden terms a "spatial history" (6). History is a totalizing concept that makes a definitive and unifying claim on temporal narrative and often implies progress and continuity. Instead of history, this book identifies a genealogy of the discontinuous "emergence" of dominant spatiality in American fiction (Foucault, "Nietzsche" 148). As genealogy, *After Utopia* articulates a specific line of spatial emergence and does not presume to constitute a comprehensive, definitive, or representative account of spatiality in twentieth-century American fiction. At the same time, the rise of critical space that is discussed in this book can, I believe, be fruitfully related to numerous other American fictional texts. Similarly, the discussions of theoretical spatiality, which are by no means comprehensive (I do not, for instance, engage with the important spatial theory of Walter Benjamin, a further example of the spatial discourse of Western Marxist theory), highlight issues that spread through many fictional trends and tendencies. The fiction about which I write offers particularly concentrated intersections with the theory under discussion, but it does not have an exclusive relationship with the multiple perspectives on spatiality that are articulated by the theorists whom I discuss. The connections between the argument of this book and other instances of American fiction are best considered in terms of Wittgensteinian family resemblance. In other words, different components of the following discussions are relevant to other examples of American fiction to varying degrees. The arguments I present can be extended most fully to texts that are located within the same general fictional areas as the texts that I prioritize. For example, the Gramscian concern with relations between cultural hegemony and social space that we see in the fiction of Dos Passos and Herbst are also evident in Depression-era writings by Tillie Olsen, Myra Page, and Henry Roth. As illustrated by various African American novels, the pertinence of certain elements of the argument of *After Utopia* can extend beyond these fictional zones. Novels by Richard Wright and Ralph Ellison articulate a displacement of Marxist historicism in favor of the analysis of urban space that resonates with Goodman's *The Empire City*. Further, the fictional texts of authors such as Nella Larsen and Chester Himes explore the dialectics of urban space in ways that can be linked to the writing of Lefebvre. Some of the arguments in this book could also be used to rethink groupings of American fiction. The midcentury spatiality of McCarthy and Goodman could, for instance, be expanded to include texts such as B. F. Skinner's *Walden Two* and Ayn Rand's *Atlas Shrugged*. Overall, the argument that follows occupies an analytical place between isolated readings of specific texts and symptomatic pronouncements on broad areas of American literary history. I regard the temporal narrative of *After Utopia* as one significant strand of genealogical transformation in American fiction, but I do not doubt the validity of other fictional genealogies and believe that encounters between the arguments of this book and other sequential treatments of American fiction could be productive.

As a means of promoting reorientation within ideas of American literary genealogy, the emergence of critical space that I trace establishes connections among writers with varying critical reputations and texts that are infrequently brought together in scholarly analysis. These two aforementioned scholarly effects are, I believe, the result of the privileging in scholarship of aesthetics over politics and the ongoing separation of these two dimensions of literary study. The separation of aesthetics and politics fosters distorted critical readings and excessively rigid periodizations. For example, readings of "postmodern" American fiction, such as that of Pynchon or Gaddis, often prioritize formalist issues in ways that homogenize the texts being considered and define the terms in which the "politics" of these texts are understood. As a consequence, such texts are cut off from the political aspects of fiction of other periods of American literary production. The privileging of aesthetics over politics has exacerbated divisions among areas of American fiction by marginalizing authors such as Upton Sinclair and Josephine Herbst for a perceived lack of aesthetic innovation. Herbst does receive attention from literary scholars of the Depression era, but these analyses are usually hermetically sealed off from other American fiction. The reputations of midcentury writers such as Mary McCarthy and Paul Goodman suffer because the texts of these authors do not fit into those dominant aesthetic or political critical paradigms that are linked to other periods in the twentieth century. Goodman is an especially interesting case. His fiction is deeply invested in aesthetic experimentation and political action, but his aesthetics are not really "postmodern" and his politics deviate from the major literary-political identities associated with socialism, communism, and anti-Stalinism. By engendering a map of twentieth-century American fiction that is characterized by widely differing reputations and discrete zones of study, these critical trends inhibit various types of scholarly coarticulations. The selection of authors discussed in this book is designed to cut through the effects of these critical biases upon periodization and reputation. The analysis seeks both to reassess critically celebrated writers such as Dos Passos and Pynchon and to recover the significance of authors such as Herbst and Goodman. More precisely, the book seeks to achieve each of these goals by means of the other. For example, the analysis of the representation of urban space in *The Empire City* leads me to provide a reading of the various models of social space presented in *Gravity's Rainbow*. I therefore argue that the interrelated discussions of authors with varying reputations and from different fictional areas is a necessary means of developing paradigms of American literary genealogy.

After Utopia also develops the concept of "critical space" as a means of subverting the lopsided scholarly dichotomy of aesthetics and politics in fiction. "Critical space" refers to fictionalizations of spatiality that identify, analyze, oppose, and imagine alternatives to the forms of social domination implemented by American capitalism. As suggested by the social emphasis of critical space, *After Utopia* is not primarily concerned with either physical geography or theories of "spatial form" (Frank 9).[5] At the same time, critical space is not synonymous with "the politics of space." In the fiction of London, Sinclair, Dos Passos, and Herbst, depictions of social space are informed by these authors' commitment to political identities such as socialism, communism, and syndicalism, but such depictions are irreducible to spatializations of political identity. The act of fictionalization shifts narrative spatiality beyond the bounds of political ideas, but this movement does not mean that textual spaces lose their critical and analytical efficacy. Rather, critical effects derive at times from social descriptions that are expressions of narrative strategies and characteristics—in short, fictional aesthetics. It is because the critical spatiality of fiction is linked to but not wholly identifiable with politics and aesthetics that it subverts the dichotomy that has influenced maps of American fiction. In the fiction discussed in the last three chapters of this book, critical space is both more central and less tied to political identity than in the writing of London, Sinclair, Dos Passos, and Herbst. In other words, the analysis of social space increasingly displaces political commitment. The issue of anarchism plays a crucial role in these developments. In the pre-1939 texts studied in this book, anarchism has a number of functions. These functions are frequently prominent, but they are often linked to the spatiality that remains subordinate to notions of naturalist and dialectical history. In Goodman's *The Empire City*, the turn to spatial analysis is to some degree a replacement of political allegiance based on dialectical history with anarchist politics. Pynchon's *Gravity's Rainbow* shares Goodman's preference for anarchist spatiality over versions of leftist historicism, but this novel has a more ambivalent relationship to anarchism than is apparent in *The Empire City*. The novels of Gaddis, Didion, and DeLillo share the prioritization of spatial analysis that dominates *Gravity's Rainbow* and *The Empire City*; while these texts do not explicitly engage with anarchism, they address forms of power that transcend state politics and thus deal with issues that are central to the anarchist imagination. The fact that anarchism drives much of the preoccupation with spatiality in twentieth-century American fiction means that it occupies a privileged place in the rise of critical space and acts as a reminder of the important role played by fictional politics in the issues discussed in this book.

Representations of utopia are difficult to find in recent and contemporary American fiction. Dystopias, not utopias, define much of the spatiality of current fictional production. Yet the spatial problematic that is central to many American fictional texts of the post-1945 era bears the legacy of utopianism. For all its absurdity, impracticality, and narrative tedium, late-nineteenth-century utopian fiction is characterized by a powerful spatial imagination that accords great significance to the synchronic and simultaneous relations between social events. The goal of this book is to trace the aftermath of utopianism's spatial commitment. In the early-twentieth-century fiction discussed in the following chapters, utopianism's spatiality is firmly subordinated to the dynamics of history and serves as inspirational refuge rather than total social vision. Contrastingly, the late-twentieth-century fiction that I subsequently assess mutates such restricted utopianism into a mature form of critical space. In a sense, these late-twentieth-century fictional texts return to the totalized perspective on social space that utopian narratives articulated at the end of the nineteenth century. But instead of proffering idealized alternatives to the effects of American capitalism, the fiction of authors such as Gaddis and Didion is primarily devoted to spatial analyses and critiques of capitalistic effects. The social expanse of the critical space of late-twentieth-century fiction is in crucial respects opposed to the idealized totalities of utopian fiction, but both types of fiction articulate spatial formulations that travel and metamorphose throughout twentieth-century American fiction.

[1]

Utopian Naturalism in Conflict

Jack London and Upton Sinclair

By the beginning of the twentieth century, the late-nineteenth-
century boom in utopian American fiction was in decline. Yet the
spatial imagination that informed these utopian texts did not disappear. Rather, it migrated to socialist fiction, such as that of Jack London
and Upton Sinclair. The novels of these authors invert utopian fiction's combination of subordinate historical processes and dominant
spatial representations. Whereas the nineteenth-century utopianists
reacted to the damaging effects of American capitalism by imagining
fully fledged utopian worlds, London and Sinclair portray limited
and provisional spaces that contain utopian traces and thus prefig-
ure the future societies toward which historical processes tend. Both
authors prioritize depictions of historical progress that are indebted
to their naturalist inclinations and their understanding of socialist
politics. They share literary naturalism's emphasis on deterministic
forces, but they transform this concern into socialist models of history. The versions of socialist history imagined by these two authors
also reflect varying tendencies in Marxist culture. At times, the deterministic historical movements depicted by these authors echo the
dialectical materialism of the later Engels, George Plekhanov, and
Karl Kautsky. To varying degrees, London and Sinclair also strive to
evoke the dialectical interaction between economic materialism and
the robust subjective activism of the working class. The combination
of economic conditions and subjective intervention accords with positions held by Georg Lukács and Ernst Bloch. Similarly, there are significant parallels between the social spaces portrayed by London and
Sinclair and the utopian dimension of Bloch's writing. In *The Principle*

of Hope, Bloch frequently proclaims "the progress of socialism from utopia towards science" (2: 620), but he supplements this movement with a return to utopianism. Bloch's commitment to utopian space was firmly subordinated to his vision of dialectical history, but his ideas differed sharply from the antiutopianism expressed by Lukács in *History and Class Consciousness*. The novels I read in this chapter are discussed in relation to the theories of Lukács and Bloch.[1] Lukács's ideas provide insight into the models of historical process in the fiction of London and Sinclair; Bloch's *The Principle of Hope* offers numerous concepts that highlight the utopian spatiality of such fiction.[2] These novelists are committed to the primacy of naturalist ideas of history and causality, but they also articulate subordinate visions of utopian space. By reinscribing utopianism within models of historical process, these authors create a discourse of critical space from which many twentieth-century American fictional texts subsequently depart.

In order to assess some of the central features of the fiction addressed in this chapter, it is useful to examine theories of American literary naturalism. Discussions of naturalism frequently overlook the texts of London and Sinclair. These authors fit none of the "three waves" of naturalism proposed by Donald Pizer—the 1890s of Crane, Norris, and Dreiser; the 1930s of Dos Passos, Farrell, and Steinbeck; and the 1940s and 1950s of Bellow, Mailer, and Styron—and in consequence they are omitted from Pizer's analyses (16). Yet London and Sinclair's relation to socialism involves an engagement with some of the most significant issues in the study of naturalism. Attempts to isolate the definitive characteristics of naturalism may cite the use of documentary reporting or the presence of lower-class "brutes" as characters, but the determinisms of heredity, biology, chance, or social and economic forces are most often perceived in this defining role. Even critics who disparage determinism as an overworked notion in naturalist criticism fail in their own work to expel its significance. Pizer, for example, criticizes John J. Conder's focus on determinism but notes that naturalist writers rely upon the "oblique expression" of "abstract deterministic ideas" (25), and Mohamed Zayani's criticism of Walter Benn Michaels's explanation of naturalism in terms of economic determinism chides Michaels for ignoring biological determinism (14). Despite the importance of determinism, naturalist texts rarely lack an element of autonomous subjectivity, because even where autonomous characters are absent, such narratives enact reformist appeals that imply the free will of author and reader. Following Oscar Cargill and other critics, Charles C. Walcutt identifies "pessimistic determinism" as the chief characteristic of naturalism, but he notes that in many novels this characteristic exists in "tension" with authorial optimism (23–24, 29). Walcutt's argument is typical of studies that suggest naturalism's determinism is compromised by or opposed to the presence of free will. Conder takes issue with Walcutt's dichotomy of pessimism and optimism by arguing that naturalism has a "philosophical coherence" that is based, in Walcutt's terminology, on a concept of optimistic determinism (4). For Conder, the Western philosophical tradition, identified primarily with Thomas Hobbes, that regards humans as both determined and free "represents the tradition within which American literary naturalism grows" (16). Conder argues for the location of naturalism within this tradition, in which causal determinism produces the free actions of the subject.

The importance of the conjunction of determinism and free will gives economic determinism a privileged place among the many forms of determinism that are apparent in naturalist fiction. George Becker argues that since naturalism is "ideally all middle" ("Introduction" 29), any writing that is teleological, such as socialist realism, is antithetical to naturalism, a point reiterated by Malcolm Cowley (446). Yet, as Richard Lehan notes, Emile Zola, one of the major influences on American naturalism, considered social determinism to be as significant for the novelist as scientific determinism (530). As well as being the most important source for social and economic determinism in naturalist fiction, Marx's writings predate the work of Darwin, Spencer, Zola, and others and thus constitute the original intellectual resource for naturalism. According to Harold Kaplan, Marx's writings epitomize the naturalist synthesis of free will and determinism. For Kaplan, Marx's writings embody what he names the "Naturalist Ethos" (13), or the replacement of a belief in absolute moral values with a belief in force as the guarantor of moral worth, which in Marxist dialectics entails the deterministic creation of a truly communist "ethics of freedom" from the "ethics of necessity" of our precommunist world (18). Kaplan states that communism represents for Marx the overcoming of the opposition between Hegelian subjectivity and economic objectivity, the union of naturalism and humanism, and the combination of "a powerful fatalism with an intense urge to do battle" (19). While Kaplan acknowledges other practitioners of the naturalist ethos, such as Freud and Sorel, he posits that "most of the imaginative constructions of political and literary naturalism that we know" are based on the Marxist paradigm of the dialectics of socioeconomic determinism and class struggle (115). As in Conder's theory, naturalism here emerges as the unfolding of subjective free will out of objective determinism, and the fact that Marx allies himself in *The German Ideology* with a Hobbesian theory of power underscores the shared philosophical premises regarding subject-object relations in these two theories of naturalism (106–07).

The unity of economic determinism and free will described by Conder and Kaplan is integral to the utopian naturalism of London and Sinclair. These authors attempt to portray the seamless emergence of subjective radicalism from objective economic conditions. It is this conjunction that connects the fiction of London and Sinclair to Marxist theory. Whereas Kaplan identifies the naturalist ethos with general aspects of Marxism, the conjunction of free will and determinism that is evoked in the fiction of London and Sinclair can be linked more specifically to Marxist critics such as Plekhanov and Kautsky. In *Fundamental Problems of Marxism*, Plekhanov addresses the issue of the " 'leap' from necessity to freedom" (91). Plekhanov negates the dualistic perception of this model of historical transformation and states that dialectical materialism involves the production of human freedom from economic necessity. Much of Lukács's *History and Class Consciousness* consists of an attack on the viewpoint articulated by Plekhanov. In particular, Lukács derides the conjunction of economic determinism and utopianism that he identifies with the theorists of the Second International, especially Kautsky.[3] The utopianism that Lukács criticizes in social democracy is primarily that associated with scientific socialism as an inevitable process; for Lukács, such economism is itself an expression of a subjectively generated utopian ideal and is not worthy of being named dialectical theory. The deterministic utopianism criticized by Lukács is a central feature of key texts by London and Sinclair. As a corrective to the economism of social democracy, Lukács appeals to the working class as "the identical subject-object of history" and proclaims the interventionary power of the Communist Party (*History* xxiii). In Lukács's formulation, economic circumstances create the conditions for revolutionary activity but do not guarantee its success. Lukács therefore identifies two distinct roles for subjectivity in versions of history: the "bad" subjectivized economism of social democracy and the "good" subject-object relation of revolutionary communism. London and Sinclair have significantly different relations to the two versions of subjectivity proposed by Lukács. Also, the dialectical naturalism of their novels is modified by utopianized representations of social space. As in Bloch's *The Principle of Hope*, the utopian spaces of London and Sinclair are examples of "concrete utopia" (1: 146). For Bloch, this term refers to the intimation of the future that is assured by Marxist dialectics.[4] Concrete utopia is a principle of hope that Bloch identifies in the cultural artifacts of Western history. Characterized by "open space" and "forward dawning" (1: 141), Bloch's principle guides humanity toward the "factually-objectively possible" (1: 225). By describing concrete utopia in terms of "space in process" and "virtual paradises" (1: 305), Bloch strongly and consistently defines this principle of hope in spatial terms. As a spatial representation that shows the path to the future, concrete utopia shares the spatiotemporal structure of utopian naturalism. In the fiction of London and Sinclair, Bloch's spatial utopianism, Lukács's revolutionary subjectivity, and deterministic naturalism are combined in various ways, and the combination of these elements produces an unstable amalgamation. Points of conflict among these issues emerge and become more pronounced as the careers of London and Sinclair develop. While both writers seek to produce broadly similar versions of utopian naturalism, the differences between the conflicts that arise in their fiction and the ways in which they respond to such conflicts reflect fundamental variations in their representations of critical space.

Jack London is still best known for adventure stories, such as *The Call of the Wild*, *White Fang*, and *The Sea-Wolf*. In these naturalist tales,

London evokes the individual's attempts to contend with the deterministic power of biology and the environment. These two aspects of the fiction correspond with his reading of Friedrich Nietzsche and Herbert Spencer, the philosophers, according to London, of individual prowess and scientific law, respectively. Since the power of the individual is associated with racial characteristics, London's interest in racial biology serves as the scandalous connection between objective determinism and subjective will. These novels are wholly naturalistic in that nature is portrayed as a force within the struggle between the individual and its deterministic conditions; neither nature nor social relationships exist as utopian spaces that are external to this naturalistic conflict. From the late 1890s London was a committed socialist, but it was only with *The Iron Heel* (1908) that he wrote a novel in which socialist ideas of history are central to the deterministic forces that he portrays. In this novel, London's extant philosophical affiliations are reconfigured in terms of a socialist theory of history. The conjunction of economic determinism and revolutionary subjectivity serves the mediating role between environment and individual that is granted to racial biology in some of London's other fiction. In addition, London's socialist naturalism involves a transformation in his representation of space. London replaces nature as a determining force with representations of natural and social space that provide refuge from and inspiration for the struggles of economic history. Spatiality thus becomes Blochian concrete utopia. As Jeanne Campbell Reesman argues, it is preferable to think of London's fiction in terms of "fine distinctions" rather than "a mess of contradictions" ("Prospects" 134). The perspectives on history and space in *The Iron Heel* are contradictory, but they constitute a rich structure of legible differences that are identifiable with tendencies in naturalist and Marxist culture.

The Iron Heel is written as the journal of Avis Everhard, the wife of socialist leader Ernest Everhard, who recounts events that take place in an imagined future between 1912 and 1917. A member of an upper-middle-class family, she comes to empathize with Everhard's socialist views at the same time that she falls in love with him. The novel describes conflicts between capital and labor in the United States that result in the eventual victory of the Oligarchy, a totalitarian state under the control of capitalist interests. As a futuristic vision of the potential horrors of capitalist society, *The Iron Heel* is often described as a dystopia. But unlike George Orwell's *Nineteen Eighty-Four*, a novel with which *The Iron Heel* is often compared, London's narrative is not primarily concerned with the spatial representation of the intersecting attributes of dystopian society. The novel's dystopian world is portrayed as a moment within a historical process, and Avis's narrative abruptly halts following the failure of the Chicago Commune, an uprising against the Oligarchy. The narrative ruptures that Alessandro Portelli discusses are crucial to the narrative's portrayal of history as more of a work in progress than a finished artifact (183). The textual frame of *The Iron Heel* consists of a series of footnotes written from the vantage point of a future in which the Oligarchy has been succeeded by an idyllic utopian society. Authored by Anthony Meredith, the fictional editor of Avis's text, these footnotes evoke the utopian future in a highly oblique manner. This narrative strategy indicates that the novel is much more concerned with expressing the process of history than enumerating the details of either dystopian or utopian society. The marginalization of utopia also reflects the uncertainties and conflicts that haunt London's understanding of history.

In numerous respects *The Iron Heel* typifies the naturalistic fiction that Lukács criticizes. From his earliest works, such as *Soul and Form* and *History of the Evolution of the Modern Drama*, Lukács attacked naturalism, yet it was through his literary criticism of the 1930s that Lukács made his most sustained and influential criticisms of naturalism. Famously, Lukács argues that, prior to 1848, bourgeois critical realism, epitomized by Balzac, shared the creative revolutionary energy of the bourgeois class. Written by authors who were immersed in contemporary public events, critical realism portrayed the interaction between "typical" yet nonstereotypical characters (*Historical* 36), such as the heroes of Walter Scott's fiction, and the important historical trends of their day. After 1848, when the bourgeoisie's revolutionary spirit devolved into capitalist apologetics, critical realism was succeeded by the naturalism of Zola, in which the passivity of clichéd characters before a barrage of irrelevant details and deterministic forces mirrored that of their authors. Lukács frequently notes that Balzac's politics were royalist, whereas Zola's political views were closer to Lukács's own, but this does nothing to mitigate his critique of the reified nature of subjectivity in naturalism. Lukács's criticisms of literary naturalism are continuous with his attacks on social democracy in *History and Class Consciousness*. For Lukács, social democracy is characterized by a combination of subjective utopianism and determinism. By collapsing subjectivity into objectivity, social democracy robs economic conditions of their ability to foster subjective revolutionary action and reduces subjectivity to bourgeois fatalism. Lukács's writings on naturalism are therefore part of a system of thought based on the distinction between authentic and inauthentic models of subject-object relations. The limitations of naturalism in Lukács's account are due to an inauthentic combination of subjectivism and objectivism. June Howard observes that in Lukács's criticism "naturalism is an objectivist negation of realism" (25), but it is important to note that for Lukács naturalism is a subjective and utopian idealization of the historical process as objective determinism. In the case of both literary naturalism and social democracy, reified empiricism and abstract theories of determinism are nothing more than subjective fancies.

The naturalist determinism that is reiterated in *The Iron Heel* exemplifies the subjectivized objectivity that Lukács loathes. London's articulation of deterministic history occurs through inert narrative passages, which are devoid of the dynamics of dialectical struggle that they ostensibly propose. Even though Everhard takes issue with the bourgeois values of Avis's father and his associates, the fact that these appeals to determinism occur in settings such as Avis's home and a gathering named the Philomath Club suggests their bourgeois nature. Also, the novel's opening chapters evoke numerous deterministic motifs. By describing Everhard as a Nietzschean natural aristocrat who is descended from an old American family, London suggests a quasi-biological basis for his protagonist's "masterfulness" (25). Similarly, those who testify against a laborer who is injured at work do so because they are "all tied to the merciless industrial machine" and are driven by the "instinct to protect" their families (55). Most prominently, Everhard cites Herbert Spencer to claim that all social phenomena are explicable in terms of scientific law and fact. In the name of Spencer, Everhard rails against specialization and advocates the synthesis of all knowledge, and it becomes clear that, for

London, class struggle is the higher synthesis that unites the range of deterministic forces: "We say that the class struggle is a law of social development. We are not responsible for it. We do not make the class struggle. We merely explain it, as Newton explained gravitation. We explain the nature of the conflict of interest that produces the class struggle" (28). Yet Everhard's Hobbesian view of naturalistic history is not borne out by subsequent narrative events. As Eric Homberger argues, *The Iron Heel* consists of "two distinct books" (16), one that describes the optimism of conversion to socialism and another that portrays the ineffectivity of socialist attempts to combat the Oligarchy. In the transition from the first to the second of these narratives, those other forms of naturalist determinism that class struggle had originally synthesized become more prominent. Specifically, the Marxist vision of future society is couched increasingly as a Nietzschean appeal to Spencerian processes. Everhard believes in the ultimate victory of the working class because of its "primitive strength" (154), which signals a reversion from the determinism of class struggle to that of biological power. London's protagonist continues to make successful predictions about the outcomes of events and refers to the inevitability of the defeat of the Oligarchy, but his comments rely on Spencerian notions of scientific fact and evolution rather than the emergence of proletarian freedom from economic determinism. Also, Everhard's vision appears more as a reflection of his individual greatness than as a statement of the collective will of the working class. As the determinism of class struggle becomes untenable, Everhard's appeal to the surety of future revolution increasingly relies on a subjectivized call to biological, evolutionary, and individualistic factors.

The narrative transition identified by Homberger also involves a shift from economic determinism to Lukács's theory of revolutionary subjectivity. Several chapters in *History and Class Consciousness* are relevant to the revolutionary turn in *The Iron Heel*. In his essays on Rosa Luxemburg, Lukács expresses divergent views that reflect a tension in his overall outlook on revolutionary activity and the process of history. "The Marxism of Rosa Luxemburg" celebrates Luxemburg's critique of the economic determinism of German social democracy. For Lukács, Luxemburg's *The Accumulation of Capital* accurately criticizes the idea of the expansion of capitalism according to fixed laws, "unproblematically and without a World War." Luxemburg believes that the progress of capitalism cannot be economically determined, but she never doubts "the theoretical certainty of the coming social revolution." Lukács praises Luxemburg's concept of "the spontaneous mass movement" because she allies this to an understanding of the party as the "bearer of the class consciousness of the proletariat and the conscience of its historical vocation" (*History* 32, 37, 41). In his "Critical Remarks on Rosa Luxemburg's 'Critique of the Russian Revolution,'" Lukács alters his evaluation of Luxemburg. Now she is regarded as someone who wishes to minimize the role of the party and who "overestimat[es] [. . .] the spontaneous, elemental forces of the Revolution." Luxemburg is aware that the revolutionary transition to socialist society is subject to "crises and reversions," but her idealization of "the organic character of the course of history" signals a relapse into deterministic fatalism (*History* 279, 277). Lukács's essay "Legality and Illegality" is connected to these assessments of Luxemburg. Here, Lukács insists that true revolutionary activity involves legal and illegal means, and he criticizes the " 'direct action' of antiparliamentarianism" as an anarchistic approach that ultimately reinforces bourgeois power (*History* 265). Anarchist direct action and Luxemburg's spontaneism are closely related because they both deny the fully mediating role of the party. In Lukács's account, economic fatalism and anarchistic nihilism both conspire to thwart effective revolutionary action.

In the latter chapters of *The Iron Heel*, Everhard exhibits several Lukácsian characteristics. The growing strength of the Oligarchy creates an economic crisis that engenders mass support for the Democratic Socialist Party. The Socialists are successful in the elections of 1912, and Everhard is elected to Congress. Because they interpret these events in terms of "theoretical social evolution" and regard the Oligarchy as a theoretical aberration (175), Everhard's fellow party members are confident of the imminent defeat of the Oligarchy. However, Everhard realizes that the Oligarchy will not be removed by the peaceful bourgeois method of democratic elections, and he instead acknowledges that a violent confrontation is inevitable. He therefore abandons the determinism of social democracy and adopts the revolutionary position of Lukács. He continues both to work in Congress and to foment revolution and thus shares Lukács's commitment to legal and illegal activity. Like Lukács, Everhard is aware that history proceeds in a discontinuous manner. At the same time, he retains his belief in "slow social evolution" (225). In this and other respects, London's novel accords with Lukács's positive view of Luxemburg. The two major successes of the uprising against the Oligarchy are the general strike and the creation of the Fighting Groups. Both of these achievements represent spontaneous uprisings that are coordinated by Everhard and the other party leaders. For example, Avis describes the general strike as a "colossal frolic" that "appealed to the imagination of all" (214), and she notes that the machinists spontaneously joined the strike out of "sheer desperation" (213). However, *The Iron Heel* turns increasingly toward the view represented by Lukács's criticisms of Luxemburg. The spontaneism of the Fighting Groups often breaks free of centralized control, and one unit in particular, the 'Frisco Reds, is described as a group of "fanatics, madmen" (280). The critique of spontaneism is most apparent in the novel's finale. As the revolutionists are preparing their First Revolt, the Oligarchy provokes an uprising in Chicago. During the chaos that ensues, "the people of the abyss" are described as "a raging, screaming, screeching demoniacal horde" (326, 327). By describing the lower classes of Chicago in such dehumanized terms, London suggests that the people of the abyss lack political agency, and thus he refutes the theory of spontaneism. Along with his repeated criticisms of the direct action of bomb-throwing anarchists, London's narration of the Chicago Commune reflects a belief in the need for revolutionary control that is also expressed by Lukács. Moreover, London shares the tension that is apparent in Lukács's critique of Luxemburg. He recognizes the power of spontaneous mass movements, but he will not relinquish a commitment to centralized leadership.[5]

London's novel thus moves away from its initial deterministic outlook in two ways. On the one hand, the narrative resorts to noneconomistic versions of determinism. On the other hand, London evokes the need for revolutionary control of contingent events. The conflict between these two perspectives exerts considerable pressure on the narrative, and London intimates a desire to reject all models of history as a means of escaping such contradictory impulses. Such a view is reinforced by the reflections of James Smith, one of those who testifies against the injured worker in *The Iron Heel*: " 'I wanted to become a naturalist,' he explained shyly, as though confessing a weakness. 'I love animals. But I came to work in the mills. When I was promoted to foreman, I got married, then the family came, and . . . well, I wasn't my own boss any more' " (52). In this passage London portrays various forms of determinism as a trap: the biological determinism of family life has imprisoned Smith in class struggle and economic history. It is also an ironic passage because Smith identifies the position beyond determinism as that of the naturalist. London's wish to negate history is often couched in Nietzschean terms. For example, at the novel's conclusion, Avis can adhere to an optimistic vision of socialism only by attaining "a star-cool altitude" and "a passionless transvaluation of values" (327, 327–28). Paradoxically, Avis is able to believe in history only if she removes herself from it and perceives the world from an Olympian distance. The increasing pace of narrative events also suggests a restless view of history. "History was making fast" (169), London repeatedly states. However, as "the flux of transition" turns into the chaos of the Chicago Commune (297), aspects of models of history are called into question. On more than one occasion, Avis is unable to distinguish between the different sides that battle in Chicago. In these instances the credibility of the dialectical oppositions of history collapses. Garthwaite, Avis's colleague, expresses disbelief in narrative and historical models: "I know I'm making a mess of rescuing you, but I can't get head nor tail of the situation. It's all a mess. Every time we try to break out, something happens and we're turned back" (341).[6] The abrupt curtailment of the narrative of Avis and Everhard similarly articulates an abandonment of the narrativization of history. While London's novel is superficially consistent in its advocacy of socialist revolution, it articulates a variety of positions—the determinism of class struggle, a belief in noneconomic naturalistic processes, the conjunction of spontaneism and party control, the insistence on party authority, and a negation of historicity—that indicate the incessant conflicts of his naturalist imagination and presage subsequent developments in his fiction.

The Iron Heel includes representations of space that are coarticulated with the novel's models of history and determinism. London's representation of utopian space and its relation to theories of history are characterized by oppositions and ambiguities. Bloch's theorization of utopia highlights these spatial aspects of London's novel. In *The Principle of Hope*, Bloch intends to reinfuse utopianism into Marxism without undermining the gains made by Marxist science. It is a precarious balance that sees Bloch distinguishing between positive and negative versions of utopianized space. He makes ongoing criticisms of the "abstract utopian socialism" of well-known nineteenth-century figures such as Edward Bellamy, William Morris, Saint-Simon, Charles Fourier, Robert Owen, and others (1: 146).[7] Of course, Bloch commends the transformative impulse of nineteenth-century utopianism, but he believes abstract utopia is guilty of bypassing history and rushing too quickly into depictions of ideal societies: "The abstract utopias had devoted nine tenths of their space to a portrayal of the State of the future and only one tenth to the critical, often merely negative consideration of the present. This kept the goal colourful and vivid of course, but the path towards it, in so far as it could lie in given circumstances, remained hidden" (2: 620). Bloch is also critical of the rural impulse in nineteenth-century utopianism. He suggests that the English utopianism of William Morris and John Ruskin reacted to the emphasis on business and industry in Bellamy's *Looking Backward* by imagining a "de-feudalized" form of "re-agrarianization" that would return to the rural English past (2: 614). As always in *The Principle of Hope*, the appeal to a utopian past negates the future possibilities of concrete utopia. Bloch's comments on Morris and Ruskin are components of his complex treatment of the relation between nature and utopia. One of the most interesting instances of this conjunction refers to landscape painting. Bloch states that such painting includes the "dead space" of the foreground. He then asks: "Where does the landscape begin? Where does coherent objectification start? We can only answer: beyond detrimental space, at a distance from it, precisely at the point where the darkness of immediacy together with its outskirts begins to stop." The adjacency of foreground and landscape means that "the Here-space as *spatial foreground* can ultimately cross over into landscape, can as it were conclude with it." The capture of landscape by the dead space of foreground engenders a reified and "objectified landscape" that denies the possibility of future possibilities and induces passive contemplation (1: 296, 297). Through this analysis Bloch suggests that representations of natural landscape can have the same negative effects as abstract utopias. Elsewhere, Bloch identifies nature with concrete utopia. His discussion of Leonardo da Vinci's paintings contrasts with his verdict on landscape painting. For Bloch, Leonardo's paintings represent "a space in which sculpture ends, only light is divided, into almost unknown objects" (2: 800). In other words, the natural landscape in these paintings fuses with the human figures and trails off into indistinct shapes that evoke the utopian future. At other times Bloch celebrates the "feeling of nature" and argues that "nature mythology" represents concrete utopia, not the archaic past (3: 1341, 1342).

London's concern with deterministic history means that at times he shares Bloch's critique of spatiality. In the debate at the Philomath Club, Everhard insists that socialism does not seek a return to a Rousseauistic state of nature. In stating that "the return to nature and socialism are diametrically opposed to each other" (91), Everhard suggests that socialism involves a historical process that is at odds with the static and spatial notions of Rousseau. Associations with natural space also splinter the opposition to the Oligarchy. The farmers of the Grange Party break ranks with the Socialists and are impatient for revolutionary activity. Amid the violence triggered by the Oligarchy, a religious revival "proclaiming the end of the world" leads "hundred of thousands" of people to "fle[e] to the mountains" (234, 235). Similarly, Native Americans remove themselves to "swamps and deserts and waste places" in preparation for "the coming of a Messiah of their own" (236). After the failure of the First Revolt, "terroristic organizations" that were "hopeless about the future" appeared "in the mountains of the Great West" (353n). In all these examples, rural-spatial identity is accompanied by a sense of apocalyptic immediacy and despair that foreshortens the historical process. In Bloch's terms, London identifies nature with abstract utopia and dead space. But the qualified determinism that becomes apparent in *The Iron Heel* necessitates a revision of London's representation of critical space. As London wavers between a Lukácsian awareness of revolutionary contingency and a reversion to noneconomic determinism, he mobilizes representations of utopian space to bolster his optimism of the future. These idealized spaces inspire the movement of socialist history and thus are integral to London's utopian naturalism. Throughout the narrative, nature provides spatial refuges in which the socialists practice utopian social relationships and prepare for forthcoming revolutionary activity. Most obviously, the Glen Ellen refuge serves this concrete-utopian function. The refuge is "another world" (293), where the socialists realize art, leisure, and ideal social relationships. As in Bloch's discussion of Leonardo's painting, the natural space of the refuge suggests the utopian possibility of the future. After the cataclysmic demise of the Chicago Commune, Avis and Everhard arrive "in the green country" (350), where he is inspired to prophesy once more the success of the future revolution. Such renewal of revolutionary belief underscores the concrete-utopian function of nature. Despite such moments of synthesis, however, the novel's historical processes and utopian spaces are frequently in conflict. When she is first exposed to socialist ideas and working-class experience, Avis says, "I was delighted with the unselfishness and high idealism I encountered, though I was appalled by the vast philosophic and scientific literature of socialism that was opened up to me" (100). While Avis's attraction to utopian idealism and distaste for naturalist determinism are bourgeois tendencies that Everhard criticizes and rectifies, her comments reflect the unstable conjunctions of the novel. The broad parameters of utopian naturalism remain intact throughout *The Iron Heel*, but, as London's descriptions of political refuges illustrate, utopian space is sometimes represented with more certainty than the historicity to which it is elsewhere opposed and conjoined.

While London was an avowed socialist for much of his writing career, the positive advocacy of socialist positions in *The Iron Heel* is atypical of his fiction. In the fiction that follows *The Iron Heel*, London moves away from a socialist version of utopian naturalism. His socialist commitments are most evident in his short stories, but even here he emphasizes particular aspects of *The Iron Heel*'s utopian naturalism rather than coarticulating these elements. In "South of the Slot" and "The Mexican," for example, London embodies socialist principles in specific individuals and does not portray either the working class as the group subject of history or class struggle as its deterministic mechanism. These stories also lack the utopian spaces of *The Iron Heel*. In contrast, "The Dream of Debs" and "Goliah" are futuristic utopias that marginalize the naturalist determinism that dominates much of London's fiction. "The Dream of Debs" makes some gestures toward class struggle, but its main emphasis is the distinction between the utopian experience of the working class and the dystopian world of the upper class, which is made apparent by a general strike. To the extent that its utopianism is due to the individual genius of a Nietzschean "scientific superman" (106), "Goliah" utilizes one of the forms of determinism that appears in *The Iron Heel*; but London's reliance on "Energon" (101), a mysterious form of energy that brings about utopian society, reflects his impatience with naturalistic historical processes. Among London's later fiction, it is the novels, not these stories with overt socialist elements, that represent most fully the conjunction of historical process and utopian space. However, these novels shift away from the socialist form of utopian naturalism that is apparent in *The Iron Heel*. In novels such as *Martin Eden* (1909) and *The Valley of the Moon* (1913), London reworks and reiterates aspects of the earlier novel in an attempt to simplify and resolve its conflicts of utopian naturalism.

Martin Eden is a very different novel from *The Iron Heel*. Whereas the earlier novel advocates positive visions of history and space, the later one is a largely critical account of the ineffectuality of forms of utopian naturalism that do not lead to socialist commitments. By removing the utopian naturalism of class struggle and socialist space from the narrative, London reinscribes many of the conflicts of *The Iron Heel* as a critique of nonsocialist perspectives on causality and space. As Howard argues, *Martin Eden* "self-consciously" explores "many of the elements of naturalism" (61), but it is important to note that such reflexivity applies to the ambiguities and contradictions of *The Iron Heel*, and the repetition of situations and themes enhances this sense of critical reinscription. The shift from advocacy to critique also simplifies the conflicts of London's writing. Freed from the responsibility of advocating a form of socialist textuality, London portrays the conflicts of *Martin Eden* as a broad incommensurability between nonsocialist forms of utopianism and naturalism. Even though the sensibilities of the novels are almost wholly reversed, London's interest in representing models of utopian naturalism in fiction is sustained, and such continuity suggests that London's textual interests are as strong as his political commitments.

The critical space of *Martin Eden* emphasizes the ways in which political utopianism can be undone. As in *The Iron Heel*, this novel commences with a visit by London's working-class protagonist to the bourgeois home of the woman he will love. Everhard is critical of the social environment that he visits and is able to convince the members of Avis's social milieu that his ideas are superior to theirs. In contrast, Martin is dazzled by the bourgeois space of Ruth Morse and willingly accommodates himself to its norms. While for Bloch the goal of concrete utopia is to presage humanity's arrival at its "homeland" (3: 1376), he is critical of "household remedies" that seek to realize utopia via bourgeois domesticity (2: 891). Martin's awestruck response to Ruth's home typifies the displacement of concrete utopia by household remedies that Bloch describes. Martin becomes aware of a social dualism that is symbolized by his name. He is known in working-class circles by his first name, but in Ruth's home he is addressed as Mr. Eden. By emphasizing Martin's surprise at this form of address, London suggests that the difference between Martin's first and last names reflects a division in his character. "Martin" is associated with the naturalist facts of working-class life, and "Eden" connotes his susceptibility to idealized bourgeois space; the disjunction between these terms illustrates Martin's inability to synthesize the naturalist details of his experience with a vision of utopian social space. The dualism of Martin's experience is exacerbated by his idealization of Ruth's social milieu. For Bloch, idealization usurps the utopian function by transforming goal-directed activity into an "irrevocable" attempt to satisfy the "reified demands" of "the ideal Object" (1: 166). Caught in the idealized contrast between his own world and Ruth's, Martin is unable to see that both spaces are the effect of related processes of economic history. After encountering a meeting of socialists, anarchists, and other radicals, he visits the public library to read books by the writers whose names he has overheard. Because the texts are too taxing, he instead reads poetry, which he finds more pleasurable. The lure of Ruth's aesthetic and poetic sphere thus serves as an obstacle to an analysis of the historical and spatial aspects of working-class experience. It is also significant that Martin does try to read a book by one author whose name he heard, Helena Petrovna Blavatsky's *The Secret Doctrine*. Since it is the dense prose of this text that turns him away from political theory and toward poetry, Blavatsky's writing, along with the several other references to theosophy in London's narrative, serves an important role. In Bloch's analysis, "theosophical colportage" can assist the utopian function by presenting "tensions, inter-worlds, even archetypes which have been overlooked" (3: 1188). Similarly, London's association of theosophy with the radical spheres that Martin never fully embraces suggests the radical possibilities noted by Bloch. However, theosophy is primarily associated with the poetic and idealizing tendencies of Ruth's world. Also, theosophy's language of multiple worlds reflects the utopian dualism that inhibits Martin's political consciousness. As illustrated by Martin's "vision of a world without end of sunlit spaces and starry voids through which he drifted with her" (129), London often evokes Martin's dreams of life with Ruth in an otherworldly realm in language that is tinged with theosophist vistas.

As the narrative proceeds, Martin and Ruth's moments of poetic intimacy increasingly occur in pastoral environs rather than the domestic interior of Ruth's home. Rooted in the utopian iconography of nature, their poetic space is strengthened. However, the stability of this poetic space comes under threat from tensions between Martin and Ruth. Each of them regards utopian space as the basis of different naturalist principles, neither of which exemplifies Bloch's definition of concrete utopia. Whereas Ruth associates aesthetics with leisure and consumption, Martin wishes to be a professional writer as a way of escaping poverty. Martin's goal is to synthesize the empirical facts of his experience with the poetic sensibility that he learns with Ruth. Yet Ruth hopes that Martin's experience of poetic space will inspire him to better himself in accordance with the individualism of the self-made man. When Ruth's family discovers that Martin has attended a radical meeting, the conflict between the engaged couple becomes a permanent separation. Martin then goes in search of other social spaces, but even though he claims that he has "the bump of location" (128)—a strong spatial and geographical sense derived from his seafaring experience—the meanings attached to these spaces make this project difficult. In *The Principle of Hope*, Bloch states that the "geographical" utopia of "Eldorado-Eden [. . .] comprehensively embraces the other outlined utopias" (2: 793). Bloch arrives at this conclusion because he believes that "discovering definitely wants and is able to change things" (2: 749). In London's novel, Martin's last name suggests that his real and imagined voyages are equated with larger utopian pursuits, but, unlike Bloch, London regards the geographical utopia as a denial of concrete utopia. There are several illustrations of the false utopia of the sea. Early on in the novel, Martin fails to discover the treasure that he seeks on his voyages. Also, after he has lost Ruth, Martin's plan to sail to the South Seas and find an island paradise ends up in failure and suicide.[8] On occasion, Martin does regard seafaring in terms of naturalist class struggle. For example, he identifies sea labor with the naturalist struggle against captains and underwriters, "either of whom could and would break him and whose interests were diametrically opposed" (78). However, such conceptions of life on the sea are infrequent and unrepresentative.

Martin's attachment to Ruth means that he fails to engage with working-class space. While this aspect of the novel ostensibly reflects London's critique of Martin's bourgeois affiliation, it also, to reverse Fredric Jameson's formulation, represents an antiutopian textual unconscious. In other words, London's textual strategy suggests an inability to represent the concrete utopia of working-class space. Compared with the idealized figure of Ruth, the working-class environment engenders a feeling of "spiritual nausea" in Martin (87). His transitory thoughts about going to "the grass-walled castle in the Marquesas" with Lizzie Connelly, a working-class woman, suggests how the spaces of working-class life and seafaring voyages are similarly unreal to him (426). In Bloch's writing, geographical utopia leads to concrete utopia, but in *Martin Eden* the possibilities of working-class space are subsumed by geographical fantasy. Working-class experience also means that nature and pastoral space fail to attain a utopian meaning for Martin. Bloch identifies several versions of pastoral "Sunday space" in painting (2: 815). These include the celebratory "Eternal Sunday" of Breughel and the "bottomless boredom" of Manet's landscapes of leisure (2: 813, 814). Also, Bloch describes Arcadian images of nature as "dangerously isolating" attempts to hide from social space (2: 915). London shares Bloch's sense of the dangers of Sunday pastoralism and Arcadian escape. When he works with Joe Dawson at the laundry at Shelly Hot Springs, Martin's Sunday is one in which exhaustion prevents an appreciation of nature (198). He is attracted to Joe's Arcadian vision of the life of the hobo: "Whole herds of moments stole away and were lost while their careless shepherd gazed out of the window at the sunshine and the trees" (205). However, these images are nothing more than a fantastical compensation for the drudgery of work. Martin attempts a return to working-class pastoral space when he visits the Bricklayers' Picnic at Shell Mound Park, but his continued attachment to Ruth means that he does not regard the working-class picnic as a concrete utopia. He can only appreciate such spaces when they are gone. For example, he describes the radical discussion group that he visits with his friend Russ Brissenden as a "paradise," and he thinks of his working-class life as "the Paradise he had lost" (453, 477–78). When he is among these spaces, his attachment to the spatiality he associates with Ruth prevents him from viewing them as scenarios of socialist possibility.

Martin never commits himself to socialist or working-class space because he lacks a theory of history with which it could be coarticulated. His ignorance of politicized models of history frees London from the contending and contradictory positions that are evident in *The Iron Heel*. Though Martin encounters many naturalist theories, he fails to embrace the socialist history of class struggle. Martin's experiences of history and space are interwoven. When he reads Herbert Spencer, he is elated to discover the theory of evolution. Initially, his belief in Spencerian theory displaces the reality of working-class space: "At table he failed to hear the conversation about petty and ignoble things, his eager mind seeking out and following cause and effect in everything before him" (149). As the novel progresses, Martin seeks to integrate his spatial experiences into the deterministic theories that he embraces. Thus a version of utopian naturalism is produced that denies socialist history and working-class space. He has "a basic love of reality" (118), a fidelity to the details of his working-class experience, but only in so far as these details contribute to a Spencerian synthesis. When he sees the cherry juice on Ruth's lips, he realizes that she is also "subject to the common law" (139). Martin believes that love is the ultimate "cosmic" force (106), and this experience convinces him that it is possible to unify the naturalist force of love, Spencerian fact and law, and the aesthetic sense that is associated with the social space that he shares with Ruth. Martin is not content with a theory of utopian naturalism that applies to his own experience; he also seeks to establish a literary form to represent "saints in slime" (168). His story, "Adventure," best illustrates the conjunction that Martin has in mind because in this piece "beauty" is the utopian inspiration and support for the dominant principle of evolutionary force (171). When she hears this story, Ruth appreciates its "beauty" but not its naturalism. Ruth's response expresses her antipathy to Martin's realism, but it also intimates the conflict that is inherent in both his literary project and his wider commitments. Also, as Martin becomes more successful, deterministic law gives way to individual will, which suggests a conflict between the forms of naturalism that Martin attempts to combine.

In *History and Class Consciousness*, Lukács discusses ideas that offer insight into the connections among Martin's various thoughts. When he meets Ruth, Martin undergoes "moral revolution" and "reform" (81, 82). According to Lukács, "[e]conomic fatalism" and " 'ethical' reformation" are "intimately connected" because they equally deny the function of revolutionary subjectivity (*History* 38). Lukács speaks with specific reference to reformist socialism, but his comments are also relevant to the conjunction of Spencerian determinism and moral reform associated with Martin. By overlooking the role of subjective mediation in processes of change, these theories induce passive contemplation. Similarly, Martin's obsession with Spencer engenders passive aestheticism. Lukács states that "the contemplative attitude of the bourgeoisie became polarized into two extremes: on the one hand, there were the 'great individuals' viewed as the autocratic makers of history, on the other hand, there were the 'natural laws' of the historical environment" (*History* 158). Additionally, Lukács defines "the conscious activity of the individual" as the object of history and the proletarian class as its subject (*History* 165). As in Lukács's account, Martin's "contemplative attitude," his deification of the individual will, and his adherence to Spencerian evolution are all facets of the same bourgeois subjectivity. That Martin has been used by Ruth's mother as an "instrument" to make Ruth "conscious of her womanhood" indicates that, as in Lukács's writings, the great individual is more object than subject (212). As illustrated by his attachment to various bourgeois philosophies, Martin's beliefs cause him to negate socialism and prevent him from arriving at a stable form of utopian naturalism. On several occasions he describes himself as the enemy of socialism, and when he regards Brissenden as typical of the failings of socialism, he resorts to images of biological naturalism: "He was the figure that stood forth representative of the whole miserable mass of weaklings and inefficients who perished according to biological law on the ragged confines of life" (390). Martin opposes socialists because they "dream of a society where the law of development will be annulled" (391). For London, this dogmatic adherence to deterministic law prevents Martin from realizing that socialist naturalism overcomes the dualism of law and individualism within which he himself is trapped. Following the loss of Ruth and suicide of Brissenden, Martin's belief in both evolutionary law and individual might becomes enervated. These theories ultimately fail him, and he is left with neither an inspirational model of social space nor a viable conception of the process of history. His experience epitomizes how the attempt to forge ideas of utopian naturalism in the absence of socialism leads to conflict and then destruction.[9]

In his later fiction London abandons the socialist position that is explicit in *The Iron Heel* and implicit in *Martin Eden*. In *The Valley of the Moon* (1913), London maintains his textual commitment to utopian naturalism, but his departure from socialism rids him of the need to resolve the complexities that inform the politics of his earlier fiction. Like *Martin Eden*, *The Valley of the Moon* utilizes the familiar utopian and naturalist ideas that are evident in *The Iron Heel*. It restates, simplifies, and inverts many of the positions of *Martin Eden*, and, in so doing, it articulates a utopian naturalism that is more cohesive than those of its predecessors. In *The Valley of the Moon*, London forfeits the idea of space as a model of the future in favor of a utopian space that is identified with specific locations. This empirical approach to spatiality enables London to assess the relation between particular urban, national, and natural spaces and naturalist principles. By portraying utopian space in achieved terms, London depicts a nonsocialist space that is linked in certain respects to Bloch's abstract utopia. London's textual strategy also brings the function of spatiality closer to that of historicity and thus enhances its status. The distinctiveness of *The Valley of the Moon* is evident in its treatment of gender and class. Male characters in *The Iron Heel* and *Martin Eden* are identified with naturalist traits, and female characters are associated with utopian ones; the subordination of utopianism to naturalism exists in part through an equivalent subordination of the feminine to the masculine. In *The Valley of the Moon*, London adheres to his ideology of masculine power and the overall structure of his masculine-naturalist and feminine-utopian ideas, but he also attributes naturalist and utopian motifs to both genders and accords greater significance to spatiality as the narrative progresses. In earlier novels the duality of proletarian males and bourgeois females underscores London's privileging of naturalist elements over utopian ones. The two main characters in *The Valley of the Moon*, Billy Roberts and Saxon Brown, are both members of the working class, yet their descent from American pioneers qualifies both their working-class identities, enhances the status of social space in the novel, and suggests an alternative to the naturalist determinism of class struggle.

The shifting variations of utopian naturalism in London's earlier work are replaced in *The Valley of the Moon* by a critical opposition. One pole of this opposition involves a critique of urban space and socialist politics. Through the narrative's spatial emphasis, London now identifies with the critical views of Martin Eden. The opening sections of *The Valley of the Moon* focus on Billy and Saxon's working-class environment in Oakland. The hardship of Saxon's work at the laundry is not contrasted with depictions of proletarian utopian space, and the utopian characteristics of the Bricklayers' Picnic, where Billy and Saxon become acquainted, are quickly marred by violence. Primarily through the character of Tom, Saxon's socialist brother, the idea of socialist space exists in the novel as a dream of government land. As Billy and Saxon discover, such land no longer exists, which suggests not only the bankruptcy of socialist utopian space but also its divorce from models of history. It is typical of *The Valley of the Moon* that its critique of socialism should take the form of spatial, not historical, representation. Disillusioned with the labor struggles that define life in the city, Billy and Saxon go in search of land to farm and pursue a renewed conjunction of utopian naturalism. Saxon has a stronger understanding than Billy of the spatial and historical attributes of labor politics, which enables her to save them both from further deterioration. She identifies the problems of labor with the city, realizes the futility of Billy's union activities, and takes the initiative in deciding to search for a rural retreat.[10] That her mother was a poet adds to Saxon's utopian characteristics. Through the distinction between Saxon and Mercedes Higgins, their neighbor, London stresses that Saxon does not desire a wholly abstract or static utopia. Unlike Mercedes, who regards the inequalities of princes and peasants as part of the eternal and feudal order of things, Saxon sympathizes with the plight of the working class and seeks an alternative space within which causal principles other than those of class struggle can be asserted. Saxon is inspired to find another social space after she traverses the beaches of the Oakland area, where she forages for food when Billy is in prison. As she and Billy walk through the countryside of Northern California, Saxon, in keeping with the ideals of government land, initially desires a large acreage for their utopian farm. But through numerous encounters with different rural locales, they realize that they should look for a smaller piece of land that can be intensively farmed using modern scientific ideas. It is this form of utopian naturalism, supported by the abhorrent racist naturalism of Anglo-Saxon supremacism, that London advocates in *The Valley of the Moon*. By stating that this ideal farm must be close to markets, he makes a further distinction between this utopian naturalism and the pure space that, once again, is associated with government land. However, London emphasizes that Billy and Saxon's ideal space is leisurely rather than commercial, which ensures that its utopian aspects are not compromised.

The critical space of *The Valley of the Moon* has varied connections to Bloch's writings. Saxon's pursuit of a form of utopianism that differs from that of Mercedes is similar to Bloch's tirades against "feudal statics" (1: 139). Yet the Anglo-Saxon racism of the novel falls foul of the "ancestor worship" that, according to Bloch, transforms future-oriented utopias into regressive ones (1: 135). These seemingly contradictory tendencies are related because Billy and Saxon seek to advance into a utopian future by using principles that they identify with an ancestral past. Billy and Saxon's attitude toward nature further illustrates the often close resemblance between socialist concrete utopia and deviations from it. One of the key concepts of *The Principle of Hope* is Bloch's theorization of the dialectics of nature. Bloch's spatial emphasis leads him to theorize the role of nature in facilitating and limiting the extent of human utopia. He claims that nature undergoes the same dialectical processes as those that characterize the history of human activity. As nature affects human society, so too human activity transforms nature. The goal of this process is the co-utopianization of nature and human society. Bloch recognizes that "the former pioneering will in America" exemplifies the subjective factor that is necessary for the realization of utopia, but he observes that American capitalism "has no relation to nature at all, not even an aesthetically mediated one" (2: 683, 695). In *The Valley of the Moon*, Billy and Saxon's scientific farming exhibits the will of the pioneer and the co-transformation of nature and human society. However, London's concern with process has shifted wholly from history to scientific farming. As a result, the historical process is foreshortened, and Billy and Saxon achieve only an individualized abstract utopia that is entwined in capitalist transactions. In Bloch's terms, Billy and Saxon therefore have no relation to nature beyond that of objectification and exploitation. The conclusion of *The Valley of the Moon* indicates the distance traveled by London's utopian naturalism. The conflicts among the various historical processes articulated in *The Iron Heel* have been reduced to the science of farming. Similarly, Billy and Saxon's abstract utopia dramatically simplifies *The Iron Heel*'s ambiguous treatment of utopian space. London remains committed to representations of the conjunction of naturalist processes and utopian space, but his rejection of socialism overhauls the characteristics of this conjunction.

There are many connections between Jack London and Upton Sinclair. Both authors were committed to socialism and the principles of literary realism, and they were each other's advocates. Also, the same issues are central in their fiction. Like London, Sinclair engages with the naturalist conjunction of free will and determinism and seeks to synthesize ideas of history and representations of space into a form of socialist textuality. Yet the specific aspects of their political and literary preoccupations are very different. In writing that precedes the explicit socialist fiction of *The Iron Heel*, London represents the contending forces of instinct, environment, and heredity in challenging natural settings. London's utopian naturalism is a development of these earlier concerns: naturalist principles are extended to encompass the process of class struggle, and distinctive locales are charged with idealized social meanings. In contrast, Sinclair was led to naturalism by socialism. Early in his career Sinclair wrote dime novels and historical romances, both of which, according to Alfred Hornung, were genres that "displaced and delayed" the realization of naturalist literature in the United States through their respective ideologies of laissez-faire Social Darwinism and nostalgic escapism ("Political Uses" 333, 334). Following his conversion to socialism in 1904, Sinclair transformed key aspects of his earlier work to produce a literature of utopian naturalism. Sinclair replaces Social Darwinism with a socialist determinism and empiricism founded in Zola's naturalism and German social democracy, and his escapist romance turns into a spatial utopianism derived from anarchist and socialist traditions. These different approaches to and conceptions of literary principles result in major distinctions between the fiction of London and that of Sinclair. Because London's textual interests arise from a broad context of naturalist representations of history and space, he responds to the conflicts of his fiction by articulating alternative forms of utopian naturalism. Just as his earlier fiction often involves struggles among naturalist forces, London's turn toward a socialist form of naturalism is informed by political conflicts, such as the tension between his revolutionary aspirations and the gradual reformism of social democracy. London responds to such conflict by turning, ultimately, to the conjunction of scientific technique and American natural space. Unlike London, Sinclair remains singularly committed to a form of naturalism that is based on social democratic ideas of history and space. Yet Sinclair's fiction is characterized by conflicts between his socialist model of utopian naturalism and issues such as the exigencies of political action and different perspectives in the radical tradition. These conflicts suggest the incompatibility of Sinclair's ideas of history and space and threaten the utopian naturalism to which he is committed. Sinclair responds to such conflict by seeking to reconstruct socialist textuality rather than abandoning it for other versions of utopian naturalism.

Sinclair's relation to Lukács differs from that of London. Whereas London's *The Iron Heel* articulates several models of historical process, Sinclair's fiction primarily adheres to the deterministic naturalism that Lukács attacked. In his literary criticism of the 1930s, Lukács raises issues that highlight many attributes of Sinclair's writing,[11] and in his attacks on the naturalist sensibility in fiction, Lukács often singles out Sinclair's writing. For Lukács, Sinclair's naturalism results in "coldly-calculated all-good and all-bad stereotypes" and the denigration of "art to the level of children or uneducated peasants" (*Studies* 8, 257). Also, Lukács states that fiction such as Sinclair's is guilty of "psychologism," a practice of bourgeois writers "who are not directly connected with material production" and who thus perceive "existing reality [. . .] as 'mechanical,' 'soulless,' and dominated by 'alien' laws" (*Essays* 46, 47). While appearing as the opposite of psychologism, "reportage" is, for Lukács, its complement. Writers indulge in reportage when they seek to discredit capitalism by identifying "certain isolated facts" and emphasizing "empirical reality" (*Essays* 50, 48, 51). A fictionalized version of journalism, reportage attempts to negate subjectivism in favor of the objective facts. However, writes Lukács, "The subjective factor they [the writers of reportage] push aside appears in their work as the unportrayed subjectivity of the author, as a moralizing commentary that is superfluous and accidental, an attribute of the characters that has no organic connection with the plot" (*Essays* 49). The return of moralizing subjectivity accounts for the psychologism of reportage. Of course, Lukács's discussion of reportage reiterates his critique of Zola. He describes Zola's empirical approach as one in which the "solitary observer" will "spend a few days" in a chosen setting, record the facts of this setting, and render them in fiction as a "grey statistical mean" that is drained of dialectical energy (*Studies* 90, 91). As well as being moralizing and empiricist, the fiction discussed by Lukács also idealizes objective historical process as "tendency" and reduces the author's political intervention to a "demand." As Lukács insists, the representation of deterministic tendency in fiction is due to "the unliquidated legacy of the Second International." He further states that tendentious fiction often includes "an elegiac or outraged sentiment simply tacked on afterwards" (*Essays* 41, 44, 148). Moral, empiricist, sentimental, and deterministic qualities are therefore closely linked in Lukács's analysis.

The literary characteristics noted by Lukács are central to Sinclair's representation of history and space. These characteristics are especially prominent in Sinclair's *The Jungle* (1906). Similar to the role of *The Iron Heel* in London's career, *The Jungle* represents a departure point in the trajectory of Sinclair's utopian naturalism. But whereas *The Iron Heel*'s conflict among various forms of naturalist determinism is simplified in London's later fiction, tensions associated with the conjunction of history and space in *The Jungle* become more prominent in Sinclair's subsequent writing. *The Jungle* refers to the range of naturalist forces that are evident in *The Iron Heel*, but, unlike London, Sinclair offers a consistent appraisal of their validity. Sinclair wrote *The Jungle* for publication in *The Appeal to Reason*, a prominent socialist journal, and in 1904 he spent seven weeks conducting research for the novel. Using the empirical details that he observed in Chicago, Sinclair recounts the hardships endured by Jurgis Rudkus and his family of Lithuanian immigrants in Chicago's stockyards. *The Jungle* exemplifies the tendentious novel of reportage criticized by Lukács, and Sinclair's tendentiousness is fully revealed in Jurgis's conversion to socialism. Prior to this experience, Sinclair depicts a series of false causes or determinisms in the experiences of Jurgis's family.[12] When he first arrives in Packingtown, Jurgis believes that his formidable physical strength and mental willpower will enable him to succeed in financially supporting his family. However, a succession of misfortunes caused by capitalist exploitation undermines the power of both biological determinism and individual will, as the industrial system of Packingtown forces Jurgis deeper into economic hardship. A culminating moment in this process occurs when Jurgis, exultant after walking home through a blizzard, injures his ankle while at work. By narrating that "the soul of Jurgis was a song, for he had met the enemy and conquered, and felt himself the master of his fate" (110), Sinclair intimates the falsity of Jurgis's fleeting self-confidence: Jurgis is not a "master" and "conqueror," "fate" is not the force governing his life, and the "enemy" is not the natural force of the blizzard that makes it difficult to get to work. Depriving Jurgis of his ability to work, this event triggers a new level of suffering among his family—alcoholism, sexual abuse, imprisonment, death—and dramatizes the triumph of the conjunction of chance and the industrial machine over Jurgis's mind and body. As Sinclair's protagonists realize the hopelessness of their lives, they continue to attribute their misery to the blind fatalism of the inexplicable workings of chance. When Ona, Jurgis's wife, tells her husband how she was abused by her boss, Connor, she deterministically prophesies what will happen next: "I am going to have a baby—I am getting ugly. He told me that—twice, he told me, last night. He kicked me—last night—too. And now you will kill him—you—you will kill him—and we shall die" (147). As such scenes illustrate, Sinclair's portrayal of Ona deploys the sentimental and moralizing elements appraised by Lukács.[13] Sinclair evokes Ona's mordant fatalism as an adjunct to the folkways of his illiterate Lithuanian immigrants, who believe in cursed houses, regard factory supervisors as ghosts and witches, and describe settlement workers as fairy godmothers. The imagery of forests, fairy tales, and supernatural agents that permeates *The Jungle* evidences the hold that folklore has on the imaginations of these formerly forest-dwelling characters. For Sinclair, nostalgic thoughts of Lithuania are evidence of a mystified consciousness that is unable to penetrate through fanciful imagery to the brutal and exploitative realities of economic determinism.

Jurgis fails to understand that it is the deterministic force of the industrial-capitalist machine, more so than that of chance and fatalism, which has overpowered his will and biology. Mark Seltzer uses the term "The Naturalist Machine" to designate the importance of technology for the naturalist sensibility (25). Seltzer characterizes naturalism by its "radical entanglement of relations of meaning and relations of force, and [. . .] radical entanglement of writing, bodies, and mechanics" (15), and he argues that the collapsing of the human body (as in Jurgis's case, an amalgam of biological determinism and free will) and industrial machinery into a single technological discourse is the fundamental attribute of naturalism (15). In accordance with Seltzer's thesis, bodies and machines are incorporated in *The Jungle* into the singular logic of Packingtown's system of differentiated tasks: the factories have been designed according to the dimensions of the machinery, not the human employees; workers are unable to appreciate or even notice the changing seasons because they are "tied to the great packing machine and tied to it for life" (100); Ona's stepmother "was part of the machine she tended" (132); and Jurgis's entire body is coated with the disgusting particles of the fertilizer works. The representation of the power of industrial capitalism's Naturalist Machine to trump other explanatory forces in *The Jungle* is enhanced by the literary strategy noted by Michael Brewster Folsom, whereby Sinclair initially imputes to industrialism " 'value-free' significance and 'natural' (nonhuman) origins" (241). Sinclair's evocation of industrial might also presages his treatment of the deterministic force of history, because, as Folsom argues, Sinclair's socialism takes advantage of the qualities of industrialism that initially mystify Jurgis (242). William A. Bloodworth suggests that the relentless and detailed hardship Jurgis suffers produces a naturalistic effect in the novel but that as Jurgis loses his family, moves away from Packingtown, and becomes a socialist, the novel's naturalistic qualities evaporate (55). However, Jurgis's conversion to socialism is continuous and consistent with the bulk of the novel, as one form of determinism is transformed into another. From the outset of *The Jungle*, socialist history seeks to assert itself within the impervious consciousness of Jurgis and his family, yet critics such as Bloodworth view the appearance of socialist rhetoric as a forced imposition on the narrative and neglect the textual presence of a socialist historical awareness and its relation to the progress of Jurgis's experience.

The tendentious force of socialist history is apparent in the midst of the novel's treatment of false determinisms. The early speech made by the Lithuanian neighbor Grandmother Majauszkiene, "a socialist, or some such strange thing" (66), describes the history of the house bought by Jurgis's family and intimates the type of history that is asserted in *The Jungle*. The fact that Jurgis's family responds to these revelations by regarding themselves as "victims of a relentless fate, cornered, trapped, in the grip of destruction" indicates the difficulty this model of history will have in gaining recognition (69). The determinism of the Naturalist Machine first starts to falter when Cousin

Marija Berczynskas joins a trade union after the canning factory is shut down, an event that denaturalizes the industrial system and signals the appearance of history: "Marija would about as soon have expected to see the sun shut down—the huge establishment had been to her a thing akin to the planets and the seasons" (84). Paralleling incidents and descriptions such as these are moments that reveal Jurgis's lack of historical awareness. Throughout the tale, strikes and shutdowns have little impact on Jurgis, who "lived like a dumb beast of burden, knowing only the moment in which he was" (137). When tried in court for attacking Ona's assailant, Connor, Jurgis assumes he will have time to make his case, but he is denied this possibility by the judge; this experience exemplifies how time and history have been eliminated in Jurgis's world. In prison Jurgis is not cognizant of causal and historical forces, and he has "no wit to trace back the social crime to its far sources—he could not say that it was the thing men have called 'the system' that was crushing him to the earth; that it was the packers, his masters who had bought up the law of the land, and had dealt out their brutal will to him from the seat of justice" (156). When the Socialists threaten to bring historical forces to bear on static and plutocratic city politics, the corrupt machines of Chicago Democrats and Republicans enlist Jurgis to undermine the socialists' growing power. Even here Jurgis remains oblivious to the stakes of history, and it is only when he accidentally stumbles across a socialist meeting that the materialist process of history is revealed to him. Following this meeting, Comrade Ostrinski unveils to Jurgis the socialist victory assured by the deterministic forces of democratic class struggle: "Every Socialist did his share, and lived upon the vision of the 'good time coming,'—when the working class would go to the polls and seize the powers of government, and put an end to private property in the means of production. No matter how poor a man was, or how much he suffered, he could never be really unhappy while he knew of that future; even if he did not live to see it himself, his children would, and, to a Socialist, the victory of his class was his victory" (302). In accepting Ostrinski's vision of slow, dialectical change, deferred class victory, and optimistic determinism, Jurgis breaks free of the false explanations of individualism and the determinisms of biology, fatalism, and the capitalist machine. While

Jurgis's revelation is sudden in the sense that he had shown no prior tendencies toward socialism, it entails the culmination of a lengthy textual process.

Some commentators, such as Folsom (257), have posited the psychological implausibility of Jurgis's conversion, but these and other critics neglect Sinclair's attempt to unite subjective and objective forces. Hornung argues that Sinclair cannot make up his mind whether to present a naturalism of individual power or of corporate power, but the socialism of *The Jungle* is both a corrective to these determinisms that have been shown to be flawed over the course of the narrative and a synthesis of individualism and industrialism ("Literary Conventions" 28–30). Just as for Bloodworth *The Jungle* departs from naturalism when empirical hardship gives way to socialist optimism, other critics, such as Howard (159), interpret this departure in terms of the exercise of free will and denial of determinism apparent in Jurgis's conversion. However, Jurgis's action represents a union of economic determinism and individual activism, as he relinquishes the stubborn individualism he had previously lived by and capitulates to the materialist force of history. In making Jurgis's exhilarating sense of freedom a result of his identification with socialism, Sinclair creates a form of naturalism that conforms to what Kaplan calls the collapsing of freedom into necessity in Marx or what Conder describes as the collapsing of free will into determinism in Hobbes. As has been suggested, this naturalist synthesis differs from that advocated by Lukács, who argues that the true subject of history and the bearer of class consciousness is the revolutionary party and not the empirical and psychologistic subject. Instead, Sinclair's fictionalization is consistent with Lukács's descriptions of social democracy. According to Lukács, social democracy fetishizes reified empirical facts, emphasizes psychological consciousness rather than class consciousness, ignores social totality and issues of working-class organization, perceives democratic gradualism as a deterministic law, and consequently denies the role of violence in revolution. In *The Jungle*, Sinclair also portrays a gradual democratic victory that is devoid of violence, and his emphasis on Jurgis's psychology rather than the working-class organizations that were active in Chicago in 1904 indicates that his idea of the synthesis of subject and object accords with that attributed to social democracy by Lukács.

As in London's fiction, Sinclair's representation of naturalistic process in *The Jungle* relies on depictions of utopian space. Since they contain traces of the realm of freedom that will succeed the time of necessity, these spatial representations are examples of Blochian concrete utopia. Many of Bloch's ideas are particularly relevant to Sinclair's representations of spatiality. In *The Principle of Hope*, Bloch distinguishes between the "No-Longer-Conscious," which refers to the Freudian unconscious, and the "Not-Yet-Conscious," "a future consciousness which is only just beginning to come up" (1: 115, 116). As components of the same psychic system, the No-Longer-Conscious and the Not-Yet-Conscious can be mistaken for one another. In Bloch's terms, the No-Longer-Conscious is "the peculiar hiding-place of the Not-Yet-Conscious" (1: 133). The Not-Yet-Conscious is accompanied by the "Not-Yet-Become," which Bloch describes as "a space of concrete anticipation" (1: 127). The presence of the Not-Yet-Become indicates that social space carries traces of the future and thus is discontinuous and fragmented. Bloch's musings on non-Euclidean geometry focus on the multiplicity of social space, and he is fond of tropes, such as the image of the rose in Dante's poetry and the depiction of the Madonna in the Sistine Chapel, that subvert notions of spatial homogeneity and collapse "nearness and distance" into "situationless landscape" (2: 822, 837). The notion of fragmentation is central to Bloch's theory. In cultural representations, spatial fragmentation reveals a "hollow space" of "unrounded immanence" (1: 219). The fragmented or unrounded quality of these representations enables them to gesture toward the utopian future. In contrast, fully rounded spaces are unconnected to the future and thus are abstract utopias. For Bloch, religion offers especially keen insight into the progress toward future utopia. He states that the eschatological perspective of Christianity articulates "explosive hope" and the possibility of the "Utterly Different" (3: 1193, 1195). These aspects of Christianity communicate the revolutionary nature of utopia. The Christian notion of the "kingdom of God" highlights "the mystery of spatiality" that Bloch envisions (3: 1196). In Bloch's account, utopia entails the realization of the kingdom of God without God, or the transformation of the idea of God into the realization of atheistic utopian space.[14]

The representation of spatiality in Sinclair's fiction links at several points with Bloch's ideas. Coterminous with *The Jungle*'s movement toward socialist determinism is a quest for an ideal utopian space, or a microcosm of the social harmony that will exist at the end of dialectical time. The novel progresses through a number of potential utopian spaces, such as the ethnic community, the domestic realm, and the work site, that illustrate the falsity of the various determinisms Sinclair explores. The subordination of the aforementioned folk fatalism to industrial capitalism is enacted in the scene of the Lithuanian *veselija*, or wedding celebration, that follows Jurgis's marriage to Ona. This scene replicates Lithuanian customs and community, as clothes, music, food, and drink all transform the squalid surroundings of the "back of the yards," the horrific residential area attached to Chicago's meat-packing factories, into a version of the characters' feudal homeland. However, the terms in which this scene is described evoke its nostalgia, escapism, and utopian frailty. The "magic wand" of Tamoszius Kuszleika's violin bow might transform the scene into "a fairy place, a wonderland, a little corner of the high mansions of the sky" (6, 9), but such magical thought cannot deny industrial realities. Material poverty asserts itself as the younger guests fail to take part in the tradition of giving money to the newlyweds, and the transformative power of the *veselija* continues only as long as Tamoszius plays music and Marija Berczynskas dances. Despite their best efforts to maintain the illusion, Tamoszius and Marija inevitably tire, and when Tamoszius plays an American tune, the music is described in terms of the incessant, mechanical monotony that characterizes the lives of the industrial machine's employees. The past to which the characters are drawn is feudal and static and thus does not open onto the socialist future. Having succumbed to the temptations of the No-Longer-Conscious, the characters therefore find themselves trapped in the present.

All other spaces are equally under the power of Packingtown. The house that the family buys is built on a cesspool and is ultimately possessed by the leasing company, which emphasizes the fallibility of Jurgis's ideology of self-reliance. Incidents such as this appear to reinforce the power of the Naturalist Machine, and this is generally true of the descriptions of the industrial landscape of Packingtown as being "made" from garbage dumps impressed upon the prairie and of "Bubbly Creek," that portion of the Chicago River that runs through the district, as "a great open sewer" (92). When Jurgis leaves Packingtown for the countryside, he remains within the ambit of the determinism of the Naturalist Machine. As already noted, this machine encompasses the variegated workings of capitalism as well as the meat-packing plants, and as a rural tramp Jurgis remains under the control of capital as he encounters the insecurities of seasonal work and is forced to beg. Because Jurgis is headed toward an ideological and not simply a topographical space, the pastoral realm is insufficient for Sinclair's needs, and Jurgis is forced to return to the urban environment. Jurgis's experiences—like Martin Eden's—accord with Bloch's critique of pastoral space. Yet as well as showing the power of the industrial machine, Jurgis's pastoral experiences realize earlier instances of rural impulses, such as Jurgis's inadvertent movement toward the countryside after leaving prison and his employment with the Harvester Trust, and accelerates the urgency of *The Jungle*'s concrete-utopian problematic. Back in Chicago, Jurgis visits a panoply of spaces within the extra-Packingtownian urban capitalist system, such as bars, evangelical gatherings, and Republican meeting halls, before encountering the socialist gathering that typologically foreshadows the ideal society that the socialists believe is coming. As the place where Jurgis is initiated into the socialist history toward which the text has been moving, the socialist community is the site of the convergence of both the deterministic and the utopian dimensions of the novel. By describing the socialist community as "the fourth dimension of space" (304), Sinclair shares Bloch's emphasis on the discontinuous and non-Euclidean social space of concrete utopia.

Despite the convergence of the historical and spatial aspects of *The Jungle*, there are points of tension in Sinclair's combination of these elements. Like London, Sinclair associates utopianism with feminine characteristics, and such tension is embodied in Jurgis and Ona, "one of those incongruous and impossible married couples with which Mother Nature so often wills to confound all prophets" (4). The conflicts of Sinclair's utopian naturalism are clearest in the transition from deterministic to spatial utopianism in the novel's concluding chapters. In chapter 28, Jurgis converts to socialism as a result of the unnamed speaker's articulation of the conditions involved in determining a socialist revolution and his appeal to socialists to precipitate such a revolution. As well as articulating the fusion of subjective will and objective determinism, this chapter brings consciousness and spatiality together in a manner that is similar to Bloch's theorization of the Not-Yet. However, in chapter 31, the concrete utopia of this historicist vision is displaced by the debate between Comrade Lucas and Nicholas Schliemann regarding the details of what utopian society will look like after the socialist revolution. Spatiality, which had been subordinate to historicity throughout the novel, now becomes dominant as Sinclair imagines the possibilities of abstract utopia. In Bloch's terms, fragmented space has given way to fully rounded space. That Schliemann is a "philosophical anarchist" (325), who refers to Kropotkin's ideas about the political effects of the spatial distribution of rural and urban areas, suggests the link between utopianism and anarchism in Sinclair's spatial imagination. Of course, Bloch's ideas often run close to anarchism and chiliastic immediatism, but he overtly derides the abstract utopianism of nineteenth-century anarchists. For Bloch, anarchists such as Proudhon not only bypass historical processes but also fail to acknowledge class struggle. In his most vociferous moments in *The Principle of Hope*, Bloch castigates Proudhon for imagining a utopian society that consists of identical petit-bourgeois individuals who therefore have no need for law or state. The abstract utopia that Sinclair invokes at the conclusion of *The Jungle* exhibits the Proudhonian characteristics that irritate Bloch. Sinclair's presentation of abstract utopia is also filled with references to Christianity. As noted, Bloch shares Sinclair's interest in the utopian dimension of Christianity, but, unlike Bloch, Sinclair does not quite attain the removal of religion from the kingdom of utopia. In a reversal of the movement of *The Iron Heel*, Sinclair's narrative additionally replaces Jurgis's working-class milieu with the bourgeois interior in which proletarian voices are marginalized. The anarchist, Christian, and bourgeois aspects of Sinclair's novel thus combine to displace the deterministic process of history.

In his subsequent fiction Sinclair adheres to the model of utopian naturalism that is evident in much of *The Jungle*, but the conflict between history and space that is apparent at the novel's conclusion becomes increasingly manifest in novels such as *King Coal* (1917), *Oil!* (1927), and *Boston* (1928). *King Coal*, which was inspired by the Ludlow Massacre and strikes among mineworkers in Pueblo, Colorado, in 1913–14, puts the theories of *The Jungle* to the test by showing, from the perspective of protagonist Hal Warner, the pressures generated by a confrontation between coal camp bosses and workers. The son of a wealthy coal-mine owner, Hal sympathizes with the miners and is consequently led to live and work among them incognito. Throughout the story, the mining community tries to obtain its legal rights to a "check-weighman" and various safety considerations (85). The more vocal and unified this group of immigrant mining families becomes, the more they are subjected to violence and intimidation by lackeys of the coal camp bosses. The ensuing conflict is characterized by contending perspectives that complicate the optimism with which *The Jungle* concludes. As a result of the exigencies of class struggle, the workers take a passive role in the conflict: they are "child-like people" who must be guided by orators and organizers such as Hal and the "heroic seven" of the union committee, which is itself subservient to the United Mine-Workers of America (306, 312). Whereas in *The Jungle* the acts of will undertaken by Ostrinski and, to a lesser extent, Jurgis are the outcome of their own experiences of economic determinism, the hierarchically arranged leadership in *King Coal* is divorced from its naturalistic roots. The division between subjective and objective aspects of radicalism is most evident through the character of Hal, who responds pessimistically to the setbacks faced by the union and exhibits utopian tendencies that are unrelated to working-class experience. For example, Hal frequently refers to the Irish working woman Mary Burke as Joan of Arc or a "wild rose" (26), and he is attracted to secretive labor activity because of the "romance" of the stories of revolution he has read (106). In *The Jungle*, poetic images are often associated with discredited forms of naturalism, such as a belief in fate, and the presence of such images in *King Coal* also reflects a qualification of the novel's economic determinism. For Lukács, naturalism frequently tries and fails to use symbolism as a way of overcoming the contradictions of subjectivism and objectivism (*Essays* 162). In

King Coal, the utopian symbolism voiced by Hal is equally unable to restore the dialectics of naturalism. The optimistic determinism of *The Jungle* is voiced by Jim Moylan, the union secretary, who refuses to allow the miners to go on strike and tells them to organize patiently until the time "when the big strike comes" (378). Previously concerned with action and the imposition of his will, Hal learns from Moylan's words and the miners' inactivity that history is being determined by more powerful forces than himself. Yet in comparison with *The Jungle*, *King Coal* exhibits a textual rupture between Hal's willfulness and the mineworkers' uncompromising passivity, which exacerbates the fragmented qualities of the novel's naturalist vision. Also, the fact that Hal derives from and returns to his bourgeois capitalist class illustrates Lukács's claim that the objectivism of literary naturalism, despite its protestations to the contrary, reinscribes "the abstract surface of the capitalist economy" (*Essays* 154).

Like the elements of its historical outlook, the critical space of *King Coal* is more fragmented than that of *The Jungle*. The coal camps' isolated Rocky Mountain location means that the system of capitalist power, which encompasses churches, doctors, militia, media, and politicians, is more integrated than it is in *The Jungle*. Whereas in *The Jungle* a socialist network could thrive, in *King Coal* virtually all the workers' conversations and meetings are monitored and censored by the mine supervisors. Such surveillance threatens the possibility of utopian space. However, some retreats are evident in the novel's discontinuous social space. For example, the "tipple," where the miners' loads of coal are weighed, is evoked as the "one place in the camp [. . .] where they could not keep silence, where their sense of outrage battled with their fear" (44). Also, the homes of the Italian Socialist Minetti and "Big Jack" David are retreats in which the miners' radicalism can be renewed. For Bloch, domestic space can exemplify the discontinuity of social space by engendering a "small infinity" or vastness that functions as concrete utopia (2: 834). Sinclair's descriptions of the miners' homes are charged with the effect discussed by Bloch. But unlike the utopian colony or even the meeting hall, these are occasional and vulnerable utopias dependent upon stolen moments in time. Denied a stable spatiality, Sinclair's utopianism appeals to the physical and conceptual aspects of the

American landscape, as evoked in Hal's statement that "[t]he land belongs to the company, but the landscape belongs to him who cares for it" (25). The rugged mountainous landscape is beyond the utilitarian domain of the coal camps and is a place where Hal can speak with other radicals and renew his commitment to the miners' cause. As in Bloch's description of the mountainous landscape in Goethe's *Faust*, Sinclair portrays the sublime landscape as a trope for "infinite striving" toward the socialist future (2: 823). Hal's comments on the landscape also suggest his wish to return to the "real" America of freedom and equality that has been usurped by industrial capitalism. As the miners proclaim, "We're going to stand by the union, all of us, till we've brought these coal-camps back into America!" (359). The proclamation of nationalist space subverts concrete utopia and reflects the novel's fragmentation of utopian space. The sense of fragmentation is further suggested by the representations of anarchists. In *The Jungle*'s conclusion, Sinclair imagines that Schliemann's theoretical ideas of spatial anarchism are compatible with the socialist politics that he represents. In *King Coal*, the anarchist demands of the "spontaneous revolutionist" named "Dutch Mike" and the anarchosyndicalists are suppressed because they represent a threat to Sinclair's deterministic theory of history (16). The challenges of labor conflict do nothing to lessen Sinclair's commitment to the coarticulation of deterministic history and utopian space, but they do affect its nature. Sinclair depicts locales that lack the total social vision characteristic of utopian socialism, and he articulates a vision of history that is more reformist than revolutionary. These two attributes are embodied in Hal, who is closely associated with the utopianism of nature and insists that the miners should claim only the implementation of existing laws rather than the creation of a new industrial relationship. In keeping with the views of Lukács and Bloch, Sinclair's reformism strengthens his deterministic sense of history, and his ideas of utopian space embody tendencies that negate concrete utopia.

In *Oil!* and *Boston*, Sinclair remains committed to social democracy, but his utopian naturalism endures an increased amount of fragmentation and reconfiguration. The protagonist of *Oil!* is Bunny Ross, the son of a wealthy oil magnate in Southern California, who becomes a socialist and gets involved in labor disputes in the oil industry and debates among radicals. Whereas Hal is a member of the upper class who is fully immersed in working-class life, Bunny remains in his father's milieu for much of the narrative. This perspective disrupts the coherence of Sinclair's naturalist textuality. Sinclair describes World War I as a deus ex machina that distorts the clash between labor and capital, and Bunny's subjective interventions are similarly tangential to the main lines of class conflict. Bunny is sympathetic to the plight of the oil workers and takes a theoretical interest in socialist history, but, unlike *The Jungle* and *King Coal*, *Oil!* is not a novel in which socialist commitments derive from the details of proletarian experience. There is, in other words, a split between the empirical and deterministic components of Sinclair's naturalism. This division indicates that Sinclair's naturalism turns against itself. His departure from an empirical basis to Bunny's radicalism echoes Lukács's critique of social democracy's reliance on reified facts. Yet, as Lukács notes, Sinclair's distance from class struggle in *Oil!* enhances the naturalistic weakness of the novel: the narrative offers only "a rapprochement to the revolutionary proletariat that arises from the critique of bourgeois society, but which up till now has developed only into a criticism of the bourgeoisie, not into a real coalescence with the revolutionary class, so that it remains stuck halfway even as a simple critique of bourgeois society, a mechanical and not a dialectical critique" (*Essays* 55). The impact of World War I also causes Sinclair to critique the democratic gradualism of the socialists whom Lukács attacks. Bunny is persuaded of the error of supporting the war by Paul Watkins, a member of the family whose land Bunny and his father buy in order to mine oil. As worker, soldier, and political activist, Paul is given credibility and authority by Sinclair, and he is the mouthpiece for political and scientific deterministic theories. Paul teaches Bunny that the future power of the working class is assured by the simple and certain process of class struggle. However, this moment of accord belies the rift that occurs among the novel's radicals. Sinclair reduces all of the novel's different radical views to the distinction between Third International communism and Second International socialism. Paul voices the communist viewpoint, and Bunny vacillates between this revolutionary position and the democratic and evolutionary "long vision" of the socialist Chaim Menzies (429). Sinclair expresses sympathy for both these theories of history as an attempt to attain a unified radical position. Yet he can attain such unity only by depicting Paul's communist views as a variant of naturalist determinism. Ostensibly an advocate of revolution, Paul does not articulate the subject-object dialectic that characterizes Lukács's position in *History and Class Consciousness*. Even though Bunny ultimately chooses the socialist path, his indecisiveness obscures the clarity of the novel's political vision. Initially, he allies himself with socialism rather than communism so as to appease his father's distaste for violence. Also, at the novel's conclusion, deterministic statements function as warnings about the threat of communist violence rather than as assurances of an egalitarian future. Both these instances reveal how Sinclair's espousal of socialism lacks the naturalist force and certainty of its earlier manifestations.

Sinclair modifies the spatial politics of *Oil!* in relation to his revised treatment of history. While he lacks empirical proletarian experience, Bunny has a sensitivity to utopian space that forms the basis of his subsequent radicalism. The declining significance of the empirical details of proletarian experience is therefore balanced by the rising significance of spatiality. Early in the novel, Bunny romantically regards the Watkins family as exotic and is attracted to Paradise, their ranch, as a pastoral retreat. When Paul tells him to "remember Paradise" in order to understand the novel's political events (266), Paradise functions as the utopian support for class struggle. Yet the narrative qualifies the utopian function of Paradise. As its name suggests, Paradise is portrayed in symbolic terms. According to Bloch, the symbol "religiously forms the archetypes" because it "is consistently assigned to the *Unitas* of a meaning" (1: 161). In *Oil!* Paradise has a religious and symbolic meaning that is self-contained and is thus uncoupled from concrete utopia's orientation toward future possibilities. Paradise is a distinctive space in Sinclair's fiction because it appears as both concrete and fully rounded utopia. Therefore, the possibility of untainted concrete utopia is marginalized. At times, spatiality serves a dystopian role in the novel. The Watkins ranch becomes an oil field, and Sinclair emphasizes how capitalist power entails such spatial transformation. As exemplified by the pastoral descriptions of Vernon Roscoe's "Monastery" and Eli Watkins's religious community (311), the utopian function itself works against the interests of the novel's radical groups. Also, spatiality becomes an alternative to the politics of historical struggle. Following his father's death, Bunny uses the money he inherits to finance a utopian educational colony. The socialist Chaim Menzies opposes the idea of a utopian colony because this would entail a departure from class struggle, which indicates that Bunny's plan is not simply a reflection of his socialist commitments. Rather, Bunny's decision indicates that he resolves the conflict between socialism and communism by turning from historical struggle to abstract utopia. While Bunny proposes that members of the colony would spend time in prison and thus participate in the historicist struggles of labor, *Oil!* differs from Sinclair's other novels because its spatiality is based on a qualification of his naturalist textuality. As the representation of spatiality becomes more significant and complex in this novel than in others by Sinclair, the coherence of the text's utopian naturalism is undone.

The displacement of historicity by spatiality that is evident in *Oil!* is even more prominent in Sinclair's *Boston*. Published just a year later than *Oil!*, *Boston* combines a narrative of the case of Nicola Sacco and Bartolomeo Vanzetti with the story of Cornelia Thornwell, an upper-class Bostonian woman who chooses to live and work among the city's working class. Sinclair's overt purpose is to suggest that a corrupt legal system causes the unjust conviction and execution of Sacco and Vanzetti. Yet *Boston* is also a study of the relationship between anarchist and other radical theories. Through Cornelia's contact with Sacco and Vanzetti's anarchist milieu, Sinclair attempts to integrate anarchist and socialist thinking and recapture the political synthesis of *The Jungle*. This project is made difficult by the conflict between Sinclair's commitment to democratic socialism and anarchist tactics, organization, and philosophy. The utopian anarchism that Sinclair imagines as an extension of social democracy in *The Jungle* becomes, in *Boston*, disconnected from Sinclair's socialist views. Sinclair's representation of anarchism therefore makes manifest the latent conflicts of *The Jungle*. The distinction between anarchism in *The Jungle* and in *Boston* also modifies Sinclair's relation to Bloch's critique of anarchism. As we have seen, Bloch pillories Proudhon's petit-bourgeois individualism. For Bloch, Proudhon's individualism is "in the case of Bakunin or Kropotkin [. . .] blurred in the larger world of fire or love" (2: 571). Bloch concedes that Bakunin opposed Proudhon's bourgeois apologetics, yet he reiterates his critique of anarchism's hatred of the state and opposition to any form of process beyond putschism. In terms that Bloch uses throughout *The Principle of Hope*, anarchism imagines a utopian future, but it is limited to the "Front" of existing society and cannot reach out to the "Novum" of future possibilities that mediate between the capitalist present and the utopian "Ultimum" (1: 198).

In *Boston*, Sinclair abandons bourgeois anarchism and emphasizes the tendencies that, for Bloch, mute individualism. Specifically, Sinclair portrays Vanzetti as an advocate of Kropotkin's communal love and Sacco as a revenant of Bakunin's fiery violence. As in Bloch's analysis, the anarchists in *Boston* reject the idea of history's Novum. In terms of Sinclair's utopian naturalism, the anarchists postulate an absolute as opposed to petit-bourgeois individualism that undermines the emergence of subjective free will through deterministic processes. Vanzetti explicitly opposes studying and making history because he claims that such activity makes people "conservativo, timido" (1: 53). For Vanzetti, the utopian future cannot be compromised by participation in political processes. Cornelia repeatedly criticizes the absolute rupturing of history and utopianism in anarchist thought and claims that Vanzetti offers no method for realizing the ideals to which he adheres. The anarchists' individualism also causes them to negate the social space that is integral to Sinclair's utopian naturalism. In one scene the socialist Culla asks Vanzetti for the names of anarchists whom he would like to invite to a socialist picnic. Vanzetti refuses because the anarchists function in a clandestine, anonymous, and individual way that denies the utopian function of socialist spatiality. Unlike the subordinate utopianism of socialism, the anarchist appeal to utopian space seeks to completely realize the ideals of future society and therefore contributes to the denial of an activist theory of history. The immediate utopianism of the anarchists is associated with natural space. Vanzetti in particular imbues natural landscapes with the values of freedom and equality that the anarchists believe will permeate the promised land of future human society. Also, such space is identified with the Italian pastoral landscape that Sacco and

Vanzetti have left behind. However, such idealized space is powerless to hinder the dystopian space of Boston society; in terms of Sinclair's spatial imagery, Italian pastoralism is destroyed by Roman imperialism. In the language of Bloch, the landscape of the past is a romanticized "land beneath the veil" that serves as "the most powerful block" to the realization of concrete utopia (1: 136, 137).

Despite Sinclair's critique of some of the ideas of Sacco and Vanzetti, his increasing commitment to representations of utopian space results in a considerable and overt identification with aspects of anarchist theory. The anarchists' suspicion of history permeates the novel. Throughout the narrative Vanzetti correctly predicts the course of events and is described in prophetic terms. The prophetic antihistoricism of the anarchists is therefore legitimized by Sinclair. While Sinclair's critique of Sacco and Vanzetti moves toward Bloch's tempered views of anarchism, his shift from determinism to prophecy fails to accommodate the revolutionary subjectivity of both Lukács and Bloch. In particular, Bloch is hostile to both "social-democratic automatism" and the "[l]unacy" of seers, prophets, and occultists (1: 148, 2: 627). The cooling of Sinclair's relation to deterministic theory is also apparent in the trial of Sacco and Vanzetti, where he evokes the difficulty of sustaining a causal model that incorporates all the details of the case. As well as exposing the false causal model that is put forward by the prosecution, Sinclair suggests that any attempt to establish a total causal narrative will fail because "there were not cells enough in the human brain to hold all the details" (1: 349–50). This view departs from the strong deterministic theories that are evident elsewhere in Sinclair's fiction. At numerous points in the novel, Sinclair demonstrates the ineffectuality of "formulas" that are applied to events as a way of explaining them (1: 365). The formulaic theories that inform naturalist fiction are also subject to critique. The experience of Powers Hapgood, a character who, like Hal and Bunny, goes to live among the working class, "smashe[s]" the "categories" of "scientific minds" (2: 698), and Sinclair likens this effect to that endured by the theories of Herbert Spencer, whose "idea of a tragedy was a generalization killed by a fact" (2: 699). Of course, Spencer's Social Darwinism is consistently opposed by Sinclair, but this incident suggests the incoherence of naturalism's coarticulation of empiricism and determinism. The limited nature of the representation of natu-ralist determinism in *Boston* is most apparent through the characters of Cornelia and Joe Randall. Cornelia is the vehicle for the factual, muckraking aspect of the novel, and, like Sinclair, she seeks to over-come the division between capital and labor, opposes violence, and believes in the validity of democratic politics. Yet as the court case unfolds and the credibility of the legal institution crumbles, Sinclair questions Cornelia's and his own opposition to anarchism. Joe is a strong socialist presence in the narrative. However, he rarely voices the optimistic determinism of social democracy that is sounded in Sinclair's other novels, and he succumbs to Vanzetti's pessimism. At the novel's conclusion, Sinclair's adherence to socialism is evident in his appeal to the working class "to take Joe Randall's advice" (2: 747), but his commitment is not expressed in the naturalist politics of his earlier fiction. Also, Joe is identified with political spaces that constitute alternatives to historicity. Joe and Betty Alvin have a fact-finding "sociological honeymoon" in a factory (2: 469), and, as in the conclusion of *Oil!*, Sinclair's protagonists manage a socialist labor college. As in the anarchist theory that he criticizes, Sinclair's appeal to utopianism displaces and compensates for his uncertainty about the course of socialist history. While Sinclair disagrees with many aspects of anarchism, the narrative of *Boston* reflects an imbalance between spatial and historical aspects that is also apparent in his rep-resentation of anarchism. Sinclair's attempt to unify socialism and anarchism sunders the components of concrete utopia and shatters the viability of naturalist determinism.

According to Lukács, anarchism is related to the conflicts of so-cial democracy and naturalist fiction. In his debate with Bloch on expressionism, for example, he states that the aesthetic of naturalism and modernism "forms an anarchistic pendant to the evolutionary theories of reformism" ("Realism" 55). Sinclair's fiction exemplifies the association between anarchism and naturalist reformism made by Lukács because even though he sometimes takes a critical stance toward anarchism, his own utopian naturalism increasingly resem-bles anarchist positions as its confidence in deterministic history and inspirational social space decline. Sinclair remained a socialist and never renounced the political ideas represented in *The Jungle*, but the developments in his writing mean that their utopian and naturalistic qualities become distanced from each other. In contrast, London remained committed to a cohesive textual articulation of utopian naturalism. The conflicts in London's writing involve the different forms that utopian naturalism takes rather than an antagonism between its two constituent elements. In London's fiction the central conflict is between those forms of utopian naturalism that express socialist politics and those that do not. As *The Valley of the Moon* suggests, the integrity of London's utopian naturalism was achieved at the expense of socialist textuality. Despite differences in the nature of the conflicts that are evident in the writing of London and Sinclair, both authors imagine and reimagine the naturalist processes that Lukács criticizes. While Sinclair and London are committed to versions of Blochian concrete utopia, they rarely embrace the subject-object dialectic that both Lukács and Bloch advocate. Nevertheless, the theories of Lukács and Bloch highlight the nuances and trends that are apparent in the fiction of these authors. The strongest general trend that we can see in the novels of London and Sinclair is the growing importance of representations of critical space. The struggles among London's various naturalist allegiances are resolved when he arrives at a version of naturalist process that is centered upon the physical space of the California landscape; for Sinclair, the attempt to integrate the anarchist politics of space into his socialist views results in the spatial qualification of deterministic theories of history. In many respects, London and Sinclair represent opposed treatments of the conflicts of utopian naturalism, but the tendency toward according greater prominence to spatiality that is evident in the writing of both authors reflects their shared participation in a trend that informs much twentieth-century American fiction.

[2]

Hegemony, Culture, Space

John Dos Passos and Josephine Herbst

Like the novels of London and Sinclair, the 1930s fiction of John Dos Passos and Josephine Herbst offers representations of critical space that are entwined with articulations of left-wing politics. However, Dos Passos's and Herbst's representations of spatiality significantly differ from those of London and Sinclair. Such differences are reflected in part by the context in which the fiction of Dos Passos and Herbst was produced. Both these authors exemplify the intellectual and political commitments of the Popular Front that permeated and defined American culture in the Depression era. As Michael Denning states, the Popular Front was "more a historical bloc, in Gramsci's sense, than a party, a broad and tenuous left-wing alliance" (6). As well as being epic histories of American culture and society, Dos Passos's *U.S.A.* (*The 42nd Parallel* [1930], *Nineteen Nineteen* [1932], and *The Big Money* [1936]) and Herbst's Trexler trilogy (*Pity Is Not Enough* [1933], *The Executioner Waits* [1934], and *Rope of Gold* [1939]) reflect the expansive and variegated political bloc of the Popular Front. Whereas London and Sinclair articulate a socialist perspective that carries traces of both economism and utopianism, Dos Passos and Herbst express anarchist and syndicalist tendencies but lack complete identification with socialism, communism, or other strains of American radicalism.[1] The decentered politics of *U.S.A.* and the Trexler trilogy engenders representations of history and space that depart from the utopian naturalism of London and Sinclair. Despite their historical sweep, these novels retreat from the models of radical history, such as Second International socialism and revolutionary Leninism, that inform London's and Sinclair's novels. Dos Passos and Herbst do reconstruct models of historical transformation, but these versions of history are devoid of teleological optimism. Simultaneously, representation of spatiality in *U.S.A.* and the Trexler trilogy abandon the utopian impulse. These two issues are related. In the fiction of London and Sinclair, utopian spatiality is coarticulated with strong representations of history. The weakened versions of history in the novels of Dos Passos and Herbst result in similarly qualified representations of spatiality. Yet depictions of social space are more important and more closely linked to issues of history in the writing of Dos Passos and Herbst than in that of London and Sinclair. Issues of historical transformation are caught up in the struggle for hegemony among a wide array of cultural, economic, and political spaces. As the struggles of history are mediated through social space, the critical and analytical aspects of spatiality displace the utopian function that is apparent in the novels of London and Sinclair.

The following discussion of Dos Passos and Herbst is informed by the Marxist theory of Antonio Gramsci. There are numerous differences between Gramsci and these American novelists, but a reading of Dos Passos and Herbst in terms of Gramsci's ideas usefully draws out the distinctive aspects of the representations of history and space in *U.S.A.* and the Trexler trilogy. Like Lukács, Gramsci was a stern critic of deterministic theories of history, yet Gramsci's separation from the sureties of dialectical history is more pronounced than that of Lukács. Gramsci's position on theories of history varies over the course of his writing, but the negation of economism is consistent. Some of the key attributes of Gramsci's notions of history are articulated in his earliest political writings. In one of his most important early texts, "The Revolt against *Capital*," Gramsci boldly claims that the Russian Revolution "explode[s] the critical schemas [. . .] of historical materialism" and disproves the need for fixed historical stages in the progress toward revolution (33). More so than Lukács, Gramsci emphasizes the role of subjective will in forming history. In a departure from Lukács, he emphasizes the subjective interpretations that direct history: "[I]t is not the economic structure which directly determines political activity, but rather the way in which that structure and the so-called laws which govern its development are interpreted" (38).[2] Gramsci insists that the causal processes of history are a complex amalgam of economic, political, and cultural factors that vary from nation to nation. As a result of his keen awareness of national difference, Gramsci recognizes the prevalence of "political superstructures" in Western democracies that "makes the masses slower and more prudent, and therefore requires of the revolutionary party a strategy and tactics altogether more complex and long-term" than those of the Russian Revolution (131). Gramsci's critique of determinate ideas of the progress of history extends to the notion of the inevitability of "favorable conditions" for revolution (220).

Gramsci's varying ideas on the role of the party in revolutionary history are especially pertinent to the fiction of Dos Passos and Herbst. In his writings on the Factory Council movement that took place in Turin in 1919–20, Gramsci's doubts about the certainties of history inform his advocacy of the workers' takeover of factories. At this point in his career, Gramsci was influenced by the spontaneism of Rosa Luxemburg and the syndicalism of Georges Sorel.[3] As a reaction against the indeterminacy of the future, Gramsci proclaimed a spontaneous proletarian movement that would undertake the syndicalist tactics of the appropriation of the workplace. Of course, Gramsci overtly criticizes the economism of syndicalism and acknowledges that Factory Councils are to be subservient to a centralized party, but he clearly celebrates working-class activism "from below" and even states that the Factory Councils constitute an anarchist "organization of power" (100).[4] More so than his earlier texts, Gramsci's prison writings emphasize the importance of the party as a Machiavellian "modern prince" (240), a galvanizing revolutionary myth. Yet Gramsci associates the party with "the sphere of complex superstructures" and "not only a unison of economic and political aims, but also intellectual and moral unity" (205). Whereas Gramsci's disdain for deterministic history previously led him to advocate the immediate and spontaneous takeover of factories, now it results in a theory of cultural hegemony as a slow and incremental preparation for revolution. His prison writings explore the role of cultural mediation and leadership as a means of advancing revolutionary possibilities. For example, his theory of "historical bloc" refers primarily to the mutually determining interaction of economic base and cultural superstructure (192). Also, his "methodological" distinction between political society and civil society highlights the role of intellectuals in using cultural institutions to attain consensual hegemony over populations (210). However, Gramsci also emphasizes that cultural hegemony can work against revolutionary interests. In his reading of the Italian Risorgimento, the struggles for power in the process of national unification in the late nineteenth century, Gramsci states that the Moderates had intellectual hegemony over the Action Party and thus were able to achieve a "passive revolution" of "revolution/restoration" (250, 270). For Gramsci, passive revolution denotes a societal transformation in which key elements remain unchanged. Most notably, he defines the transition to Italian fascism as a passive revolution in which the implementation of a planned economy did not alter capitalist business practices. In his writings on "Americanism and Fordism," which powerfully resonate with the novels of Dos Passos and Herbst, Gramsci suggests that the Fordist planned economy of the United States also exemplifies a passive revolution that relies on cultural hegemony over many aspects of workers' lives.

The interplay of ideas of history and space is one of the most prominent characteristics of Gramsci's writing. His shift away from strong models of history leads him to a lateral analysis of, in Edward Soja's terms, "the spatiality of social life under capitalism" (*Postmodern* 90). Gramsci repeatedly anchors his ideas in specific forms of social space, such as urban and rural regions, nations, sites of economic production, and cultural institutions. These spaces do not simply provide concrete examples of the ideas Gramsci presents. Rather, they determine the nature of those ideas. In his writings on the Factory Councils, for example, the autonomous space of the factory is necessary for the realization of working-class spontaneism. Unlike Ernst Bloch, Gramsci is critical of all conceptions of utopian space. However, his description of the Factory Councils as a "delimited territory" of "proletarian republics" that realizes "the shop-floor *way of life*" bears traces of utopian spatiality (98, 91). Elsewhere, Gramsci states that the national circumstances of culture and economics should influence the nature of political activity in different countries. His discussion of the "Southern Question," the issue of the relation between Italy's rural south and urban north, is of course his most extended treatment of the importance of the exigencies of particular national spaces. The distinction between Gramsci's views on the Factory Councils and his construction of the Southern Question suggests that his turn to cultural hegemony is accompanied by a recasting of notions of spatiality. Yet there are significant continuities in Gramsci's thought. One of the great benefits of the Factory Councils, he claims, is the way in which they enable workers to become technicians who can use their creativity to improve production. Temporal progress is here figured as technical development. In his discussion of the Southern Question, he states that the industrial workers of the north can unite with the southern peasants through the dissemination and development of technology. Technology is therefore integral to the realization of hegemony, the formation of a historical bloc, and, as in the Factory Councils, the movement of history. Gramsci's awareness of the complex social terrain of Western democracies, which is exemplified by his writings on the Southern Question, forms the basis of his insistence on the need for the mediations of cultural hegemony. His emphasis on the contours of society means that his spatial language is not simply metaphorical. In his celebrated theorization of a transition from a "war of manoeuvre" (or "war of movement") to a "war of position" (226), he describes the state as an "outer ditch" and the superstructures of social space as "a powerful system of fortresses and earthworks" (229). For Gramsci, the war of position, a struggle for hegemony on the terrain of cultural superstructures, is the most appropriate form of resistance to capitalism in modern Western democracies. He states that the war of movement, which he identifies with strikes and other forms of class conflict on economic terrain, remains important but is subordinate to the war that takes place across the uneven cultural landscape of social space.

John Dos Passos's odyssey from communist fellow traveler to Cold War conservative remains one of the most compelling developments in twentieth-century American fiction. In *U.S.A.*, Dos Passos's representations of history and space reconfigure the paradigm of utopian naturalism in ways that help to explain the course of his political transformation.[5] Toward the conclusion of the trilogy, Dos Passos concedes, "[A]ll right we are two nations" (*Big* 413).[6] Also, in the fictional sections devoted to Ben Compton, one of his major characters, he quotes well-known excerpts from Marx and Engels's *The Communist Manifesto*, such as "The history of all hitherto existing societies is the history of class struggles" (*Nineteen* 369). According to Barbara Foley, statements such as these reflect a historical perspective that informs the entirety of Dos Passos's trilogy. Foley contends that Dos Passos was the foremost pioneer of the radical "collective novel" (425) and that critics denigrate "the extent to which [his] conception of historical contradiction is shaped by a Marxist notion of class struggle" (425). Foley concedes that Dos Passos did not ordinarily employ the terminology of class analysis, that his main protagonists were not heroic proletarians, and that his allegiance to the Communist Party was partial and occasional. Rather, Foley's argument rests on the nature of narrative unfolding in *U.S.A.*, which she believes to be that of a dialectical historical determination that overpowers individual wills. Discussing the conclusion of *The Big Money*, Foley writes, "The trilogy's movement towards closure is decisive. But narrative momentum derives more from the teleology of public events than from patterning internal to the fictional stories" (435). In many respects, Foley's argument is convincing. The public narrative of *U.S.A.*, as contained in the Newsreel sections, exerts a strong influence on the fictional tales. However, numerous factors in the novels complicate the credibility of the teleology of class struggle. Foley argues that much proletarian literature of the Depression era was written at a time when many believed a socialist revolution was imminent (viii), but there is very little sense in *U.S.A.* of excited anticipation regarding impending revolution. The issue of cultural mediation dominates the narrative and undermines any teleological or naturalist tendencies that characters may express. Dos Passos's negation of deterministic history in favor of cultural mediation is heavily indebted to the influence of Thorstein Veblen.[7] Yet Veblenian concepts do not account for the entirety of *U.S.A.*'s imagining of historical process. Reading *U.S.A.* in relation to Gramsci enables us to address a range of issues, such as the intersections of history, culture, nation, region, and language, that lie beyond the scope of Veblen's concerns.

An analysis of *U.S.A.*'s representation of labor activism highlights the relation between Dos Passos's and Gramsci's ideas of history. As has been suggested, Dos Passos shares Gramsci's rejection of the idea of a deterministic outcome to history. The failure of most forms of labor activism illustrates the absence of teleology in *U.S.A.* Like Gramsci, Dos Passos portrays trade unions as ineffective agents of historical transformation. For Gramsci, the centralized nature of trade unions means that they are divorced from the life of the working class (93). In his narrative of George Barrow, Dos Passos evokes unions in terms that share Gramsci's perspective. Dos Passos portrays Barrow as a demagogue of the American Federation of Labor. He represents labor in negotiations with business interests, but his immersion in the milieu of business separates him from those he represents. In *The 42nd Parallel*, he visits Mexico as part of negotiations that concern the oil industry. Barrow is a "mediat[or]" between labor and business (308). He works with J. Ward Moorehouse, who has established an advertising agency that is involved in "this new unexploited angle of the relations between labor and capital" (231). Moorehouse is therefore also a mediator, and the purpose of his work with Barrow is to nullify labor unrest. Barrow's wish to meet with "stable labor elements" in Mexico and his advocacy of the social democracy of the Second International are portrayed as betrayals of labor that result from an excess of mediation (279). When he meets Ben Evans, an itinerant American worker, Barrow describes him as "just the man this investigator [Moorehouse] would want to meet to get an actual working knowledge of conditions" (282). Rather than bringing his experiences with the working class to his negotiations with business, he seeks a token worker to facilitate Moorehouse's understanding of the oil industry in Mexico. The process of labor representation and transformation is inverted and thus subverted. In Gramsci's account, mediation via cultural hegemony is the process by which a historical bloc and historical transformation are pursued. Barrow's mediating activity is restricted to the economic sphere and does not engage with politics or culture. Also, he does not seek to mediate among different sectors of the working class. By stalling the process of history, his actions have the opposite effect of that articulated in Gramsci's theory of hegemonic preparation for revolution.

Dos Passos's representation of the Communist Party echoes much of his treatment of George Barrow and expresses Gramscian concerns. Throughout his writings, Gramsci defends the vanguardist role of the

Communist Party, yet at times he criticizes the party's centralized authority. He opposed the Comintern's policy of the United Front because he thought that national circumstances in Italy prohibited a combination of socialists and communists. Moreover, he described the policy of the United Front as an idealization that "has in no country found the party or the men capable of concretizing it" (126). A privileging of the will of the party over that of the working class leads, for Gramsci, to passivity, and he states that the structure and function of the party must never become absolute: "The truth is that historically a party is never definitive and never will be" (130). He also criticizes the internecine conflicts of the Communist Party in the Soviet Union. In these respects, Dos Passos's criticisms of the Communist Party share Gramsci's concerns. The narratives of Ben Compton, Don Stevens, and Mary French articulate key aspects of Dos Passos's critique of communism. At the time of the Soviet Revolution, Don states, "[W]e're on the edge of gigantic events," thus expressing the belief that communism is the motor of history (*Nineteen* 194). As a result of "Lenin and Trotsky's victories in Russia," Ben similarly claims, "[t]he tide's going to turn" in favor of American labor (*Big* 398). However, Dos Passos discredits these views by portraying the communists' adherence to "party discipline" as more of a mechanism for policing left-wing orthodoxy than an agent of historical change (*Big* 472). The expulsion of Ben Compton from their organization illustrates the self-destructiveness of the communists' notion of the fixed nature of the party. Also, Don Stevens's "defeatist" mentality" (*Big* 409), which results from the communists' failure to instigate a general strike in protest against the death sentences imposed upon Sacco and Vanzetti, reflects the party's inefficacy. Tactical inefficiency is also evident in Mary French's dealings with Ben Compton. He tells her about "how hard we'll have to work when we have soviets in America," but Mary thinks "they'd do better work if they didn't always try to do so many things at once" (*Big* 400). Mary's comments suggest that communist tactics lack specificity, but at other times she accords with the communist viewpoint. When Ben Compton is expelled from the party, she calls him "a stool pigeon as well as a disrupter" (*Big* 476). Because they combine a critique of communist tactics and an articulation of the policing function of communist party orthodoxy, Mary's experiences encapsulate Dos Passos's critique of the disjunctive qualities that he attributes to communism.

As already noted, Dos Passos's radical sympathies in *U.S.A.* are aligned with anarchists and syndicalists. Yet such sympathies are weakened by the introduction of pretensions to historical progress. Dos Passos's varying treatment of American syndicalism is most evident in the story of Mac. In *The 42nd Parallel*, a member of the Industrial Workers of the World (the Wobblies), Mac traverses the western United States and Mexico and becomes involved in Wobbly-organized labor activism. Despite the identification of Mac with the Wobblies, he is introduced to radical politics by a man named Bonello, one of several Italian anarchists in *U.S.A.* The anarchist core of Mac's radicalism asserts itself whenever he encounters the necessity of historical deferral. He goes to Goldfield, Nevada, to participate in a miners' strike. At a meeting that Mac attends, Big Bill Haywood, the famous Wobbly agitator, proclaims that "the day had come to start building a new society in the shell of the old and for the workers to get ready to assume control of the industries they'd created out of their sweat and blood" (92). While an enthusiastic anarchist, Mac has a sardonic response to Big Bill's words that reflects Dos Passos's inability to imagine the radical transformation of history. Mac tells Fred Hoff, a fellow Wobbly in Goldfield, that he intends to leave Goldfield for a while and get married. Hoff responds by saying, "A wobbly oughtn't to have any wife or children, not till after the revolution" (93). As well as being determined by personal circumstances, Mac's decision to leave Goldfield exemplifies an anarchist rejection of the authority of historical process. Through the continuation of Mac's narrative, Dos Passos expresses his attachment to Wobbly syndicalism. Yet syndicalism is most often affirmed when it is expressed in vague terms. Charley Anderson, one of the most important characters in the trilogy, dreams of Wobbly activism that would be "a big revolution like the American Revolution only bigger" (347). Charley's invocation of syndicalist revolution is evoked in the terms of national tradition that are of central concern to both Dos Passos and Gramsci. However, Charley's proclamation appears authoritative precisely because he is uninvolved in any practical opposition to capitalism. More specific forms of revolutionary syndicalism are usually met with criticism. For example, Ed Schuyler tells Dick Savage, another important character in *U.S.A.*, that "he had it on good authority the syndicates were going to seize the factories in Italy the first of May" (*Nineteen* 336). Dick rebuffs Ed's statement by saying that the end of World War I means the end of revolutionary fervor in Europe. Additionally, Dos Passos's representation of Grassi, an Italian anarchist who worked at "the big Fiat factories at Torino" (*42nd* 350), does not refer to the important role that the Fiat automobile plant played in the Factory Councils of 1920. Such an absence reveals Dos Passos's preference for the anarchist disdain for all types of historical process over the syndicalist program for the occupation of factories. Dos Passos holds the Wobblies in high regard, but he cannot embrace syndicalist-leaning projects such as the Factory Council movement that Gramsci advocated.

Dos Passos's aversion to representations of historical process is due to his awareness of the role of mediation in society. Like Gramsci, he realizes that class conflict is mediated through social practices and cultural institutions. But whereas Gramsci regards mediation as a means of establishing hegemony and preparing the way for revolution, Dos Passos portrays cultural mediation as a qualification of revolutionary progress. The representation of journalism in *U.S.A.* typifies Dos Passos's ideas about the relation between culture and revolution. Throughout the trilogy, journalistic activity is associated with labor struggles. For Gramsci, journalism is "the most dynamic part of th[e] ideological structure" of society (380). Because it is connected to many areas of society, journalism, for Gramsci, is a powerful force for establishing cultural hegemony and is one of the most significant elements of the war of position. Gramsci believes that "a spirit of scission" is required to turn journalism into an "integral" form that will enlarge public identification with the working class (381, 383). In contrast, Dos Passos opposes journalism to the establishment of radical hegemony. As a linotype operator, Mac often works for newspapers. Yet his employment at the *Los Angeles Times* and the *Mexican Herald* is linked to domestic comfort and a lack of radical activity. When Mac first arrives in Juarez, Mexico, he is told, "The situation is very confusing here. . . . Our townworkers are very organized and are classconscious, but the peons, the peasants, are easily misled by unscrupulous leaders" (*42nd* 113). In *U.S.A.*, as in Gramsci's discussion of the Southern Question, the main problem that radicals must solve is that of the relation between industrial workers and peasants. But rather than engendering the hegemony that could unite the lower classes, the *Mexican Herald* is portrayed as a potential target of revolutionary action. Elsewhere, Dos Passos depicts the journalistic war of position as a component of the war of movement. Denied its own sphere of operation, the journalistic war of position in these cases also fails to achieve cultural hegemony. During a strike in Pittsburgh, Mary French writes publicity and journalism for radical activists. She tries to persuade "metropolitan newspapermen" to publish stories that are not biased against the agitating workers, but her attempts do not succeed, and she realizes "that the highpaid workers weren't coming out and that the lowpaid workers were going to lose their strike" (*Big* 121, 122). As a manifestation of the war of movement, the strike creates an environment in which workers are brutally repressed and a historical bloc cannot be formed. When Mary becomes George Barrow's secretary, her journalistic work devolves into a form of mediation that has lost touch with the goals of radical activism. The highly repetitive work that Mary does for Barrow exemplifies the inability of such writing to advance the process of history.

In Dos Passos's representation of labor struggles and journalism, the movement of history is thwarted. Yet elsewhere in *U.S.A.* cultural mediation is a very effective mechanism for the advancement of capitalist interests. Much of Dos Passos's trilogy is concerned with the critique of a dynamic of history that is driven by forms of capitalist hegemony. In pursuing this critique, Dos Passos suggests that class struggle is blunted and undone by the existence of a third class that mediates between workers and owners. The harmful effects of this mediating class are expressed by Tim O'Hara, Mac's uncle, at the outset of *U.S.A.*: "And who gets the fruit of our labor, the goddam businessmen, agents, middlemen who never did a productive piece of work in their life" (*42nd* 13). Dos Passos's antipathy to certain types of mediation constitutes one of the two main ways in which his writing is influenced by Veblen.[8] Veblen consistently rails against sales, publicity, advertising, consultancy, and financing as the professions of a distinct class of "middlemen." One of the functions of this mediating class is to articulate values of consumption that disrupt binary class relations. For Veblen, "The motive that lies at the root of ownership is emulation," because, according to Veblen's anthropology, ownership began as the predatory seizure of goods for the purpose of proving superiority in the barbarian phase of culture (17). Further, Veblen states that consumer emulation is driven by the desire for leisure-class values. In accordance with these theories, Dos Passos portrays the status-driven practice of conspicuous consumption as being most vigorously pursued by the class of corporate financiers. In the biographical section on J. P. Morgan in *U.S.A.*, Dos Passos refers to Morgan's passion for antique objects and literary classics in "the original manuscript" (*Nineteen* 292). According to Veblen, a taste for handcrafted goods and original books is indicative of the emulation of leisure-class values (161–64). Similarly, Charley Anderson, the engineer turned financier, occupies a "[h]alf-timbered Tudor" house, which signifies the stockbroking class's identification with preindustrial aristocracy (*Big* 270). Conspicuous consumption is also an attribute of the other mediating professions. Moorehouse's success as a publicity agent is motivated by aristocratic emulation as well as the accumulation of wealth. He takes golf lessons, wears English clothes, and, most significantly, becomes highly conscious of the status connotations of cars. Moorehouse's interest in golf is telling because this sport affects the leisure-class rusticity and pastoralism that Veblen attributes to horse racing and lawn keeping (134, 142–44).[9] By showing how mediators on behalf of capital themselves succumb to capitalism's cultural charms, Dos Passos suggests that business interests are winning the war of position.[10]

Along with his critique of mediating professions, Veblen's consideration of the social role of engineers also influences Dos Passos's *U.S.A.* Because they understand the machine process of cause and effect, industrial engineers, according to Veblen, ought to be the guiding force of historical transformation. In Veblen's estimation, engineers constitute a counterclass that is opposed to publicity and sales figures and corporate financiers and that overcomes mediation-as-wastefulness by resorting to mediation-as-revolution (the engineers mediate between machine knowledge and the rest of the population). Dos Passos shares Veblen's respect for engineers, but in *U.S.A.* the engineers are neither a Veblenian revolutionary class nor the creative proletarian technicians that Gramsci observed in the Factory Councils. Rather, they succumb to the lure of the cultural hegemony that is sought by the mediators of capital. The narrative of Moorehouse exemplifies the ways in which industrial technology comes under the sway of capitalist mediation. In Pittsburgh, Moorehouse is responsible for making Bessemer products attractive to the public. His thoughts manipulate and distort technical details by turning them into elements of advertising and promotional rhetoric. Moorehouse's later role as mediator between the interests of labor and capital is simply an extension of his occupation as salesman, as he acts as a publicity agent for industrial concerns. The class of publicity agents to which Moorehouse belongs is related to that of the corporate financier or investment banker: the financier mediates between a parasitic class of wasteful and superfluous absentee industrial owners and a productive class of technologically knowledgeable industrial engineers. Dos Passos's most extended treatment of the financier is, of course, Charley Anderson in *The Big Money*. In Veblenian terms, the essence of Anderson's narrative is the transformation of a knowledgeable and productive engineer into a superfluous and wasteful financier. One of the key moments in this trajectory occurs when Anderson is fired from a car repair shop in New York and subsequently finds employment as a salesperson for a car dealership. From this moment, Anderson's ties to the hands-on world of machine knowledge become less and less substantial, and he devotes an increasing amount of time and energy to stockbroking rather than engineering interests. Anderson's transition from engineer to financier is most graphically illustrated in his dealings with Bill Cermak, his engineer. While Anderson indulges in an occasional, drunken, and sentimental identification with Cermak, his more entrenched conviction is that engineers and workers are subordinate in importance to management, investors, and absentee owners, and he justifies this belief by invoking an ideology of nationalism and, ironically, technological progress. Whereas the case of Moorehouse illustrates how business concerns manipulate technical knowledge, Anderson's narrative indicates that even the engineer can become the agent of corporate mediation.

The model of historical process that emerges from *U.S.A.* is one of cultural mediation. Dos Passos offers no support for naturalistic theories of history, and he makes no guarantees about the future. He bemoans the way in which mediating forces, such as the party and journalism, undermine the effectiveness of the activism of the working class. As in Gramsci's analysis, Dos Passos's awareness of the importance of cultural hegemony is matched by an attraction to unmediated forms of direct action. But unlike Gramsci, he believes that capitalist mediation is much more successful than its lower-class opposition. Dos Passos's treatment of history is embedded in his critical representation of social space. More precisely, the limitations of Dos Passos's imagining of historical transformation are due in part to the complexity and instability of social space in the trilogy. The spatiality of *U.S.A.* echoes Gramsci's conjunction of the specificities of nation and region with the uneven cultural terrain of civil society. There are significant differences between this model of spatiality and that of London and Sinclair. In the fiction of the latter authors, the localization of industrial power creates the possibility of alternative, utopian spaces that are free from the taint of industrial systems. In *U.S.A.*, industrial power is no longer completely localized. Instead, industrial decentralization, abetted by the increased significance of transportation and advertising, has made the locus of capitalist power hard to discern. Put differently, capitalism is realized through the contours of Gramscian civil society. In *U.S.A.*, the trends of decentralization and mobility threaten the possibility of utopian spaces. Where such rural idylls are evoked, they are usually places of danger and apoliticism, which are effects of the colonization of social space by transformations in transportation technology. But despite his discrediting of the possibility of an alternative, untainted, utopian space of political opposition, Dos Passos adheres to representations of spatial retreat. He continues to believe that values associated with the rural homestead are the means by which American society can be improved. However, this space is the site of decentralized Jeffersonian yeomanry rather than a socialist utopia. Dos Passos's many references to farms and phenomena such as Frank Lloyd Wright's plans for Broadacre City reflect the sustained importance of idealized spaces in *U.S.A.* While these spaces are not holistic utopias, they serve as inspirational supports for Dos Passos's attempt to salvage a progressive model of history from the domain of capitalist hegemony. In this respect, the basic spatiotemporal structure of the fiction of London and Sinclair is retained. Yet Dos Passos fails to attain a coherent coarticulation of radical history and spatiality, and his turn toward regressive and conservative forms of rural and national space in his later career is a mark of such failure.

Transportation is a key element of civil society in *U.S.A.* Through the exigencies imposed by transportation, the war of position in the trilogy becomes a literal war of movement. According to Gramsci, an emphasis on developments in transportation technology can lead to a misguided form of economic reductionism. For example, he criticizes writings that perceive "the social influence of the aeroplane" and "the subject of petroleum" (213, 214), two issues that are of great significance in *U.S.A.*, as evidence of the determining influence of the economic base. As suggested by his comments about the "problem [. . .] of the railwaymen" as a "national political problem" rather than a trade union issue (134), Gramsci assesses the significance of transportation in terms of the contours of social space not technological determinism. In the trilogy's opening and closing sequences, Dos Passos evokes the overarching importance of transportation in *U.S.A.* in these Gramscian terms. The introductory segment, entitled "U.S.A.," which Dos Passos wrote for the single-volume publication of the trilogy, corresponds with "Vag," the final section of *The Big Money.* This correspondence is not simply a retrospective attempt to impose unity on disparate material; rather, it directs the reader to elements that are prominent in virtually every section of the trilogy. In "U.S.A.," a young man, exhausted from physical labor, walks alone through the city streets. The streets are empty because all the other city dwellers are cocooned in technologies of transportation: streetcars, buses, trains, elevators. The only people he sees are prostitutes and winos, workers repairing transportation technology, and "two sallow windowdressers" (*U.S.A.* v), busily maintaining the vicarious consumer culture that will devastate labor solidarity as Dos Passos's trilogy proceeds. The young man's head is "swimming with wants" (*U.S.A.* v), suggesting that he too has fallen victim to the hegemonic phantasms of consumerism. At the conclusion of *U.S.A.*, this young man reappears as "Vag." Due to the developments in transportation technology that *U.S.A.* charts, Vag now inhabits a transformed geographical landscape. Instead of a city of streetcars and trains, Vag occupies a suburban space where the transportation networks of automobiles and airplanes dominate the terrain. The plane that drones overhead represents the dominant power network that connects cities together and bypasses the variegated rural landscape of the United States. The rural areas between the cities are Vag's domain and, Dos Passos intimates, the repository of those values that might possibly resist the dominance of "Power Superpower" (*Big* 464). Yet these technological developments have increased Vag's alienation and disenfranchisement. The "ads promised speed" (*Big* 493), but Vag is even more static now than at the outset of *U.S.A.* Where he was previously able to walk through the city streets, he is now fully immobile, a hitchhiker on the suburban highways; where the pedestrian was previously tolerated as a rightful urban inhabitant, the vagabond is now beaten, kicked, and driven to the outskirts of the city. Vag's head still swims, but this is no longer compensated for by the nourishing sound of urban speech, the "stories," "yarns," and "tales" that formerly reminded him of the succor of family solidarity (*U.S.A.* vi). Technologies of mobility, and the business interests and monopoly capitalism for which they are a sign throughout *U.S.A.*, have isolated lower-class individuals, depriving them of both the possibility of mass organization and the communal culture of storytelling.

Between these two vignettes, Dos Passos portrays geographical mobility as a compulsion that encompasses large-scale immigrant movements and individual displacements and threatens the possibility of ongoing, localized solidarities.[11] Gramsci states that humans "become conscious of their social position, and therefore of their tasks, on the terrain of ideologies" (196). In *U.S.A.*, the notion of the terrain of ideology is literalized. Characters such as Mac, Joe Williams, Charley Anderson, and Dick Savage are drawn into radical activity and then thrust from it by the exigencies of mobility. These movements affect the characters' ideological thoughts and thus are an essential component of the war of position that Dos Passos portrays. Despite the fact that he has considerable firsthand experience of how monopoly business interests thrive in wartime, Joe Williams has but a flimsy allegiance to labor solidarities. Joe's plight is a consequence of constant naval movements, which undermine protracted radical inquiry at the same time that they offer tangible evidence of how war stimulates certain trades in contravention of official political allegiances. Over time, the former tendency obliterates the latter, for Joe simply does not stand still long enough to develop a substantial radical sensibility. Following an altercation with a petty officer, Joe absconds from the U.S. Navy and joins the merchant navy. He is so disorientated by constant movement that even after working for a United Fruit Company vessel, his radicalism is dimmed rather than enlivened: on his journey from the Caribbean to Liverpool, Joe is oblivious to the larger forces of monopoly, trade, and war even as he facilitates them. The desire for self-improvement, which in Joe's case means the attaining of a second mate's license, fully replaces any radical thoughts he may have. Similarly, Charley Anderson's pursuit of the big money expels all traces of radical opinion, but the first, crucial stages in his descent from radicalism occur with reference to transportation motifs. Anderson joins Monte Davis in various Wobbly strikes, but as soon as a truck driver is going his way, he accepts the ride and abandons his IWW activities. Also, his adventures and education with Grassi are curtailed when the latter must take a boat to Argentina following the United States' entry into World War I. Through his repetitious characterization, Dos Passos suggests that relentless spatial movements prevent the formation of class blocs and promote ideologies of individualistic social mobility.

In his prison writings Gramsci defines "historically necessary" ideologies as those that "form the terrain on which men [sic] move" (199). Gramsci's interweaving of ideological and spatial concepts suggests that the working class's realization of its "historically necessary" ideology is inseparable from the formation of social space. At several points in *U.S.A.*, radicals attempt to form spaces of ideological realization. However, these spaces are vulnerable to attack by "Power Superpower." The "anarchist picnic" in Camera Eye (41) is described as "a nice afternoon we sat on the grass and looked around le geste prolétaire" (*Nineteen* 365). As a moment of radical solidarity, the anarchist picnic is flawed because it is evoked as an ineffective riposte to the might of industrial technology and the power of journalistic hegemony: "But God damn it they've got all the machineguns in the world all the printingpresses linotype tickerribbon curling iron plushhorses Ritz and we you I? barehands a few songs not very good songs plûtot le geste prolétaire" (365). The radicals in this scene succeed in forming a terrain upon which their ideological views can be expressed in cultural form. However, these cultural expressions fail to establish the hegemony that is necessary for a historical bloc, and they are reduced to nothing but proletarian gestures. In the war of position between the forces of capital and labor, the culture of capitalism is dominant and isolates radical opposition in its ideological terrain. Following this scene, the spatial dispersals effected by technologies of transportation undermine the possibility of the formation of ideological spaces. The Wobblies' attempts to create spaces of ideological opposition are especially susceptible to violent assault. Along with a group of Wobblies, whose headquarters are "like a picnic ground," Ben Compton is driven "[o]ut in the woods where the country road crossed the railroad track" (382). In this pastoral setting, Compton and his associates are beaten up by a sheriff and his deputies. Throughout the scene, the harmful presence of railroad technology is affirmed, as when, for example, Compton "tripped on a rail and fell, cutting his arm on something sharp" (383). This scene is quite obviously no anarchist picnic, and neither is the scenario of the biographical section on Wesley Everest. The Wobblies "said the forests ought to belong to the whole people" (399). But rather than being the utopian setting of radical principles, the woods are where Everest is chased and caught by a gang of Centralia employers before being castrated and hanged. Like the Wobblies, Mac, and Vag, Everest is a nomadic pedestrian. That the employers take him to his execution in a "limousine" indicates the importance of transportational control in the destruction of oppositional ideological terrain (402).

As well as subverting oppositional space, capitalist power produces its own spaces of ideology and culture. Sites that might appear as utopian retreats in U.S.A. are revealed to be gardens of power. Dos Passos's critique of utopian idylls is consistent with Gramsci's views. Gramsci describes the revolutionary will as "an impulse acting in a straight line towards the maximum destination, without jaunts into the green meadows on the wayside to drink a glass of cordial fraternity, softened by the greenery and by tender declarations of respect and love" (39). Like Gramsci, Dos Passos regards self-enclosed rusticity as being antithetical to revolutionary activity. At Port of Spain, Joe Williams and Warner Jones visit the Blue Pool, an apparently idyllic retreat that reminds Joe of a happy outing in the country he once took with his sister. Joe seeks a place to swim and observe monkeys, but he finds instead a scene of colonial and aristocratic power upon which he dare not intrude. In this scene, the forces that are hostile to labor enact their ideological and cultural norms in seemingly utopian space. The process by which the idyllic retreat undermines radical activism is suggested by Dick Savage's wartime experiences. As he proceeds by ambulance across the continent, Dick comes across several rural escapes: the garden at Récicourt, the Argonne woods, and Italian scenery. In each setting Dick becomes indolent, and his sense of aesthetic pleasure is aroused. Drunk on nature and architecture, Dick's radical thoughts wither away. When he meets a group of sailors who complain that the war is corrupt, Dick does not respond; whenever he does consider such views, his thoughts immediately turn to the beauty of his immediate surroundings: "He didn't give a damn about anything any more. It was sunny, vermouth was a great drink, the towns and toy churches on the tops of hills and the vineyards and the cypresses and the blue sea were like a succession of backdrops for an old fashioned opera" (*Nineteen* 168). Dick continues to express radical opinions. However, his thoughts are couched as a fantasy of escape that is disconnected from the realities of social space. For example, he has "a daydream of himself living in a sunscorched Spanish town, sending out flaming poems and manifestoes, calling young men to revolt against their butchers, poems that would be published by secret presses all over the world." While these reflections imagine the spatial basis of radical cultural expression, they prevent Dick from observing "the suburbs of Paris or the bluegreen summer farmlands sliding by" (181). The dream of revolutionary poetry does not qualify Dick's capitulation to the hegemony of bourgeois culture, which is assured by moments of aestheticism and nostalgia. Rather than being spaces where the radical community can be strengthened, idylls such as the Blue Pool and Dick Savage's retreats are places of distraction and inactivity. They generate a cultural hegemony that is opposed to the interests of labor. They are nostalgic, not revolutionary.

Dos Passos's treatment of rural space is not limited to his critique of pastoral idylls. The numerous farms in *U.S.A.* are sites of hegemonic contestation. Whereas the pastoral idyll is cut off from social space and thus cannot form the basis of radical cultural hegemony, the farm is linked to labor and industry in ways that suggest the possible generation of an oppositional historical bloc. The farm therefore becomes a potential means by which the union of industry and agriculture, an issue that concerns Dos Passos as much as Gramsci, can be forged. Dos Passos is interested in the farm as a source of cultural and technological meanings that might produce hegemonic groupings in the war of position against capital. Through the trilogy's biographical portraits, Dos Passos analyzes the various ameliorative possibilities suggested by the spatial model of the farm. Dos Passos claims that William Jennings Bryan "charmed the mortgageridden farmers of the great plains" by citing farmers, along with miners, as the embodiment of the working class (*42nd* 154). Bryan therefore succeeds in effecting the historical bloc of industrial and agricultural workers. According to Denning, Dos Passos's concern with technicians and technology is realized at the expense of rural space (177–78). However, Dos Passos attempts to imagine the conjunction of farming and technology as a means of attaining both cultural hegemony and the political unity intimated in the biography of Bryan. Dos Passos's most successful attempt to depict such a cultural force occurs in his biography of Frank Lloyd Wright. After mentioning that Wright's youth was spent in a midwestern farming community, Dos Passos describes his architectural projects, such as the unrealized Broadacre City, as attempts to overcome the "Near and Far," the city and the countryside, through the incorporation of technologies within midwestern prairies. Wright is a Veblenian hero, respectful of the possibilities of technology and machine knowledge and busy "projecting constructions in the American future instead of the European past." In Dos Passos's account, Wright "preaches to the young men coming of age in the time of oppression, cooped up by the plasterboard partitions of finance routine, their lives and plans made poor by feudal levies of parasite money standing astride every process to shake down progress for the cutting of coupons" (*Big* 387, 385). Dos Passos evokes the culture of Wright's architecture and spatial plans as a foundation upon which the rural and urban masses can unite and drive progressive history forward.

However, the coarticulation of rural and technological elements that we see in "Architect" breaks down at other points in *U.S.A.* In "The Campers at Kitty Hawk," the Wright brothers' inaugural airplane flight is evoked as a victory for rural ingenuity, which precedes the appropriation of this transportation technology by "Power Superpower." Similarly, technology and farming are at odds with one another in the biography of Veblen. Veblen's childhood laziness and hostility to farm work are a liability on his parents' midwestern farm. Veblen leaves the family farm, which is threatened by "parasite businessmen" and the need to keep up with technological innovations (*Big* 87). He vaunts the dissemination of the impersonality of the machine, but his ideas fail to attain hegemony over workers or engineers. As Dos Passos notes, Veblen retired at the end of his life to a rural setting in the hills of California. Here, rural space is portrayed as an insular alternative to Veblen's unsuccessful program of technological hegemony. Dos Passos's biography of Henry Ford shares many features with that of Veblen. Ford is raised on a midwestern farm, and while he is happy to tinker with farm machinery, he loathes farm labor. After leaving his father's farm, Ford pursues the goal of industrial efficiency, makes "his fortune by bringing the city out to the farm" (*Big* 46), and returns to the farm in his twilight years. However, there is a fundamental difference between "Tin Lizzie" and "The Bitter Drink." Whereas Veblen advocates mechanical efficiency in order to disseminate the instinct of workmanship, Ford does so to maximize investors' profits; whereas Veblen's spatial retreat is an attempt to escape the business system, Ford's return to the farm is an expression of the success of that system. Ford's reconstruction of his father's farm is an expression of nostalgia and aristocratic leisure values, where even "the old bad road" is rebuilt "so that everything might be / the way it used to be, / in the days of horses and buggies" (*Big* 49). In his writings on "Americanism and Fordism," Gramsci insists that the success of Ford's industrial system relies on the regulation of workers' behavior via the establishment of cultural hegemony. Dos Passos's narration of Ford's success also stresses the importance of cultural attributes. But, unlike Gramsci, Dos Passos is primarily concerned with the way in which Ford's cultural interests reflect a powerful construction of the meaning of rural space. Ford redefines the farm and its relation to

industrial technology and urban space in terms of reactionary, hierarchical, and individualistic values. By attaining cultural hegemony,
Ford's ideals negate the possibility of a historical bloc of workers
in town and country that, for Dos Passos, both Wright and Veblen
advocate. Doc Bingham's description of himself as being "born and
raised on the farm of plain Godfearing farming folk" illustrates the
success of Ford's cultural perspective (*Big* 442). Rather than being the
locus of labor solidarity, the farm is associated by advertisers with
conservative individualism.

As we have seen, oppositional models of history and space are consistently subverted by the war of position that takes place in *U.S.A.*
However, at the end of the trilogy, Dos Passos evokes a triumphant
vision of *national* spatiality that is coupled with a hopeful appeal to
historical transformation through *linguistic* renewal. Both concepts
are related to Gramscian concerns. Gramsci insists on the national nature of revolutionary movements and derides any formulation, such
as Trotsky's theory of permanent revolution, that is not based on national characteristics. Also, Gramsci equates "the fact of 'language' "
with culture and suggests that the quest for historical change through
cultural hegemony must also foster a "national-popular" language
(347, 345). Dos Passos's attempt to imbue American national space
with radical cultural meanings takes the form of a nostalgic return to
the rhetoric upon which he claims the United States was founded.[12]
In one of the final Camera Eye sections, a narrator wanders around
Plymouth harbor and envisions the pastoral space dreamt of by radical seventeenth-century Pilgrims: "[T]his is where the immigrants
landed the roundheads the sackers of castles the kingkillers haters of
oppressions this is where they stood in a cluster after landing from the
crowded ship that stank of bilge on the beach that belonged to no one
between the ocean that belonged to no one and the enormous forest
that belonged to no one that stretched over the hills where the deer-
tracks were up the green rivervalleys where the redskins grew their
tall corn in patches forever into the incredible west" (*Big* 390). Dos
Passos's thoughts are occasioned by the trial of Sacco and Vanzetti.
While the Italian anarchists sought "a world unfenced" (390), powerful interests in the United States are described as "strangers who have
bought the laws and fenced off the meadows and cut down the woods

for pulp and turned our pleasant cities into slums and sweated the wealth out of our people" (414). Through such contrasts, Sacco and Vanzetti are presented as true and archetypal Americans. They are also the vehicles for Dos Passos's appeal to linguistic renewal. They speak "the old words the immigrant haters of oppression brought to Plymouth" and are therefore examples of how to "rebuild the ruined words worn slimy in the mouths of lawyers districtattorneys collegepresidents judges" (391). Sacco and Vanzetti are "the men in the deathhouse [who] made the old words new before they died" (414), and thus they exemplify the negation of Doc Bingham's construction of farming values. The generation of a language that is linked to national space and cultural mediation constitutes *U.S.A.*'s most optimistic representation of historical transformation.[13] However, the language of renewal to which Dos Passos appeals does not derive from popular culture and thus does not fully conform to Gramsci's definition of the national-popular.[14] Also, Dos Passos's primarily cultural view of historical change lacks the certainty of the naturalism of London and Sinclair. Since Dos Passos's articulation of the transformative possibilities of language emerges from his representation of American national space, the notion of spatiality has a more integral role in *U.S.A.* than is true of the novels of London and Sinclair. At the same time, the nostalgic aspects of Dos Passos's appeal to national space and language express reactionary tendencies that become more prominent in his later writings.

Josephine Herbst's Trexler trilogy represents many of the social and political contexts and issues that are featured in *U.S.A.* Herbst dramatizes the struggles between capital and labor and fictionalizes the ideas and strategies of anarchists, Wobblies, and communists. Herbst's portrayals of industrial strife are subsumed by the narrative of the fortunes of the Trexler family, which extends from the post–Civil War era to the late 1930s. The familial emphasis of the narrative results in a portrayal of history and critical space that deviates from Dos Passos's concerns. The fictional narratives of *U.S.A.* lack psychological depth and emotional intensity. Dos Passos's method of characterization means that there is a dearth of revolutionary ardor among the characters who struggle against capital. Dos Passos is therefore unable to call upon the political enthusiasm of his characters in the wake of his critique of models of radical history. As a result, his reconstruction of a viable model of historical transformation turns away from working-class agitation and embraces the role of national language in the production of hegemony. In contrast, Herbst portrays the familial and personal experiences of her characters as the source of their political commitment. According to Gramsci, the formation of a national historical bloc requires the "[p]assage from knowing to understanding and to feeling and vice versa from feeling to understanding and to knowing" (349). Dos Passos's critique of history is based on intellectual "knowing" but does not undertake the passage to "feeling." Herbst articulates a more extensive critique of models of history than Dos Passos, but in her case the "knowing" critique derives from a sense of "feeling" that is constantly reasserted. Whereas Dos Passos's analysis leads to an alternative construction of history, Herbst's continual return to characters' "feeling" does not result in the promotion of a definitive idea of history. Both authors are interested in the possibility of Gramscian cultural hegemony, but Dos Passos, more so than Herbst, quickly seeks to stabilize cultural hegemony within a large-scale model of historical transformation.

In comparison with *U.S.A.*, Herbst's Trexler trilogy is less committed to the reconstruction of a singular model of history and more committed to the importance of critical spatiality. Dos Passos's emphasis on national space is replaced by Herbst with a prioritization of domestic space. The search for a form of spatiality that is conducive to radical activism occurs throughout *U.S.A.* and is only fulfilled in the final moments of the trilogy. Conversely, the significance of domestic space is asserted at the outset of *Pity Is Not Enough* and has a powerful influence on radical sensibilities in all three volumes of the trilogy. Speaking of the characters of Vicky and Rosamond Wendel, two of the most significant characters in the latter two novels of the trilogy, Laura Browder states, "The domestic sphere becomes a site for the Wendel girls' political education" (104). As Browder suggests, domestic space has a particularly important role to play in the politicization of female characters. However, domestic space also produces, sustains, and renews the political commitment of these and other characters.[15] The oral and popular culture of the domestic sphere is a central factor in this process of politicization. Herbst's treatment of the culture of domestic space is one of the most significant ways in which her relation to Gramsci's writing differs from that of Dos Passos. The conclusion of *U.S.A.* identifies Sacco and Vanzetti with Gramscian national language, but the Trexler trilogy is steeped in references to popular culture. Put differently, Dos Passos emphasizes the national component and Herbst the popular aspect of Gramsci's conception of national-popular culture. Gramsci describes popular culture as a reflection of the tastes and preoccupations of the social masses. His reflections on popular culture are informed by his theorization of "common sense" as the "folklore" of philosophy (343). The formation of a cultural and political historical bloc must, for Gramsci, take as its "starting point what the student already knows and his [sic] philosophical experience (having first demonstrated to him precisely that he has such an experience, that he is a 'philosopher' without knowing it)" (347). Gramsci states that such philosophical common sense is "absorbed by the various social and cultural environments in which the moral individuality of the average man [sic] is developed" (343). In other words, common sense is closely identified with particular types of social space. Herbst shares Gramsci's view of popular culture that is localized in particular social space as the "starting point" of radical activism. Most insistently, Herbst suggests the popular culture of domestic space is essential to the production of a radical sensibility among her characters. However, unlike Gramsci, Herbst does not develop elements of popular culture and common sense into a vanguardist form of cultural mediation that can achieve widespread hegemony and a historical bloc. The absence of large-scale cultural mediation exemplifies Herbst's reluctance to endorse any particular theory of historical change.[16]

In *Pity Is Not Enough*, the first novel of the Trexler trilogy, Herbst narrates the story of Joe Trexler, Anne Wendel's brother. Joe goes to the South after the Civil War and becomes involved in political and economic scandal. Joe makes money through railroad fraud in which local government is implicated. He sends money home to his sisters and mother in Pennsylvania; they idolize him and never completely accept the extent of his corrupt financial dealings. Much of the narrative of the novel concerns the relationship between the public sphere inhabited by Joe and the domestic sphere of the Trexler women. Through Joe's political involvements, Herbst establishes a critique of capitalist democracy as a historical mechanism. Herbst portrays how Democrats and Republicans work together to maintain corrupt systems of power that indulge in deals such as buying senators and voters. Rather than a historical system of social improvement, politics is a charade of vested interests. When the railroad speculation fraud is exposed and Joe is arrested, he discovers that his "position [is] exactly nowhere" and that "[b]oth sides" in the legal case construct him in derogatory terms (92, 97). After the case, all parties, with the exception of Joe, resume their previous political positions. Rather than a dialectical interaction between democratic parties, history is shown to be the repetition of a venal status quo. Earlier, Joe had confidence in the new history inaugurated by the war, but his loss of money and position makes postwar history appear as a "terrible time" without "cause" or "name" (105, 106). Joe's experiences cause him to despair of history. He continues to seek his fortune in the gold mines of South Dakota and on occasion appeals to Social Darwinist reasoning, but it is more usual for him to experience the disorientation that he feels when the railroad scandal bursts. His opposition to the naturalist theories of Darwin that interest his sister Anne and brother Aaron and his lack of comprehension about miners' attempts to engage in class struggle evidence his extensive abandonment of historical models. Along with Joe's descent into madness, the title of the novel and the repetitious use of "pity" to describe characters' weak responses to misfortune suggest the need for a robust historical consciousness. Yet the only models of history that we see in the novel are those associated with capitalism, democracy, and Social Darwinism. Herbst criticizes all these notions and therefore leaves her appeal to history without substance. The absence of positive historical representation in the novel reflects Herbst's hesitancy about its viability.

Herbst's representation of critical space in *Pity Is Not Enough* is more substantial than her representation of history. However, the emergence of a form of domestic space that can facilitate radical activism occurs gradually throughout the novel. At the outset of the text, the oral narration of family history that Anne Wendel gives to her daughters establishes the importance of the culture of domestic space. In this scene Anne tells her daughters the story of poor Joe as the family awaits the passing of a cyclone warning in the basement of their Iowa home. Gramsci recognizes the power of oral culture, but he associates it with an excessively "operatic" sentimentality (373), and he states that the need for "a check upon the loose expository manner of oratory reappears as soon as one raises the fundamental problem of creating a new culture on a new social base" (377). Herbst intimates a similar critique of Anne's oral narrative because she portrays domestic family space as a form of cultural retreat in the midst of the cyclone of capitalism. The absence of positive historical models in *Pity Is Not Enough* is therefore complemented at times by a utopian tendency that is at odds with Gramscian notions of the political consequences of cultural space. Also, the housing scheme in which Aaron, Anne's brother, is involved suggests the conjunction of utopian space with the naturalist understanding of history that Herbst criticizes. Herbst communicates this conjunction through her description of Flemmer, Aaron's partner, as "a man of means who had lived abroad and had mixedup ideas about the Renaissance and Darwin and the origin of species and town planning and immigrant labor" (77). Herbst's critique of the link between utopianism and domesticity is further exemplified by Anne's experience. The Trexler family moves into a house in Grapeville, New Jersey, that was built by a Mrs. Ferrol, who utopianistically named the house El Dorado. While she is in Philadelphia, Anne yearns to return to the utopian home in Grapeville. Anne's thoughts are presented as a wish to retreat from the public world into a restricted domestic environment of stereotypical gender roles: "Sometimes lately she had no desire to go to Sunday school and stayed at home instead cutting out clippings from papers about duty and the home and womanly women and she found it hard to keep her mind on these things that had nothing to do with the life that was secretly going on around her" (150). As exemplified by Anne's reactionary comments, domesticity is often portrayed as a spatial adjunct to notions of capitalist development. (For example, comments made by Mem, Anne and Joe's mother, about the importance of buying a house reflect a capitalist desire for property.) Yet Anne's experience of the home also inaugurates the trilogy's representation of domestic space as a factor in the war of position against capital. Anne is strongly identified with domestic space and must stay at home while other family members are away. Her frustration with her domestic life enables her to sympathize with striking workers. It is at this point in the narrative that the radical possibilities of domestic space begin to unfold.

Yet there are numerous obstacles to the emergence of domestic space as a source of radical hegemony in *Pity Is Not Enough*. Through the experiences of Joe, Herbst narrates how involvement in the public sphere weakens the connection to domestic space and thus retards the formation of radical political consciousness. Joe is known as "poor Joe" because he dies in poverty and insanity, and Herbst suggests that the vulnerability of Joe's character is due to his loss of connection to domestic culture. When he is first in the South, Joe writes to his sister Catherine about the importance of art and music. However, Mem notices that the quality of Joe's handwriting declines, which reflects a decrease in both Joe's bond with home and his interest in culture. After the death of Nannie Ellis, the young niece of one of his associates, Joe attempts to write poetry, "[b]ut dollar signs got tangled up with the birds on his paper" (55). The confusion of domestic space and financial ambition is also evident in his relationship with Lucy Blondell. Joe thinks, "[F]ortunes were like continents in Columbus's day, just waiting to be discovered. [. . .] The talk about continents got all mixed up in his mind with Lucy [. . .] and before he knew, he'd blurted out that she must marry him" (61). As this event illustrates, Joe adheres to spatial ideas of economic advancement that are in conflict with domestic meanings. That Joe's preoccupation with obtaining capital causes him to become impatient with Catherine's letters on the details of home life suggests how economic concerns succeed in displacing Joe's interest in domestic culture. When he loses his money and status, he turns to spatial ideas, but these are disconnected from domestic culture. He has nostalgic and sentimental ideas about childhood but not an active engagement with family members through domestic culture. Also, his spatial ideas are identified with empirical landscapes rather than social relations, and they remain imbued with connotations of capitalist success. His desire to seek his fortune in the gold mines of the west, for example, is articulated through images of the American landscape and new urban developments. Also, his failure to invest in the successful Homestake Mine is a metaphor for the break with domesticity that informs his use of spatial language.

The development of domestic culture in Herbst's novel also occurs through characters other than Joe. The difficulty and importance of nourishing domestic culture is expressed through the character of Catherine, Anne's sister. Catherine is the most bookish member of the family, and she "fe[els] the full burden of the family on her shoulders, not the financial but the moral burden, to keep the girls interested in their music [. . .] and to keep them all going with bright thoughts about the future" (144). As in Gramsci's writings, cultural development is described by Herbst as a moral imperative. When Catherine dies at a young age, it is left to Anne to shoulder the moral burden of the family and establish the domestic space that will inspire progress toward the future. As well as exhibiting a reactionary attitude toward the home, Anne displays an appreciation of domestic culture. In her time with Mrs. Ferrol at Grapeville, she reads poetry, plays music, and begins to understand domesticity in terms of cultural expression rather than the undertaking of chores assigned to women. As she tells her daughters about these experiences, she is fully aware that she is passing on an invaluable cultural resource. Herbst's references to poetry and music echo Gramsci's belief in "a modern 'humanism' able to reach right to the simplest and most uneducated classes" (369). If Dos Passos articulates the importance of technical development as described by Gramsci, Herbst expresses Gramsci's interest in humanistic education. The combination of textual and oral elements that we see in Anne's recounting of her Grapeville experience to her daughters illustrates the tempered orality that Gramsci posits in his discussion of popular culture. Herbst also suggests the importance of other forms of material culture. Anne has numerous "treasures" or "knickknacks" that preserve family memories and become pedagogical resources for future generations (179, 188). Toward the end of the novel, Herbst brings together different aspects of domestic culture to suggest their political significance. As mine superintendent, Joe is perturbed by the labor unrest caused by the trial of the Haymarket anarchists in Chicago. Yet as he reads the newspaper account of the trial, he realizes the truth of the anarchists' words and accords more value to everyday domestic life than economic aspiration. Herbst therefore connects domestic space with anarchist politics. Further, she suggests that Joe's neglect of the domestic sphere prevents him from developing his sympathy for the anarchists into a more substantial political awareness. Anne saves the newspaper story as part of her trove of keepsakes. Years later, Vicky and Rosamond read this account of the Haymarket anarchists, and their commitment to radical activism is strengthened by "the words of the dead men that leaped at them alive and vigorous" (289). As noted above, Gramsci stresses that journalism is a powerful agent in the war of position. In Herbst's novel, journalism has the effect noted by Gramsci once it is appropriated as a form of domestic material and textual culture.

The concluding events of *Pity Is Not Enough* are replicated and extended in the subsequent novels of the Trexler trilogy. The engagement with radical politics that is evident in the experiences of Joe, Vicky, and Rosamond pervades the narratives of *The Executioner Waits* and *Rope of Gold*. The greater prevalence of political struggle in the later novels reflects an enhanced engagement with representations of history. More precisely, Herbst increasingly portrays a variety of forms taken by ideas of history. The variegated representation of history in the Trexler trilogy enables us to assess further Herbst's relation to Gramsci in this area. In his comments on Lenin and utopia, Gramsci makes an especially vigorous critique of deterministic models of history. Speaking of the links between the economic base and political superstructures, he writes: "The unraveling of the causation is a complex and involved process. To disentangle it requires nothing short of a profound and wide-ranging study of every intellectual and practical activity." He then states, "In a proletarian revolution, the unknown variable 'humanity' is more mysterious than in any other event" (45, 46). According to Gramsci, the complex mediations that occur across the sectors of social space mean that the process of historical transformation is "mysterious" and virtually unknowable. The multiplicitous nature of the representation of history in the Trexler trilogy suggests that Herbst, like Gramsci, regards history as a complex process of mediation that is irreducible to any single form. At the same time, Herbst offers a critique of ideas of history and refuses to completely embrace any one of them. Herbst's critical awareness of multiple forms of causality accounts for the absence in the Trexler trilogy of the proclamation of a singular idea of history that we see in *U.S.A.* Moreover, Herbst's lack of attachment to any single model of history serves to maintain radical commitments. For Herbst, the ossification of radical tendencies into fixed ideas of history undermines the effectiveness of the struggle against capital. The issue of multiplicity also informs Herbst's representation of spatiality in *The Executioner Waits* and *Rope of Gold*. Herbst continues to suggest that political sensibilities derive from and are in dialogue with domestic cultural practices. However, the importance of rural space increases in the last two novels of the trilogy. As in *U.S.A.*, the struggle among contending meanings of rural and domestic space is central to the issue of cultural hegemony in Herbst's writing. The multiplicity that is associated with history and space itself reflects a spatial emphasis and demonstrates that Herbst's prioritization of representations of spatiality is stronger than that of Dos Passos. Also, Herbst's open-ended approach to questions of history and space prevents her from succumbing to the conservatism of Dos Passos's later career.

In *The Executioner Waits*, radical politics are centered upon the IWW. As Robert Shulman notes, the Wobblies serve the role of "grass-roots radicalism" and "militant alternative" that is played by the Haymarket anarchists in *Pity Is Not Enough* (106). For Herbst, the Wobblies are significant because they assert the Gramscian subjective will of the working class. Through her representation of the Wobblies, she therefore accords with the positive view of spontaneism and syndicalism that is articulated by Dos Passos and Gramsci. However, Herbst's perspective on the Wobblies differs from that of Dos Passos. Whereas Dos Passos values the disposition of the Wobblies but veers away from depictions of their industrial action, Herbst sympathizes but does not wholly identify with such activism. The movement from the peripheral significance of the Haymarket anarchists in *Pity Is Not Enough* to the centrality of the IWW in *The Executioner Waits* reflects Herbst's growing concern with the politics of history.[17] The radicalism of Vicky and Rosamond is nurtured by and focused upon Wobbly politics. Vicky in particular is attracted to the Wobbly tactics of direct action, and she is impatient with fund-raising activities and legal analyses of property and crime. They befriend George Gates, a formerly imprisoned Wobbly who is out on bail and who is identified with the model of historical success from which the novel's title is taken: "The Executioner waits at the door" (229). Yet Gates's apocalyptic vision of historical victory is not an articulation of historical process, and Herbst is more interested in portraying the realization of domestic cultural hegemony than validating the Wobbly theory of history. Vicky gets to know Gates because he hides in the apartment in which she lives. It is therefore the restricted domestic environment that develops Vicky's radical commitment.

Most notably through the figure of Joe Hill, the Wobblies are often associated with music and expressive culture. In *The Executioner Waits*, the power of Wobbly culture is incarnated in Ed Bates, the brother of a co-worker of Vicky and Rosamond's father. At his brother's home, Ed sings the Wobbly songs; Vicky and Rosamond are moved and inspired, and they join in with the singing. When she writes to her husband, Jerry Stauffer, Rosamond thinks of the encounter with Ed: "The songs kept repeating themselves and her pen almost swung to a kind of remembered rhythm." By giving her a vision of "[a] new world to come," the songs enable the Wobblies' historical optimism to become hegemonic. The interplay of Wobbly activism and domestic space is further exemplified by the fact that "[o]nly Ed and a street full of Wobblies singing" can eradicate Vicky's unhappy memories of her childhood past (140, 142). In this instance the future-oriented Wobbly culture that is expressed in domestic space displaces cultural memories that are painful to Vicky. At the same time, the appearance of the Wobblies in Oxtail constitutes a "crisis" in the town's "history" (109). The realization of cultural hegemony among Vicky and Rosamond is Herbst's main concern, but she does not deny the Wobblies' explicit struggle for historical transformation.

The spatial multiplicity of *The Executioner Waits* is expressed through the struggle for the meaning of domesticity. According to Gramsci, social conflicts take place "on a higher plane than the immediate world of the economy" and pertain to issues of "class 'prestige' " and "an inflammation of sentiments of independence, autonomy, and power" (208). The conflicting meanings of domesticity in Herbst's writing reflect a battle for cultural hegemony that touches on these Gramscian issues. Similar to Dos Passos's portrayal of rural space,

Herbst's narrative is keenly aware of the importance of the struggle for the hegemonic meaning of domestic space, and she suggests that radical and conservative ideas of domestic space are often difficult to distinguish. Yet Herbst's treatment of the contestation of spatial meaning is more complex than that of Dos Passos, which again suggests that the analysis of spatiality is more central in the Trexler trilogy than in *U.S.A.* Since, for Herbst, spatial experience is the source of radical convictions and historical involvements, the spatial multiplicity that she describes threatens the emergence of political consciousness. The world of capital is more organized and integrated than the buccaneering entrepreneurship of *Pity Is Not Enough*, and one of the effects of this development is the need for business interests to identify with ideas of domesticity that support their financial activities. Domesticity is therefore a means by which familial bourgeois prestige and independence is asserted. David Trexler, Anne's entrepreneurial brother, espouses "home influences" and regards family property as the natural conjunction of business and domestic attachments (4). Yet the fact that David often does not feel at home suggests that his domestic allegiances are far less substantial than his economic views. David's comments on the importance of obtaining capital for business centralization provide evidence of his more heartfelt spatial concerns. Abel Chance, the father of Jonathan Chance, Vicky's husband, similarly embodies the capitalist denial of domesticity. He creates a stifling domestic atmosphere from which Jonathan constantly seeks refuge; he also gives Jonathan and Vicky money as long as they spend it on business ventures rather than their home.

The examples of David Trexler and Abel Chance highlight the business world's contradictory relation to domesticity: on the one hand, business tries to colonize the significance of domesticity on the "higher plane" of culture; on the other hand, these characters are interested solely in economic profit. As exemplified by the experience of Nancy and Clara, Vicky and Rosamond's sisters, women undertake the struggle to appropriate domesticity as a sign of business power. Nancy and Clara uphold a sustained commitment to domesticity that is based on conventional social norms associated with religion and marriage, which act in tandem with business interests to oppose radical activism. Through her description of Clara's dream of a domestic life that will unfold "in the nice pleasant way that she had dreamed it should go" (110), Herbst criticizes the notion of utopian domestic space. That both Nancy and Vicky create family albums indicates the similarity between different versions of domestic spatiality, yet whereas Nancy has a "Memory Book" (41), Vicky seeks inspiration for the future from family mementos. For much of *The Executioner Waits*, Vicky and Rosamond are paired in opposition to their sisters. However, Rosamond succumbs to nostalgic feelings about the Trexler home in Oxtail because she and her husband Jerry Stauffer are "never at home" (182). Also, she seeks such a refuge as an escape from labor debates. In Gramsci's terms, she fails to associate domestic space with the prestige of the working class. Because radical conceptions of domestic space do not achieve hegemony in Rosamond's experience, she lacks cultural support for her political views and thus retreats from activism.

Unlike these other characters, Vicky and Jonathan's domestic experiences nurture their political involvement. Their ongoing support for the Wobblies is associated with their creation of a home in Iowa, which is often described as an island apart from the other forces they confront. The time that Jonathan spends at the working-class homes of the Krauses and Schultzes solidifies his identification with labor, and his possession of family letters and inheritance of his grandfather's unorthodox characteristics suggests that his behaviors are an extension of family attributes. Yet Herbst introduces nuances into Jonathan's character that intimate the limitations of domestic influence. Jonathan is consistently attracted to modernist literary culture. Toward the end of the novel, when Jonathan realizes that the Wobblies are doomed and looks elsewhere for signs of radicalism, he still cites Joyce and Proust as authorities on the progress of modern society. Jonathan's interest in literary culture suggests a departure from the cultural function of domestic space. His experience also connects in various ways to Gramsci's writing. While initially supportive of the revolutionary possibilities of the new language of Italian Futurism, Gramsci subsequently argued that Futurism devolved into fascism and had no relevance to the revolutionary movement. Gramsci also regarded fascism and American Fordism as examples of economistic passive revolution. In the family restaurant of the Vidisichis, Jonathan meets with friends and discusses modernist culture. As Jonathan later realizes, these discussions of modernist culture are obstacles to understanding the significance of political events, such as the murders of Rosa Luxemburg and Karl Liebknecht. One of his friends, Earl, works at the Ford plant in Detroit and is very fond of Rabelais. Earl is "an expert worker and he liked to think that someday he could use words with the same precision as tools" (163). Like Dos Passos, Earl has Veblenian sympathies and hopes to cause historical change through a new cultural language. However, Herbst suggests that such concerns are expressions of Fordism and are cut off from radical politics. Earl's ambitions therefore indicate that Jonathan's milieu is nothing but a cultural version of Gramsci's passive revolution. Conversely, Vicky engages with domestic space in ways that almost always nurture political radicalism.

In *Rope of Gold*, the final novel of the Trexler trilogy, Herbst evokes the effects of the Depression and the radical culture of the 1930s. The tendency toward increased involvement in political struggle that is evident in the trilogy's first two novels is also apparent in this final novel. Where *Pity Is Not Enough* invokes the Haymarket anarchists and *The Executioner Waits* concentrates on the Wobblies, *Rope of Gold* represents communist and trade union activism. In so doing, the final novel exhibits Herbst's most overt, diverse, and extended discussion of ideas of radical history and illustrates the often thwarted drive in Herbst's fiction toward establishing a secure theory of history upon which to base political action. Simultaneously, *Rope of Gold* includes Herbst's most diverse range of spatial representations, and, through developments such as the conflict between rural and urban space and the tensions caused by the gendering of public and private space, Herbst interrelates the historical and spatial aspects of her narrative to a much greater extent than in the earlier fiction. The various political perspectives that emerge from these interrelations engage with many issues that dominate Gramsci's writing. The relative merits of syndicalist direct action and cultural mediation, the vanguardist role of the Communist Party, the hegemonic alliance of industrial and rural workers, and the importance of intellectuals are just some of the Gramscian concerns of the novel. Also, Herbst associates distinct positions on these issues with particular characters.

At the opening Jonathan is a delegate for farmers who endure economic strife. Throughout the novel Herbst portrays the farmers as "a house divided" between both conservatives and radicals and long-standing rural families and those who are newly arrived from the city (84). Jonathan realizes, "The farmers around him seemed to be living in feudal ages and to have taken for granted their position as underdogs to the little bankers who in turn took their orders from the city" (166). As in Gramsci's analysis of southern Italian peasants, economic crisis in this novel does not automatically bring about a transformation in consciousness, and the persistence of feudal patterns of thought suggests the need for intellectuals, such as Jonathan, to create hegemony among the farmers. He tries to get the farmers to work toward the future and ignores those who advise him "to shake out of the idiocy of rural life and come to the city where the real struggle of the proletariat would begin" (41). However, Jonathan's envious feelings toward Jackson, one of the farmers, suggest that he is disconnected from those he seeks to represent: "Jackson's way seemed so much more inevitable than his own. This particular moment in history fitted Jackson like a glove, whereas Jonathan felt he would need trimming to fit anywhere" (17). Jonathan finds it difficult to overcome the farmers' entrenched ideas and establish the hegemony of radicalism. He consequently feels outside of history and resorts to fatalistic references to inevitability. He then turns away from the politics of rural space and becomes a "Front" for the Communist Party (239). In this position Jonathan uses the medium of culture to establish radical hegemony among the urban middle classes. However, he dislikes being away from everyday labor struggles and questions orthodox communist statements on issues such as the importance of industrial machinery. His work also takes him away from the domestic space of life with Vicky. Through Jonathan, Herbst suggests the need for cultural mediation among farmers and criticizes the separation between communist vanguardism and the spatial specificities of the working class.

Steve Carson is one of the other main characters in *Rope of Gold*. The conjunction of urban and rural politics associated with him differs from Jonathan's experience. Steve's father, Walt Carson, has endured economic hardship and family bereavement as a farmer, and he is suspicious of the influence of the city. That Walt covers the walls of his "tarpaper shack" with copies of the *Appeal to Reason* links his rural identity to socialism and domestic space (94). In contrast, Steve is eager to escape domestic life on the land and fight in the city. Incidents occur that complicate his views. For example, the indifferent support of packinghouse workers during a farmers' strike in Sioux City, Iowa, leads Steve to understand the validity of his father's suspicions. Also, his frequent homesickness causes him to rethink his rejection of domesticity. However, he resents the power of cultural hegemony among the farmers. He gets irritated when his father reads the newspaper, and he is sensitive to journalists' attempts to foster farmers' identification with capitalism by describing them as "the new pioneer and salt of the earth" (209). His critique of cultural mediation sharply differs from Gramsci's discussion of the role of hegemony in uniting industrial and agricultural workers. Influenced by the Wobblies who worked on the farm when he was young, Steve sees industrial conflict as more meaningful than the struggle for rural hegemony. He therefore shares Gramsci's awareness of the revolutionary importance of the workers' appropriation of industrial technology. Also, his commitment to direct industrial action reiterates Gramsci's championing of the Factory Councils. Steve's preoccupation with technology and direct action informs his participation in a sit-down strike at an automobile plant in Flint, Michigan. In this concluding scene of the Trexler trilogy, Steve demonstrates his commitment to radical history. While Steve's thoughts about the male nature of work reflect an insensitivity to the gendered space of patriarchal capitalism, his identification of the scene at the auto plant with "the picture at home called 'Snow Scene' " suggests that he also recognizes the importance of domestic cultural space (429). In other words, Steve's thoughts hint that his radicalism is the outcome of the hegemonic influence of domestic cultural space. In the character of Steve, Herbst combines a form of historical struggle, the unmediated appropriation of the factory, with the culture of domestic space. Steve differs from Jonathan because he rejects the historical process of cultural mediation and remains connected to the spaces of labor and home. The experiences of Steve and Jonathan offer varying perspectives on the difficulty of uniting urban and rural workers: Jonathan represents an excess and Steve a dearth of cultural mediation in this area.

As Paula Rabinowitz argues, in *Rope of Gold* Steve is structurally paired with Vicky (166). Steve adheres to historical struggle through the appropriation of the space of the factory, but Vicky's spatial concerns involve a departure from models of historical transformation. Some of the distinct aspects of Vicky's ideas and behaviors are best highlighted by the contrast between her and Jonathan. Whereas Jonathan remains attached to modernist culture, Vicky is ashamed of being more interested in Dostoevsky than the economic difficulties endured by her father. That Vicky coarticulates cultural and domestic regret reflects the close relation between these issues. Vicky's continued adherence to the importance of domestic family culture distances her from Jonathan's aesthetic concerns and their associations with leadership and representation. Compared to Jonathan, Vicky is more critical of communist activities, and her distaste for the radical theories of history proclaimed by bourgeois urban bohemians is less ambivalent. Vicky also opposes an allocation of gender roles in which men participate in the public sphere of politics and women are restricted to domestic experience. She seeks a public role, but one that is an extension of the spatial principles that she values. In *Rope of Gold*, the Trexler family history remains important to Vicky, but the relationship she shares with Jonathan is the most important manifestation of domestic space. In Rabinowitz's terms, labor and desire are equally significant to Vicky, but Jonathan's activism is conducted at the expense of his relationship with her and their Iowa home.[18] As evidenced by her journalistic assignment to Cuba, Vicky's public activities are linked to domestic and rural space. Vicky is deeply moved by her encounter with sugar plantation workers: there is seemingly no division between the personal and the political among the workers, and the scene gives Vicky a powerful sense of the presence of Joe, David, Rosamond, and Jonathan. By emphasizing the workers' domestic culture and family intimacy, their occupational claim to the land, and the secluded mountainous location of their community, Herbst evokes Vicky's experience as an amalgamation of family life and political activism. After leaving Cuba, she drives on Florida roads that Herbst ironically describes as "utopian highways" (403). Such comments indicate that Herbst does not envisage the spatiality that Vicky cherishes in utopian terms. Rather, she celebrates domestic space as a mechanism that establishes the hegemony of radical commitments among characters such as Vicky. Herbst's characterization of Vicky reiterates Gramsci's interest in journalism as a means of gaining widespread hegemony. However, the primary function of journalism in *Rope of Gold* is to put Vicky in contexts that reaffirm the political effects of domestic space. As a form of cultural mediation, journalism, along with other forms of leadership and representation, is often ineffective in this novel. In contrast with her unwillingness to endorse any model of historical process, Herbst is unreservedly enthusiastic about the powerful effects of domestic cultural space.[19]

Both Dos Passos and Herbst reject deterministic theories of history. Dos Passos is critical of communist and trade union activism, and he fails to portray Wobbly activism as a viable form of historical transformation. He maintains radical sympathies, but he regards the cultural mediation of business interests as more powerful than labor's resistance to capital. He reconstructs a theory of history by appealing to the hegemonic possibility of a renewed language of radical authenticity. Dos Passos's vision of linguistic renewal derives from his feelings toward national American space. As in the case of Jack London, Dos Passos's arrival at a coarticulation of history and space relies on ideas of American authenticity that are conducive to conservative politics. In contrast, Herbst's critique of deterministic history sustains radical commitments. Herbst understands the importance of models of history in the struggle against capital, but she is hesitant about definitively identifying with any of the various ideas of history that she represents. Her most certain statements pertain to cultural hegemony. Dos Passos inserts the concept of cultural hegemony into models of history, but Herbst's association of cultural hegemony with domestic space is separate from a commitment to any model of history. Herbst's spatial conceptualization of cultural hegemony means that she accords greater importance to critical space than does Dos Passos. Many aspects of *U.S.A.* and the Trexler trilogy are linked to the writings of Gramsci. Dos Passos, Herbst, and Gramsci all strive to adhere to notions of radical history at the same time that they acknowledge the complex terrain of social and cultural space. Of course, Gramsci never wavers from his belief in the vanguard role of the Communist Party. The shift away from such certainties on the part of Dos Passos and Herbst is accompanied by an emphasis on critical space that exceeds the spatial concerns of London and Sinclair. The fiction of Dos Passos and Herbst therefore represents a significant moment in the rise of critical space in twentieth-century American fiction.

[3]

The Divergence of Social Space

Mary McCarthy and Paul Goodman

Michael Denning describes the leftist "Cultural Front" of the 1930s as "a second American Renaissance" that "triggered a deep and lasting transformation of American modernism and mass culture" (xvi). As Denning shows, American culture in the 1940s and 1950s continued to exhibit many of the concerns of the Popular Front. Similar observations lead Alan Wald to argue that "we must refuse to cut short the 1930s at 1939" and instead consider the powerful legacy of Depression-era literature ("1930s" 18). However, it is also true to say that events such as the onset of World War II and revelations about Stalin's show trials caused the socialist and communist commitments of American writers to decline after the 1930s. It is, therefore, important to assess continuities and discontinuities between American fiction written during and after the 1930s. The epic engagements with historical transformation that we find in the fiction of Dos Passos and Herbst are largely absent in post-1930s fiction. Yet midcentury American fiction returns to the dialectical principles that play a foundational role in the historicism of early-twentieth-century radical American fiction. Like models of history, fictional versions of critical space undergo significant transformation at midcentury. In the fiction of London, Sinclair, Dos Passos, and Herbst, historicity occupies a primary analytic position and critical space serves an ancillary function. In the midcentury fiction that I discuss in this chapter, critical space sheds this subordinate function, becomes increasingly prominent, and takes on the dominant analytic role that history serves in the fiction discussed in previous chapters. At the same time, critical space vigorously engages with the utopian function that underpins much of the fictional spatiality discussed in earlier chapters. The transformation of critical space at midcentury has great significance for the analysis of twentieth-century American fiction. Because it establishes a departure point for the representation of critical space in the fiction of the later twentieth century, this moment of transformation connects all the authors studied in this book. The study of representations of critical space therefore supports Wald's view that the 1930s was not an aberrant and delimited "episode" in the history of American literature ("1930s" 18); rather, the examples of Dos Passos and Herbst indicate that fiction of the 1930s establishes issues that are integral to much subsequent American writing.

In this chapter I discuss two very different novels: Mary McCarthy's *The Oasis* (1949) and Paul Goodman's *The Empire City* (1959). These novels articulate divergent versions of the transformation of critical space in midcentury American fiction. *The Oasis* is a satirical treatment of a failed utopian colony. The utopian milieu of this brief novel highlights the prominence of critical space and the decreased significance of historicism. By including characters of various radical persuasions, including those who are committed to deterministic models of history, the novel represents the historicist perspective as a subset of the spatial treatment of its subject matter. At the same time, McCarthy's critique of the colony and satirization of utopian space reflects the abandonment of critical space's attachment to traditions of left-wing radicalism. Since McCarthy's critique of utopianism suggests that political ideals are in reality the expression of social concerns, the critical space of *The Oasis* is social rather than political in nature. *The Empire City* also represents a social rather than political version of critical space. However, Goodman's novel attempts to analyze power relations and renew left-wing critique through its representation of social space. Goodman's perspective is in key respects opposed to that of McCarthy. McCarthy adheres to a distinction between the social and political spheres, but she suggests that political pretensions mask social preoccupations. As a result, her novel is a critique of the effects of social space. Goodman also abandons both historicism and politics, but he attributes to social space the analytical resources that the authors discussed in previous chapters associate with historicism. Most important, Goodman transfers the dialectical methodology from the representation of history to that of social space. For Goodman, social space is the site of the critique of and opposition to power. Like *The Oasis*, Goodman's expansive novel undoes the identification of utopianism and spatiality. For both McCarthy and Goodman, the critique of utopianism reflects a desire to present spatial analysis in primary rather than ancillary terms. However, the novels differ in their relation to other twentieth-century American fiction. *The Oasis* represents a terminal point in the politics of American literature. The spatial perspective of the novel serves to critique the historicist and utopian concerns of American writers in earlier decades of the twentieth century. In contrast, *The Empire City* is a point of beginning in American fiction. Much subsequent American fiction also uses a spatial approach to analyze power relations in society and transforms Goodman's concerns in a variety of ways.

The discussion of McCarthy and Goodman is informed by midcentury developments in critical theory. The reading of *The Oasis* refers to the theoretical writings of Hannah Arendt. Like McCarthy, Arendt suggests that models of history are best understood in terms of spatial distinctions between the different spheres of society. While McCarthy and Arendt differ in their conclusions regarding social space, they both proclaim the demise of dialectics and Marxist historicism. During the course of the analysis of *The Empire City*, I cite the first two volumes of Henri Lefebvre's *Critique of Everyday Life*. In contrast with Arendt, Lefebvre rescues the concept of dialectics from Marxist historicism. As Martin Jay argues, Lefebvre reiterates Lukács's and Gramsci's "evocation of the concept of totality as an antidote to economism" (295). However, Lefebvre differs from these other theorists because he emphasizes the dialectics of social space. Lefebvre's spatial critique provides an incisive perspective on the concerns of *The Empire City*. Just as McCarthy and Arendt critique the legacies of Marxism, Goodman and Lefebvre establish new and influential directions in the representation of critical space.

Mary McCarthy and Hannah Arendt enjoyed a very close and long-standing friendship and conducted a written correspondence that lasted from 1949 until Arendt's death in 1975. Characterized by affection, respect, generosity, and a strong sense of common cause, this correspondence was initiated by a postcard from Arendt that read as follows: "Dear Mary: I just read the Oasis and must tell you that it was pure delight. You have written a veritable little masterpiece. May I say without offense that it is not simply better than The Company She Keeps, but on an all together different level. Very cordially yours, Hannah" (Brightman, *Writing* 1). Arendt's comments obviously express support for her friend's work, yet they also suggest intellectual connections between her own political ideas and McCarthy's *The Oasis*. In what follows I examine the relation between the critical ideas that are evident in McCarthy's novel and Arendt's writings. In particular, I discuss the extent to which these two writers use ideas of critical space to assess the limits of political action in midcentury American culture. In so doing I hope to provide a theoretical approach to McCarthy's fiction that differs from the biographical and satirical emphases that, as Kelly A. Marsh argues, inform much criticism of her writing (304). When considering *The Oasis*, one must acknowledge the importance of these established critical approaches because the novel is a satirical treatment of events and people from McCarthy's own biography. Described by McCarthy as a *conte philosophique* (Niebuhr 25), *The Oasis* is also, however, a philosophical fiction that can be beneficially examined in terms of appropriate theoretical concepts.[1] In my view, Arendt's ideas about modern society offer the most fruitful theoretical perspectives on McCarthy's novel. Studying *The Oasis* in relation to these ideas helps us both to identify the nature of McCarthy's spatial critique and to situate her novel within midcentury perspectives on political ideology.

First published in *Horizon* in 1949, *The Oasis* is based on McCarthy's involvement in the utopian politics that thrived for a short time among American leftists in the wake of the decline of Marxist historicism. In the 1940s, according to Carol Brightman, McCarthy abandoned the "doctrinaire politics" of the 1930s in favor of "the utopian tendency" of "spontaneous reactions" (*Writing* 303, 304). McCarthy's development illustrates the uncoupling of history and spatiality and the replacement of historicity with spatiality that defines the representation of critical space in midcentury American fiction. In 1948 her utopian concerns led her to found, along with the Italian radical activist Nicola Chairomonte, Dwight Macdonald, and other New York intellectuals, the Europe-America Groups. In the spirit of utopianism, this project was designed to help unify European intellectuals who were opposed to both American capitalism and Soviet communism. However, the project also included figures such as William Phillips, Sidney Hook, and Philip Rahv. Rather than abandoning historicism for utopianism, these luminaries of *Partisan Review* transferred their historicist ideals from Marxism to an unqualified anti-Stalinism. Conflicts between these two groups contributed to the swift demise of the Europe-America Groups in 1949. Frustrated in particular by the *Partisan Review* crowd's attempt to take over the EAG's treasury, McCarthy fictionalized her experiences in the narrative of *The Oasis*. In the novel, two groups of radicals, "purists" and "realists," attempt to form a utopian colony in the New England countryside. However, the mission of the colony is subverted by the inability of the group to execute political decisions. Many of the characters in the novel are based on the individuals involved in the Europe-America Groups. Most notably, the leaders of the two radical factions in the novel, Macdougal Macdermott and Will Taub, are respectively based on Macdonald and Rahv. McCarthy intended that the individuals recognize themselves in order that they might reform (Kiernan 302), but Rahv was incensed by the satirical treatment of him and threatened to sue McCarthy. The notoriety of Rahv's response has strengthened the critical association between *The Oasis* and the intellectual squabbles that McCarthy personally experienced. But in addition to forming the biographical basis of the narrative, the ultimately futile conflict between purists and realists is central to McCarthy's critique of social space and its relation to Arendt's ideas of social life.

The notion of modern society that Arendt elucidates in her writings is highly idiosyncratic. In much of her writing, Arendt describes modern society as "the social" (*Human* 38). As Hanna Fenichel Pitkin notes, Arendt's "hypostasization of the adjective 'social' into a noun" reflects her sense of the social as a voracious and destructive entity (3). Arendt's distinctive usage is also central to her analysis of the different spaces or spheres of human society. In *The Human Condition* Arendt discusses her notion in the context of two distinct and loosely unified sets of concepts. In one conceptual set, she argues that human life consists of three aspects: labor, work, and action. Labor is identified with the economic fulfillment of biological needs; work refers to the permanent artifacts that humans fabricate; and action is associated with the political arena of freedom, speech, spontaneity, and the capacity to initiate new human endeavors. The other conceptual set distinguishes between the private sphere of domestic life and the public realm of collective human intercourse. Arendt clearly contrasts the labor of the private sphere and the action of the public arena. Rather than being located in a distinct sphere of human life, work appears to link and divide these other realms: work escapes the biological exigencies of labor and attains the permanence of action, yet it shares the utilitarian quality of labor and thus is distinct from the political realm of free action. Since the rise of the Industrial Revolution in the eighteenth century, Arendt argues, the integrity of the distinction between private and public spheres has diminished. The reason for this development is that the logic of labor has exceeded its domestic domain and annexed the areas of work and action. For Arendt, "the social" refers to this transgressive enlargement of labor. Arendt states that the social is a homogeneous and lonely mode of being that characterizes modern existence and that has destroyed the private sphere and, most regrettably, the public realm. Arendt's writings on the social were conceived as part of an assessment of Marxism that would supplement her study of Nazism in *The Origins of Totalitarianism*. As is evident in *The Human Condition* and the texts collected in *Between Past and Future* and *On Revolution*, Arendt's critique of the social is primarily an attack on Marxism and the revolutionary tradition to which it is indebted. In Arendt's analysis, Marx sought to colonize the logics of work and politics with that of labor. Arendt's critique suggests that the often-opposed notions of scientific and utopian socialism are both rooted in Marxism's extension of domestic concerns into other areas of life. Moreover, Arendt posits that market capitalism and Marx's "communistic fiction" of the "socialization of man" are similarly predicated on the economistic attributes of the social (*Human* 44). In making these arguments, Arendt subsumes the historicism of Marxism within a spatial analysis of different social sectors.

The main point of congruence between Arendt's theory and *The*

Oasis is the sense that seemingly distinct political positions are in fact manifestations of the same transgressive impulse of the social. Both McCarthy and Arendt use spatial analysis to assess the role of the social. Also, they articulate their ideas about the social in relation to Marxism and accord to capitalism a significant position in this relation. In her book on Arendt's idea of the social, Pitkin distinguishes between two aspects of the social (the conformist and the economic) and notes how both of them are tied to the rise of capitalism. The conformist aspect of the social refers to the obedience to arbitrary norms that is evident in mass society. Arendt's genealogy of such conformism encompasses figures such as the Jewish parvenu and the racist bureaucrat, but, as Pitkin notes, "behind them all looms the bourgeoisie" (85). As the agents of the reduction of the political sphere to a concern with the workings of a market economy, bourgeois capitalists are also responsible for the extension of the "biological" concerns of "housekeeping" into the public sphere and thus for the realization of the economic dimension of the social (*Human* 28).

McCarthy's concern with the role of the capitalist in the existence of the social is evident in her representation of Joe Lockman. As a capitalist entrepreneur in leather goods, Joe is an anomaly among the idealists of egalitarianism at the utopian colony. Yet McCarthy's emphasis on Joe at the outset of the novel reflects his embodiment of several common and general attributes of the colonists. In the novel's first sentence, McCarthy states that Joe and his wife were the first to arrive in the colony because of their adherence to "social law" (3). McCarthy's phrase highlights the power of social norms to assume the status of fundamental principles throughout the narrative. Also, the example of Joe typifies the transgressive extensions of the social. While Joe's wish to be the first in the utopian colony is due to the competitive spirit of his business dealings, his reliance on "past" behaviors in this new setting is shared by many other characters (3). Throughout *The Oasis*, the presence of the past is a trope for the extension of social habits into the purportedly political domain of utopia. Joe's awareness of this disposition distinguishes him from the other characters. He consciously seeks an "extension of opportunity" and the others hope to escape their everyday lives (4), but none of them can shake off past behaviors and prejudices. As well as denoting the continuation of previous personal characteristics, McCarthy's description of Joe's wish to utilize the values of his "factory" and "garden" in "this heavenly mountain-top" indicates the conjunction of economic and domestic factors in the displacement of politics (3).

By describing the colony as "an anarchistic experiment" (5), McCarthy emphasizes the identification of anarchism and utopianism. However, Joe is initially unaware of the "anarchistic" nature of the enterprise, and such obliviousness exemplifies the displacement of political by social space. Rather, he is drawn to utopia because he seeks the company of artists and writers. Previously, his great "passion" for creating art led to him to take lessons at a "business man's art club" (50). Disappointed with the "sterile academicism" of these lessons (50), Joe developed his own style that coincided with that of modernist art. To Joe, the autonomous nature of his discovery of the style of modern art proves "the authenticity of the revelation" (50). In her portrayal of Joe's aesthetic interests, McCarthy reiterates that he is driven by passion and personal commitments rather than a conscious imitation of accepted taste. Yet this emphasis does not mean that Joe's ambitions fail to exhibit the conformist dimension of the social. As Pitkin notes, the social conformism that Arendt describes is "passionate" rather than cynical (186). Also, Joe thinks of his commitments as "some sort of duty laid on every man who had heard its call, a system of knowledge and perception equivalent to revealed religion" (51). Joe's understanding of modernism as a system of classification by which all should abide demonstrates its socially conformist nature. He expects the other members of utopia to be equally devoted to art and the modernist cult of the new, and he is disappointed to learn that they inhabit a building devoid of modern facilities and are not concerned with aesthetic pursuits. The social basis of Joe's personal passions are further revealed when the antitechnological aspects of the colony suggest to him that "the past thirty-five years, the whole of his adult life, had been misspent by society" (53). In this instance Joe explicitly identifies his artistic interests with the technological advances of "society."

In her representation of Joe, McCarthy combines conformist, economic, and aesthetic elements of the social. In an essay originally entitled "Society and Culture," Arendt argues that modern society has transformed art into a consumer product and thus has brought it under the sway of labor, economics, and biological necessity. For Arendt, one of the signs of the consumption of art is the "the ulterior motive of self-perfection" that characterizes the "educated philistine" (*Between* 203). Art is therefore subsumed within social space. That Joe wishes to live in utopia in order to facilitate his artistic development and "self-perfection" indicates that McCarthy, like Arendt, believes that the economistic desire to improve oneself through artistic creation underscores rather than qualifies the conformism of the social. On occasion, Joe's wish to see his economic mentality become a conformist social reality causes conflict within the utopian group. For example, the scene in which Joe frightens Will Taub reveals Joe's wish to turn his ideas of labor into a social standard. Referring to Joe's thought's about Will, McCarthy writes, "He had observed him down on the lawn and marked him with a foreman's eye, being as yet too much of a novice in intellectual circles to distinguish conversation as an authorized branch of labor" (55). Joe then frightens the unsuspecting Will by shouting "State Police reporting" and "Work or the guardhouse!" at him (56). The scene shows that Joe's dreams of aesthetic conformity are complemented by his demands for conformity to his ideas of labor.

The effects of Joe's conformism are similar to those that Arendt attributes to Rahel Varnhagen. Rahel was a Jewish woman who became a celebrated member of the Berlin salon in the late eighteenth and early nineteenth centuries. Arendt describes her as a "parvenu" whose disavowal of her Jewish identity and conformity to intellectual society engendered a disposition that Seyla Benhabib defines as "romantic inwardness" (11). Rahel embodies many of the attributes of the social, because conformism leads to a denial of the public world and political space. Of course, there are numerous ways in which Rahel and Joe differ greatly, but they share the inwardness that results from social conformism. Joe often undertakes an "interior disputation" that consists of many stereotypical idioms (6). As well as being a debased version of the external dialogue of the public sphere, this inner discourse enervates Joe's subjectivity: "He used a dozen masks, accents, patters, soft-shoe steps, to parry an invisible laughter whose source he could not locate; in the confusion of these disguises, he had lost himself" (6–7). Just as Arendt claims that the space of the social destroys public and private spheres, so too the social dimension of Joe's character involves both an absence of political awareness and a weakened sense of inner self.

The encounter between Joe and Will makes it apparent to the members of the community that Joe does not belong among them. They believe that Joe lacks their political commitments, but McCarthy's representation suggests that all characters fail to make the leap from social space to the sphere of political action. As the instigators of utopia, Macdougal Macdermott's purist followers are the novel's political idealists. Mac argues that Joe is "the antithesis of everything we stand for" (7), but he shares many of Joe's failings. Rather than doing so because of Joe's business dealings, Mac initially opposes the capitalist employer's inclusion in the group on the grounds that he is "uncivilized" (7). In other words, he is appalled by Joe's inability to conform to a norm of social behavior. Also, he displays other tendencies that are attributed to Joe. According to Arendt, culture becomes a social consumer item when it is imbued with "functionality" rather than permanence (*Between* 208). In *The Oasis* Mac feels entitled to regard himself as superior to Joe because he has given up a journalistic position and taken on the cultural trappings of "Bohemia" (8). In other words, Mac views his cultural identity in terms of its social function. Also, his attachment to functional culture is stronger than his political ideals or principles. During the colonists' debate over the inclusion of Joe, the success of Mac's arguments causes him to doubt their worth, and he first opposes then supports Joe's case. His inner discussion with himself on this issue echoes Joe's inwardness and is another example of a poor substitute for political intercourse. Also, his decision to support Joe simply restates the view of his wife, Eleanor, whose authority derives from her position in "New York society" (11). In this instance and many others, the colony's decision-making process is constrained within the limits of social space.

The purists are also linked to the economic themes of domestic work that are identified with McCarthy's bluff capitalist. Joe comes upon Will in the course of hunting for partridge, and his impulse to startle the leader of the realists occurs "with the same fatality that made him drop a pot-lid in the kitchen at seven o'clock in the morning" (56).[2] After the confrontation, he decides to make his own breakfast and floods the oil stove. All these incidents highlight the biological consumption that is central to Arendt's economic definition of the social. Much of her critique of the extension of household needs into social economy derives from her understanding of the Greeks' distinction between public and private spheres. In Arendt's account, the Greeks thought of the private sphere as a place of "deprivation" that only slaves and barbarians inhabited (*Human* 38). In modern societies, the social expansion of household concerns is responsible for the erosion of public and private spheres. McCarthy represents two distinct responses to these developments in her depiction of the aftermath of Joe's failed attempt to make his own breakfast. Katy Norell, the breakfast cook for the day, blames Joe for upsetting the communal meal. Preston, Katy's husband, is angry that she does not accept all the blame for the flooded stove and consequently feels that utopia is but "a multiplication of marriage or its projection into eternity" (66). In the public space of the dining hall, Katy feels that she has lost the privacy to "make a scene" and Preston experiences "a privacy he had sought in vain during two years of marriage" (76). Whereas Katy regrets the loss of the private sphere, Preston initially mourns then enjoys its transformation into the social realm. By defining the predicament of both characters in terms of their feelings about the prominence of the housekeeping aspects of the social rather than the foundation of their purism, McCarthy suggests that the colony's highest political ideals are restricted in significance to the extensions of the private realm.[3]

The scenes in which McCarthy represents the politics of the purists reinforce the idea that they are motivated largely by social concerns. The goal of the purists is to realize the political dreams of Monteverdi, the Italian anarchist known simply as "the Founder" (15). The role of the Founder again illustrates McCarthy's association between anarchism and utopianism. In noting that the Founder advocates ideas of "justice, freedom, and sociability" (14), McCarthy hints that the political ideas of justice and freedom might be subverted by the exigencies of sociability. Following their disillusionment with Marxist theories of history, the purists have turned to the utopian space of Proudhon and Tolstoy. The novel's title, which refers to Arthur Koestler's ideas about establishing "small libertarian 'oases'" (Kiernan 295), reflects the retention of the notion of perfect social interaction in the purists' turn to utopian space. Katy Norell, in particular, is constantly disappointed when social interactions fail to attain perfect harmony. When she reads letters from Monteverdi, she believes that she has not done enough to bring perfection into the world. In the same spirit of altruism, Leo Raphael, another of the purists, conceives a plan to bring the disadvantaged of Europe to the United States and thus establish "an internal market in an economy of abundance" (120). The conjunction of egalitarianism and economic concerns relates to another key issue raised by Arendt. In *On Revolution* she argues that the revolutionary tradition that encompasses the French Revolution and Marxism is predicated on the attempt to eradicate poverty and thus solve what she names "the social question" (53). Arendt's transcription of political and historical ideals into aspects of social space therefore extends beyond Marxism. For Arendt, the political attempt to end poverty exists in opposition to the public sphere because it seeks to achieve social goals through the private virtues of "goodness" and "compassion" (*On Revolution* 78). As illustrated by her reading of Melville's "Billy Budd," Arendt believes that goodness must never become public or else it will become unlimited in its ambition and lead to totalitarianism.[4] In *The Oasis* Leo's plan incites "altruistic fervor" among the other colonists (129). However, such altruism does not translate into political action. When they hear Leo's ideas, they feel "a fresh stirring of political hope" (129), but Leo himself insists that politicians be excluded from his proposed United States of Europe in Exile. The colonists do formulate a number of political proposals, but when they attempt to put them into practice their political energy dies out as inconsequentially as Joe's fireworks. McCarthy's narrative lacks Arendt's belief that the appearance of compassion in the public realm has totalitarian tendencies, but it does suggest that the purists' wish to solve the social question negates political action. As Katy learns by the end of the novel, the "hunger for goodness was not of this world and not to be satisfied by actions" (177).[5]

Just as McCarthy criticizes utopian radicalism in her depiction of the purists, so too does she take issue with radical theories of history in her portrayal of the realists. The group led by Will Taub is composed of former Marxists. While they have accommodated themselves to liberal capitalism, they adhere to the deterministic theory of history associated with economistic Marxism. The realists exhibit many of the characteristics that are attributed to the purists and Joe Lockman, but in their case such attributes are rooted in notions of history. Similarly, Arendt argues that ideas of history, especially Marx's model of history, serve to negate the political sphere and advance the attributes of the social. In Arendt's account, Marx associates labor with necessity and work with freedom, hopes to replace both action and labor with work, and believes that humans fabricate history according to fixed laws of production. In this analysis, the dominance of work furthers the economistic principles of the social because it propagates a meaningless cycle of violence and "instrumentality" and denies the political space of action ("Labor" 176).[6] In *The Oasis* the realists' attachment to theories of history also involves a utilitarianism that lacks justifying principles. McCarthy's novel is set in a future in which atomic war seems to be a threat; rather than viewing the colony in idealistic terms, the realists regard it as a practical measure in the face of potential atomic war. McCarthy's descriptions of Will's group as nihilistic and devoid of "positive belief" suggests the deficiency of their utilitarian motives (15). Yet they fervently cling to a determinism inherited from "scientific" socialism (19), and they scour the texts of Marx and Engels for theoretical support for their views. They are committed to causal laws of conditioning and scoff at the idea of freedom. In consequence, they hope that the colony will fail, and they regard it as "an experiment which must be conducted under rigidly controlled conditions in order that the outcome they predicted should appear as the inevitable result" (25). As in Arendt's account of Marx's theory of history, the realists' utilitarian commitment to a doctrine of causal process denies the possibility of political freedom and thus reinforces social tendencies.

The realists also have personal reasons for joining utopia. In addition to their espousal of scientific causality, they attend the colony because they wish to resist conversion to the purists' utopian views. They view the gathering as "a novelty in personal relations" and entertain the possibility of such conversion if this can be achieved "privately" and without compromising their intellectual position (15,

19). As this instance indicates, McCarthy emphasizes the duality of the realists' theoretical and personal attitudes. They have an "office self" that is arrogant and condescending toward the working class (24), and they believe that their theoretical brilliance entitles them to the promotion of such a bossy identity. The self-righteousness of this position is derived from the group's belief in the deterministic forces of history. On the other hand, they have a lazy "private" self that is evident, for example, when Will chooses not to labor in the fields of the utopian colony (24). When she writes that the "relentless law to which he [Will] reluctantly yielded was simply the code of self-protection and the desire to have an easy life" (87), McCarthy makes it clear that the character of the realists is based on this unrecognized, private, social self and not on the political identity that they espouse. The realists fail to acknowledge that their theoretical notions are a self-interested attempt to give general objectivity to their personal conduct. By repeatedly describing such conduct as "behavior" (92), McCarthy suggests that the notion of "psychic conditioning" espoused by the realists applies to their own actions but lacks the status of scientific principle that they claim for it (21). Such references also indicate that the realists' adherence to deterministic behaviorism has replaced their allegiance to deterministic Marxism.

In Arendt's writings, the dominance of conditioned behaviors, such as those exhibited by the realists, is one of the core elements of her discussion of the social. When they are stripped of their capacity for action, she argues, humans are reduced to the conditioned reflexes described by behaviorism. As Pitkin suggests, Arendt's discussion of behaviorism in *The Human Condition* links the economic and conformist attributes of her definition of the social (191). The behaviorist subject is, first, limited to the animal reactions of the sort that Arendt associates with biological necessity and household labor, and, second, maintained by the conformity and homogeneity of mass society. Pitkin notes that Arendt regarded the social conformism that she perceived in the United States as "an egalitarian subservience to peers" that signified a "post-totalitarian" state (101, 100). With its conjunction of "behavioral sciences" and "social behavior" (*Human* 45), midcentury American culture appeared to Arendt as the realization of her theorization of social space.[7] As Alan Wald argues, in *The Oasis* the realists participate in a geographical exodus that represents their separation from "the life experience of ordinary Americans" (*New York* 239). Yet the realists' routine behaviors also suggest that they epitomize the characteristics that Arendt attributes to mass society. The social space of the colony therefore replicates the norms of the social space that the colonists seek to flee.

Through her treatment of Joe Lockman, the purists, and the realists, McCarthy highlights at discrete moments in *The Oasis* the different aspects of what Arendt names the social. Yet she also depicts interactions and points of overlap among these factions and the attributes that they represent. She shares Arendt's view that the worst aspect of social tendencies is their displacement of political action, and the conjunction of the components of the social is most apparent at those times when the colony comes together to try to execute policy initiatives. Because they show how several elements of the social conspire to thwart political action, the novel's concluding events offer the best evidence of the consequences of the colony's behaviors. McCarthy's description of the "strawberry picnic" commences with a portrayal of the role of personal inclinations in Will's character (144). Because the strawberries that the group finds remind him of his youth, "[u]topia appeared as the sequel to a story begun in his childhood" (145). These private thoughts are interrupted when Will and Cynthia Taub encounter a man, woman, and child picking strawberries on the colony grounds. Unnerved, Will and Cynthia return to the main house as the others cook a celebratory meal in honor of their discovery of the strawberries. References to the strawberries and the meal obviously connote what Arendt names household activities, and the members of the colony are unprepared to deal with the intrusion of a political problem into their social life. Katy's response is particularly dominated by concerns about proper behavior. She does not know if her decision not to address the intruders is caused by "the fear of being disobeyed once she had irrevocably given an order, or from some natural democratic feeling" (153). McCarthy suggests, of course, that the former motive is the true one, yet the key issue is that Katy's preoccupation with propriety prevents her from being able to distinguish between social and political sensibilities. Katy's "aesthetic claim" that the strawberries would "rather be eaten" by the colonists than the intruders reflects the cultural dimension of conformist propriety that Joe and Mac share (155); her "stupid fatalism" expresses the same allegiance to mechanical causality and denial of the freedom of action that characterizes the realists' theory of history (157). The range of social elements that is evident in this scene also includes the idea of the equivalence of political radicalism and bourgeois capitalism. While he thinks in terms of business protocol, Joe is solely concerned with conforming to the same models of appropriate behavior as those upheld by realists and purists. Faced with the presence of lower-class intruders, the colonists realize that they are dominated and united by the norms of bourgeois behavior. They fail to come up with a response to the situation that is informed by the political principles that they voice, and the only suggestion they can propose is a social invitation to the picnic. When they discover that the intruders have left, they "privately" and therefore solitarily and inwardly accept that the political mission of the colony has now failed (168). As in the writing of Arendt and sociologists such as David Riesman, so also in this novel loneliness and uniformity characterize the human life that is restricted to social space.

As the conclusion of *The Oasis* demonstrates, McCarthy shares Arendt's ideas about the different aspects of social space and the manner in which they eradicate the possibility of political action. Yet the two writers supplement such observations with significantly different perspectives. Arendt is an unrelenting advocate of political life. For her, politics is the forum in which the human capacity for initiating new projects and for spontaneity, freedom, and distinction is manifested. She desires the elimination of social space and the reawakening of the "lost treasure" of a tradition of classical republicanism (*On Revolution* 217). The architects of the American Revolution, especially Thomas Jefferson, are the foremost representatives of this tradition. In Arendt's account, Jefferson advocated a public space of political decision making that was both irreducible to other dimensions of society and organized as a decentralized "council system" of autonomous wards (*On Revolution* 265). If the colony in *The Oasis* were run according to political actions rather than social behaviors, then it might constitute the kind of republican sphere that Arendt wishes to instigate.

In contrast, McCarthy's critique of social utopia is not primarily driven by an attempt to restore political space. Instead, she seeks to rid social experience of its political pretensions. Arendt argues that social life has no legitimate place in human life, but McCarthy is less dismissive of social behavior when it is restricted to appropriate spheres. After the crisis with the strawberry pickers, Katy understands that the difficulty the colonists encountered was due to their forced attempt to view the situation as a political problem that required a social solution. "But," argues Katy, "supposing there is no problem, but simply an event: the berry-pickers are in the meadow; the sun is in the sky. If you do not wish to eject them, there is no problem, there is simply an occurrence" (173). Arendt's appeal to politics is also predicated on the importance of singular events, but she associates the "everyday experiences" that McCarthy fondly describes with the demise of the public realm (*Human* 37). The difference between Arendt and McCarthy is largely one of discipline: one writes political philosophy and the other writes fiction.[8] In *The Oasis* it is the novelist Susan Hapgood who has a clear perception of social behaviors as meaningful instances. Nominally a realist, she is more interested in behavior as an index of personality than as evidence of deterministic history. The contrast between her and Will is most evident in the scene where both observe the arrival of the colonists. For Susan, the colonists' "domestic details" are significant in themselves, but Will's concern with "[f]acts of any kind" combine with his "naturalistic bent" to create "vast structures of conjecture and speculation" (34, 35, 36). That Susan's perspective makes her wary of the colony's political procedures indicates that, for McCarthy, a novelist's attention to the singular details of social life acts against the transgressive enlargement that Arendt attributes to social tendencies. For example, Susan appreciates Tolstoy as a novelist, not a political thinker, and she enjoys the references to Monteverdi's well-being in his letters more so than his comments on radical activism.

As Alan Wald suggests, *The Oasis* is one of a few novels that posited the "end of ideology" thesis at least a decade before sociologists such as Daniel Bell made similar pronouncements (*New York* 240). McCarthy criticizes various forms of ideological thinking and, unlike Arendt, does not seek an alternative rubric of political life. As well as exemplifying the political pretensions that McCarthy criticizes, the utopian milieu highlights the spatial priorities of the novel. McCarthy's critique of utopianism is conducted in spatial terms that are themselves the outcome of traditions of utopian representation. As critical space shifts from an ancillary to a dominant mode, it loses its utopian function and becomes almost wholly satirical in nature. There are three components of the critical space of *The Oasis*. First, social space is the object of McCarthy's critique. Second, McCarthy conducts her critique by evoking the manner in which social space colonizes public and private space. Third, McCarthy identifies the interests of the novelist with a version of social space that is stripped of its aspirations to political grandeur. In all but the last of these areas, McCarthy's writing accords with Arendt's critical theory. At midcentury these two writers shared a comprehensive vision of the ways in which the social dimension of capitalist and radical ideologies negate the possibility of political action. As well as exemplifying the unique and distinctive qualities of American literary and political culture in the 1940s and 1950s, the relation between Arendt's political ideas and McCarthy's *The Oasis* represents one of the most powerful conjunctions of literary and theoretical writing in twentieth-century American culture.

Paul Goodman's *The Empire City* rescues the notion of critical space from the satirical perspective that dominates McCarthy's *The Oasis*. Goodman's novel, which was published in four sections between 1942 and 1959, details the attempts of a group of friends in New York City to establish a sense of community that negates the alienating effects of capitalist society. Set before, during, and after World War II among characters of diverse ages and socioeconomic backgrounds, *The Empire City* portrays the conditions under which these characters alternately succeed and fail in their goals. Most distinctively, the characters' endeavors occur in the social space of everyday life and do not constitute a utopian escape from society. Also, dystopian elements continually surface in the narrative. Since Goodman also abandons the historicist emphasis on economic production, class struggle, and political power that animates much of the fiction discussed so far in this book, his representation of the dialectics of social space should be viewed as a replacement for models of historical struggle. As we have seen, critical space is subordinate to representations of history in early-twentieth-century radical American fiction. In McCarthy's *The Oasis*, ideas of dialectical history are subsumed within the project of utopian space. *The Empire City* shares McCarthy's reversal of the relative positions of spatiality and historicity, but it does so in a way that generates a dialectical rather than satirical critique of social space. The difference between McCarthy and Goodman is to a significant degree informed by their perspectives on anarchism. While McCarthy expresses her disillusionment with radical politics by satirizing an anarchist community, Goodman's representation of critical space is largely a reflection of his commitment to anarchism.[9]

During the period in which *The Empire City* was published, Henri Lefebvre developed a critical theory of the space of everyday life that shares many features with Goodman's novel. In the first two volumes of his *Critique of Everyday Life*, published respectively in 1947 and 1961, Lefebvre reorients Marxist critical theory away from history and economics and toward sociology. Among English speakers, Lefebvre is often thought of as a theorist of space because of his writings on the city and the production of space. While his *Critique of Everyday Life* does not share the theorization of the totality of social space that we find in *The Production of Space*, it should be regarded as an important contribution to Lefebvre's spatial theory. In Ian Buchanan's terms, "The locus of the everyday is space—and space is constructed by the practices of the everyday" ("Lefebvre" 127). Lefebvre states that everyday life is situated in a "social space" that includes both a subjective "horizon" experienced by individuals and groups and an objective and "relatively dense fabric of networks and channels" (II 231).[10] He also claims that the social space of everyday life is not only a neglected area of theoretical inquiry but also the domain in which both alienating effects of society and the possibility of their transformation are most apparent. His studies, which often oppose the perspective of Arendt in that they privilege social space at the expense of the political realm, are therefore equally invested in addressing the alienation and revolution of everyday life. For Lefebvre, alienation refers to the denial of both human freedom and the fulfillment of human needs and desires. Lefebvre's ideas do not invoke essentialist humanism, because they are rooted in contingent processes of history. He attacks the definition of freedom associated with individualism and privacy, yet he also opposes the concepts of mechanism, determinism, and "blind necessity" (I 174). In keeping with "the dialectical principle according to which what appears to be most internal is in fact most external" (I 174), he regards the principle of private property as a component of ideas of determinism. In contrast to these positions, he promotes the positive definition of freedom as "the development of human powers as an end in itself" (I 171). In this formulation, freedoms are specific and communal; their purpose is to satisfy those needs and desires that emerge in everyday life at distinct moments in history.

Apparent in both capitalist and socialist countries, alienation, according to Lefebvre, is both social in nature and irreducible to the sphere of economic production. For Lefebvre, the alienation that occurs in the social space of everyday life is extensive and multifaceted. As Ben Highmore argues, Lefebvre's theorization of everyday life is in part a response to the "massively accelerated modernization" and "Americanization" that occurred in postwar France (132, 133). In "The Everyday and Everydayness" Lefebvre states, "Modernity and everydayness constitute a deep structure" (11), and he aims to assess the forms of alienation that are produced by this structure. He writes that in the Soviet Union the absence of both Marxist sociology and a critical interest in alienation has furthered an entrenchment of "State ideology" (I 53). Denouncing these trends, Lefebvre regrets the absence of a socialist "style of living" that would emphasize the ethical and aesthetic aspects of everyday life (I 47), and his *Critique* is in part an attempt to rectify this lack. While he states that the working class has a privileged social position because it is especially immersed in everyday life, he departs from dichotomized class perspectives by noting that the same everyday life confronts all social classes. Yet Lefebvre describes Marxism as "a critical knowledge of everyday life" (I 148), and even though he was excluded from the Communist Party in France in 1958, he argues that the *Critique* returns to fundamental aspects of Marx's thought. In particular, Lefebvre adheres in these texts to principles of dialectical transformation that form the basis of his ambiguous treatment of everyday life. Lefebvre states that in

"Official Marxism" history and dialectics are "hopelessly confused" with each other (II 35). His aim is to disentangle these two concepts so that the dialectics of social space will be shorn of the inefficacy of strong historicist architecture.[11] Lefebvre insists on historical discontinuities, such as the ways in which everyday life lags behind technological production. Also, he is less interested in plotting a teleology of revolution than assessing the dialectical processes of everyday life in nonrevolutionary moments.

Since they share many features with Goodman's *The Empire City* and foreground tools and categories for the analysis of social space, Lefebvre's ideas about everyday life provide a useful analytical tool for assessing the details of the fictional representation of critical space in this novel. Like Lefebvre, Goodman takes an exclusively sociological perspective. There is virtually no political activity in the novel, and representations of work and economic production are minimized. Theories of history and revolutionary moments are equally absent. As the novel's opening suggests, class distinctions are also muted in *The Empire City*. The reader is immediately introduced to a social milieu that encompasses the different class perspectives of Horatio Alger, Mynheer Duyck Duyvendak, and Hugo Eliphaz. Along with his brother Lothario and sister Laura, the boy Horatio inhabits a bohemian unemployed underclass. Mynheer is a member of the European aristocracy, and Eliphaz is a wealthy bourgeois entrepreneur. Yet, as exemplified by Horatio's perception of Eliphaz as his "model hero" and the fact that he later lives with him (11), there is little class opposition in the novel. Instead, these and the other major characters of the novel struggle individually and communally to establish freedom from and opposition to the alienation of everyday life that each of them encounters.[12] As Arnold Sachar notes, in Goodman's fiction "[t]he terror of daily life is evoked by a seemingly modest observation of casual facts" (292). Most significantly, Goodman emphasizes the dialectics of social space that is also prioritized in Lefebvre's *Critique*. For both authors, dialectics refers to the incessant interaction between alienated and unalienated aspects of everyday life. Such interaction causes alienated phenomena to become unalienated and vice versa. The process of dialectical transformation means that absolute value can rarely be attributed to the ideas and behaviors that these authors describe.[13]

In the first two books of the novel, "The Grand Piano" and "The State of Nature," Goodman offers a variety of perspectives on the struggles of everyday life that are to a large degree centered on specific characters. While the characters face similar quandaries and seek similar outcomes, they differ in the manner of their attempts to negate the alienation of everyday life. Through the character of Horatio, Goodman portrays the experience of the urban space of everyday life. Horatio has succeeded in evading all forms of civic documentation. As a result, he never goes to school and instead takes his education from the urban environment. For Lefebvre education engenders alienation because it promotes both fragmentation and a mystified notion of totality, a "superficial encyclopedism" (II 68). In his descriptions of children chained to tables at school, Goodman articulates a similar critique of education. Horatio's constant movement through the urban terrain seems to provide him with a unified education, but he learns from Mynheer that newspapers do not always tell the truth. Horatio has demystified what Lefebvre names the "pedagogical" illusion, yet he falls foul of the "culturalist" illusion (II 338), the belief that cultural training is free from alienating effects. Mynheer advises him to reconsider his belief that libraries are wholly alienating and his mobile experience of social space is wholly liberating. Rather, Mynheer advises Horatio to regard everyday life as a dialectical network of alienating structures and unalienating "loopholes" (21). Mynheer's comments provide Horatio with a new context for his urban adventures. He shows Mynheer those "underparts of the city" where he feels "at home" (21). For Horatio, these spaces of alterity are often cherished as sites of queer sexual practice. Under the arches of a concrete viaduct Horatio reveals expressions of graffiti that constitute "a beautiful urban atmosphere, for the massy structures and hurrying thousands had all about them a large free space, so that there seemed to be the conditions of an almost possible existence" (23–24). Horatio realizes that everyday life is constituted by a dialectical interaction between cultural expressions of power and these expressions of unalienated living.

In the foreword to the first volume of his *Critique*, Lefebvre distinguishes between the representations of everyday life associated with Charlie Chaplin and Bertolt Brecht. For Lefebvre, Chaplin is the Tramp, the "reverse image" of the bourgeoisie (I 12), who defamiliarizes the alienated aspects of everyday life. In his reading of Brecht, Lefebvre notes that the playwright identified the "traffic accident" as the best example of the epic theater of everyday life that he sought to create (I 14). As bystanders come to judgments about what has occurred at such scenes, they indicate the ambiguous nature of their characters: in everyday life, these characters are and are not playing the roles associated with their jobs. For Lefebvre, Brecht's immersion in everyday life goes beyond Chaplin's naturalism to produce a "dramatic image" (I 23), a trope for the conditions under which conscious struggle against alienation becomes manifest. Through the character of Horatio, Goodman negotiates the positions that Lefebvre identifies with Chaplin and Brecht. Like Chaplin's Tramp, he is a reverse image of the underside of power who occupies the interstices of the Empire City. As exemplified by his approval of the incorporation of Broadway into the larger road network of the Empire, Horatio at times is unable to defamiliarize the social world with which he is presented. But when he transforms the piano given to his family by Eliphaz into a bomb and then plays on the piano "the scrawlings on the walls of heavenly tunnels" (144), Horatio demonstrates his capacity to de-alienate the objects of everyday life. Along with his "dream of the demolition of the Elevated" (107), Horatio's transformation of the piano illustrates the conscious opposition associated with the Brechtian dramatic image. On many occasions Horatio realizes that he has a necessarily contradictory relation to the Empire City, for only by participating in its life can he challenge it. As in Lefebvre's analysis of Brecht, these contradictory roles give rise to acts of judgment and dramatic opposition. The traffic accident that Horatio causes on his bicycle ride illustrates the impact he has on urban life, and his critique of war and decision to flee the soldiers who seem to be following him provide evidence of his dramatic judgment.

Horatio's narrative indicates the complexity of Goodman's representation of urban space. At times Horatio is mystified by the city. On other occasions he seeks to escape it. He also realizes that he can use the resources of the city, such as graffiti, to transform urban space.

Like Lefebvre, Goodman is also interested in forms of urban space that restrict the re-signifying actions undertaken by Horatio. In the second volume of the *Critique*, Lefebvre describes "new towns" as urban spaces in which everyday life has been reduced to the "chemically pure state" of functionality (II 78). As Highmore observes, new towns are for Lefebvre "the most unrestrained form" of capitalist alienation (113). In such spaces, everyday life is simplified, structured, and reduced to private life. In Goodman's novel, Laura, Horatio's sister, embodies a similar trend in urban space to that expressed by Lefebvre. Described as a member of the "lumpen proletariat" (57), Laura exemplifies the reverse image of bourgeois power. Unemployed, she does nothing but "enjoy the day" (34). She has a laudable appreciation of her "native neighborhood" (59), and she relishes the encounter with urban space: "What I really enjoy is the feeling of the approaches of various cities, the way the highways are banked, and what they do with the public buildings" (34, 58). However, Laura's urban interests do not lead her to the dramatic transformations associated with Horatio. Rather, she becomes the architect of a new town. As part of the war effort, Laura is required to camouflage the town from enemy aircraft. When she begins this project, she realizes the "functional" town she has built is expressive of "artificial order" (186, 185). As epitomized by the experience of domesticity, the town is a "trap" in which behavior is regulated and spontaneity is eliminated: "Whatever you wished, the house was planned for it; and when you no longer wanted it, you found yourself trapped into the motions that made you want it again—but something was wrong" (186, 188). Despite these insights, Laura continues to participate in the war effort and succeeds in camouflaging the town. Nevertheless, her friends bring her back to the Empire City, and she quickly commences a new "community plan" (267). Compared to the workings of "sane society," the "occupational therapy" devised by Laura promotes a unified and fulfilled human experience (272). Laura also builds a town square in which a marriage takes place. At this scene the community of friends is seemingly happy, but the spirit of the deceased Eliphaz suggests that these activities reinscribe the alienation of everyday life. While appearing to facilitate critical engagement with the Empire City, Laura's plans contribute to what Lefebvre describes as the " 'reprivatization' of everyday life" (II 88), the withdrawal of everyday life from public concerns.

The relationship between Laura and Mynheer highlights the extent to which characters from different class backgrounds confront the same issues pertaining to everyday life. The fluctuating meanings that are evident in Laura's relation to urban space also characterize Mynheer's interactions with art and culture. For Lefebvre the separation between works of art and everyday life is inaccurate. Not only is art derived from everyday life but the critique of everyday life that is often found in art can be "reversed" (I 87), that is, everyday life can offer a critique of art. The dynamic identified by Lefebvre is illustrated in his discussion of the aesthetic tradition that encompasses symbolism and surrealism. Lefebvre states that this literary and artistic tradition denigrates everyday life in favor of the bizarre, the magical, and the mysterious. He claims that artists such as Baudelaire are interested solely in an impoverished "lining" of everyday life, and he hopes that the "greatness" and magic of everyday life can be discovered and serve as a critique of the alienated forms of magic evident in art (I 123, 129). In *The Empire City*, Mynheer initially upholds the distinction between art and everyday life that Lefebvre criticizes. Unlike Horatio, he is aesthetically horrified by the neon sign for Luis Mendoza's roadhouse diner. Believing that "it was necessary to protect the little objects in which the Holy Spirit was congealed forever" (60), Mynheer is "disastrously committed to the preservation of *objets d'art* and other specimens of culture" (60). His project is disastrous because "in practice it was often hard to distinguish which was the spirit and which was the vandal" (60). In other words, Mynheer's separation of art and everyday life is untenable.

Mynheer begins to critique his own ideas about art at a meeting of the Committee for Post-War Art. Like Lefebvre, the members of this committee criticize the decline of revolutionary Dada into aesthetic surrealism, and they advocate "bombism" or "active dada" as a means to end the separation of art and everyday life: "The work of art that gets up on its hind legs and does something—for example, explodes in your face or exudes a poison gas" (64). Initially speechless in response to these comments, Mynheer later becomes an expert on the limitations of art. At a performance of Wagner's *The Mastersingers*,

Mynheer informs Laura that aesthetic shock has already been incorporated into the bourgeois definition of art. As a reaction to such insights, Mynheer, in his pedagogical lectures to Horace, emphasizes the subversive possibilities of everyday play. Horatio believes that his own experiences are more spontaneous and less alienated than the formal game of Subway Tag proposed in these lectures, but Mynheer clearly embraces everyday life at these moments. As a member of the Committee for Constructive Bombardment, a reconstituted version of the Committee for Post-War Art, Mynheer continues to advocate bombism. While this movement returns art to everyday life, it also relies on a form of destructiveness that, in Lefebvre's terms, reintroduces the abhorrence of everyday life. Also, bombism privileges those aspects of everyday life that are derived from artistic concerns. Mynheer succeeds in identifying those moments when Horatio becomes accommodated to the Empire City and loses his critical perspective on everyday life. However, at the end of the second book of the novel, he remains tethered to the separation of art and everyday life. He anticipates a renewal of everyday life at the war's conclusion but does so in the language of theory and reason. His views of art may have changed, but his adherence to a separate and elevated realm of thought means that, as Horatio notes, he is not "in touch with the realities of the situation" (266).

On several occasions Goodman alludes to Mynheer's wealth, but it is the narrative of Eliphaz that presents economic issues most prominently in *The Empire City*. Goodman's treatment of economics shares key characteristics with Lefebvre's discussion of money and need. Lefebvre's chief economic goal is the "rehabilitation of wealth" (I 156). In contrast to the ascetics who argue that wealth is intrinsically bad and the anarchists who advocate "equal possession for all," Lefebvre suggests that a de-individualized celebration of wealth will overcome "fetishism and economic alienation" (I 155, 153). Similarly, he criticizes the capitalist reduction of needs to the need for money, and he argues for an increase in social needs. In the second volume of the *Critique*, Lefebvre concedes the problematic nature of a theory of needs and instead suggests the importance of "desires" that are rooted in specific social "situations" (II 7). Lefebvre is able to speak positively about money and need because he insists on the uses of everyday life rather than the meanings inscribed in capitalist production. In everyday life, humans can appropriate money and need for the purposes of the fulfillment of "powers and aptitudes" and the realization of their total freedom (I 161). As in Lefebvre's analysis, Goodman's representation of economic issues departs from simple oppositions to embrace the dialectical appropriations of everyday life.

In the novel, Eliphaz decorates his home with the valuable artifacts that he trades, and his home is a "flowing environment" (27), a domestic space that has constantly changing décor and is open to the social space outside. The depiction of Eliphaz's home reflects Goodman's interest in considering economic significance in relation to the fluid contexts of everyday life. Eliphaz knows that it would be more profitable to trade his goods from a warehouse, but he insists on making his home from his wares. As he tells his daughter, Emily, Eliphaz domesticates trade in order to transform the nature of economic value: "I'm trying to make a profit, girl! But a profit not on the exchange of these commodities but on their worth, even on their use; and maybe, for all you know, even on their *real* worth, maybe even on their *real* use. How can I do it unless they are *my* things and I know what it is that I am exchanging anyway?" (27). Just as Lefebvre rehabilitates wealth as a means of opposing economic alienation, so too Eliphaz lives among his luxurious goods as a way of negating the alienating effects of exchange value. For Eliphaz the concept of use value is not abstract or inherent. Rather, it is achieved in the act of appropriation in everyday life. Eliphaz's acts of appropriation are epitomized by his collection of "*objets trouvés*" (81), a random assortment of items that includes a tennis shoe and a fishing rod. These objects are precious to Eliphaz precisely because they lack exchange value and thus can be appropriated by him to fulfill particular needs.

However, his son, Arthur, resents this collection and is especially perturbed that it includes a ten-dollar bill and thus "take[s] money itself out of circulation" (82). Arthur persuades Eliphaz to sell these objects and return them to circuits of economic exchange. Eliphaz's capitulation to Arthur's demands is consistent with his wish "to change all the use value into exchange value" (36). In other words, there is a countertendency in Eliphaz's economic dealings that privileges exchange value at the expense of use value. In order to represent "all the commodities that I have fixed in their exchange value and alienated from use forever" (85), his record of financial transactions consists solely of zeroes. As his book reveals, Eliphaz treasures wealth, but his antipathy to commodities leads him to deny the role of use value in the fulfillment of the needs of everyday life. In other words, he believes that commodities trade off an element of use value; therefore, his critique of the commodity at times involves the desire to deny "every corrupted satisfaction" and wholly negate use value (87). By the time of his death in the second book of the novel, it is clear that Eliphaz has divergent perspectives on the intersection of economics and everyday life. He celebrates "the things that are made and by nature are not sold" as "the elixir of life" (170), objects that fulfill the needs of everyday life and do not become commodities. Yet Eliphaz's fusion of trade and domestic space and his obsessive devotion to exchange value results in the enervation of everyday life.

The issue of work is central to the representations of alienation that we find in the writing of Lefebvre and Goodman. As one would expect, Lefebvre evokes the division of labor as the cornerstone of alienation. Following Marx, Lefebvre states that work under the fragmented and individualized conditions of capitalism turns the worker into a reified object: "Not only do the tools of his trade loom up before him like an alien, threatening reality [. . .] but also he becomes separated, disassociated from his own self, in his real, everyday life" (I 165). Lefebvre's reading of work and alienation is inflected in two ways. First, he states that alienation is apparent throughout everyday life, not just in the domain of work. Political alienation, as represented by an adherence to the power of the state, is for Lefebvre "the most serious type of alienation" (I 63). Leisure pursuits also have alienating effects, especially when leisure is conceived as a break from the alienation associated with work and everyday life. While acknowledging how leisure can facilitate active pursuits that undo alienation, Lefebvre notes that the separation of work and leisure exemplifies the extension of the division of labor into the realm of everyday life. Second, he posits an unalienated possibility for work. According to Lefebvre, many criticisms of everyday life are in reality attacks on the working class, and they articulate "contempt for productive labor" (I

29). In negating this view of everyday life, Lefebvre also attempts to rehabilitate work. Speaking dialectically, he claims that it is through labor that humans create "human reality" and "the human" itself (I 169). Not surprisingly, he speaks glowingly of the integration of work into everyday life in "peasant life" (I 30). He is wary of the Marxist vision of the "total man" [sic] because he thinks that such a notion is predicated on the dream of a future that is absolutely different from the present (I 64).[14] Nevertheless, he believes that work can be subsumed within an integrated and unalienated form of everyday life if it has a "social essence" and is characterized by "a humble, everyday feeling" (I 169). In the opening two books of The Empire City, work appears as an alienating activity to all of the characters, and everyday life is opposed to the realm of labor. Lefebvre states that the total critique of work as inherently alienating reflects an "anarchistic" sentiment that relies on an ahistorical, essentialist, and bourgeois definition of the subject (I 78).[15] The extensive opposition to work that we find in Goodman's narrative reflects the presence of the anarchist sentiments described by Lefebvre. However, Goodman's characters frequently articulate the desire to integrate work into everyday life, and the novel struggles to overcome alienation through the rehabilitation of work.

The experiences of Lotario, Horatio's brother, evoke the problematic nature of the withdrawal from work. More specifically, Lotario's disposition toward military service is the basis of Goodman's clearest account of the opposition to work. Goodman's references to the "civilian authority" that controls conscription as "a means of organizing society" suggests the validity of an identification of work and military service in the novel. By indicating that, in the aftermath of World War I, Lotario's campaign against war serves the interests of capitalist entrepreneurs, Goodman suggests the counterproductive nature of his position. At other times Goodman upholds Lotario's views. While his colleagues advocate an improvement to the soldiers' working conditions, Lotario remains unswervingly opposed to a military draft. Here Lotario is portrayed as a principled opponent of opportunistic reformists. Yet his draft dodging is associated with his "progressive alienation" and his utopian wish to recover the "Golden Age of his childhood" (48). When he is imprisoned for his resistance, Lotario rejects "[t]he social compact" (205). Instead of considering himself a participant in social space, Lothario now inhabits the "created space" of a prison cell (206). Described as "the state of nature" and "a world without bars" (206), Lothario's predicament is also based on a distinction between the social space that he inhabits and the world beyond this domain. After escaping from his captors, Lothario adheres to the belief that he exists in the state of nature, and he frees the animals from the zoo. The failure of the animals to exit the zoo's self-enclosed plaza illustrates Lothario's inability to integrate the state of nature into everyday life. He believes society is wholly alienated and does not realize that "society *existed*, in so far as it existed, because of elementary desires and the wonderful virtues of courage, patience, the extraordinary endurance of the people" (240). Instead of embracing a dialectical view of social space, Lothario clings to a distinction between a utopian state of nature and a wholly alienated world of work. As a result, he is reduced to silence and isolation.

Most of the characters' attempts to overcome the alienating effects of the Empire City fail in the first two books of Goodman's novel. Laura accommodates too fully to social exigencies, and Lothario is overly distanced from such exigencies. Portrayed by Goodman in states of extreme alienation, these two characters both exhibit utopian tendencies: Laura seeks to create a utopian urban space and Lothario desires the utopian state of nature. While Goodman's representation of these characters emphasizes a critique of utopianism, his emphasis on the dialectics of social space should be viewed as a transformation of the principle of utopian space. Goodman transfers the dialectical process associated with ideas of history to the realm of the spatial. As in Lefebvre's *Critique*, Goodman's representation of dialectical struggle occurs within the social space of everyday life. The principle of social spatiality derives from utopianism, but Goodman's representation of social space articulates a critique of the idea of utopia.[16] Characters such as Mynheer and Eliphaz have some success in overcoming divisions between everyday life and the areas of art and economics, but they succumb to notions of separation and thus have a limited understanding of spatial dialectics. Only Horatio is able to overcome the limitations of his friends. By immersing himself fully in everyday life, he succeeds in de-alienating the phenomena that he encounters and arriving at what Lefebvre names dramatic judgment.

At the conclusion of the second book of *The Empire City*, the other characters are satisfied with the pastoral community that they have created, but Horatio remains outside these celebrations and realizes that social space is taking a new turn in the postwar era. The final two books of Goodman's novel concern the impact of this new social formation on everyday life and its communities.

Speaking the prophecies of the deceased Eliphaz, Horatio describes postwar society as "the Sociolatry" (277). The Sociolatry aims to increase standards of living, but does so on the basis of economic concerns rather than the fulfillment of needs. By manufacturing needs and failing to satisfy desires, the Sociolatry does nothing to rectify the "historical drift" associated with everyday life (Lefebvre, II 3), the technological lag between productive capabilities and the fulfillment of needs, and instead undertakes what Lefebvre, in a term derived from Guy Debord, describes as the "coloniz[ation]" of everyday life (II 11). As well as the voluntary conformity to social roles, the Sociolatry is characterized by "personal and public peace" (277). In this phrase, Goodman suggests that the Sociolatry involves the eradication of both distinctions between public and private spheres and instances of social conflict. Instead, society becomes homogenized into "one anonymous front" (278). Goodman's vision is akin to what Lefebvre describes as "the great pleonasm," a social "tautology" in which everyday life is reduced to a banal and tedious form of "private life" (II 77). In the final two books of *The Empire City*, "The Dead of Spring" and "The Holy Terror," the Sociolatry represents a greatly intensified and integrated form of the alienation that is apparent in the first two books of the novel. Goodman's characters respond to the holistic nature of the Sociolatry by heightening their desire for community. The wish to renew everyday life through community causes the issue of utopianism to become more prominent in the narrative.

The first two books of *The Empire City* are broadly concerned with the identification of central issues in everyday life that we find in the first volume of Lefebvre's *Critique*. Similarly, the second two books of Goodman's novel engage with the specific problem of the revolution of everyday life that Lefebvre addresses in his second volume. One of Lefebvre's concerns in this latter volume is the manner in which the concept of "totality" has been appropriated for "non-Marxist" ends

(II 186). Once employed to overcome the fragmentation and fetishism of capitalist society, the concept of totality has, for Lefebvre, become synonymous with the unified and fixed nature of society. Since Lefebvre's critical project emphasizes the dialectical movement of alienated and revolutionary aspects of everyday life, any idea of static totality is anathema to him. At the outset of "The Dead of Spring," Goodman evokes the alienated totality of the Sociolatry. Goodman's perspective on social totality includes a critique of the idea of an unalienated human essence. While Lefebvre is often suspicious of the concept of total man, in the first volume of the *Critique* he dreams of "total man [sic], entirely developed, entirely won back from alienation" (I 64). Contrastingly, in the chapter entitled "On the Shore," Mynheer weeps as he sees "[t]he constellation Man" [sic] in the sky (298). To Mynheer, the constellation represents the final abstraction and alienation of humanity as "something that will not change" (299). Instead of Lefebvre's dreams of the total human, we have the unchanging alienation of humanity in its totality. When the characters get together for "Our Meeting, 1948," they seek to form an oppositional community. However, they "have exhausted the strength of fraternity" and are "frozen in criticism" (283, 285). As in Lefebvre's model of social tautology, Goodman's community of characters resembles the fixed totality of humanity that Mynheer derides. As Lothario realizes, their pitiful state is linked to their role as "passionate inventors of Utopian schemes" (286). Their attempts at utopian community have been subsumed as a private enterprise within the Sociolatry. To underscore his critique of utopian space, Goodman describes a picture of Peter Kropotkin, the "amiable geographer" and anarchist theorist (287), falling from the wall of the meeting room. The characters tentatively realize that true opposition to the Sociolatry requires critical action in the sphere of everyday life. In subsequent chapters the characters struggle between the tendencies of a utopian removal from and the critical transformation of everyday life.

Lefebvre's critique of utopianism gives us insight into key aspects of Goodman's treatment of this subject. For Lefebvre, utopianism is predicated on the notion of a "golden age" that is imagined in its totality and is attainable via a definitive break from existing society (I 58). In the novel's descriptions of experimental human communities, the utopian impulse destroys everyday life, and human relations become as impoverished as those in the society the characters seek to leave (309). This is "the period of the system" in the novel (329), the time in which the Sociolatry and its purported opposition are indistinguishable. The resilience of the Sociolatry is embodied in the views of Minetta Tyler. As did Lothario in earlier parts of the novel, Minetta erroneously believes that the horrific effects of the Sociolatry can be overcome by a return to "animal nature" and a rejection of "culture" (409, 410). The nadir of this period is the death of Laura, who is described as "the crown laurel of the everyday" (395). Yet Laura's death facilitates a turn from utopianism to the critical space of everyday life. In the mourning poetry that Mynheer collects for Laura, the critique of a utopian removal from everyday spatiality is reiterated, as in the following verse from Rainer Maria Rilke:

> But we have never, not a single day,
> pure space in front of us, that flowers
> endlessly open to; but always world
> and never nowhere [. . .] . (402)

In these lines Rilke denies the possibility of "pure space" and the "nowhere" of utopia. The rejection of utopia causes Mynheer to articulate the need to embrace everyday life, but he also realizes the dilemma that confronts them: "If we conformed to the mad society, we became mad; but if we did not conform to the only society that there is, we became mad" (407). Rather than simply accommodating to a reified version of everyday life, the characters must, if they are to find a way out of this dilemma, engage with everyday phenomena with a view toward transforming them. When the characters fly and levitate in search of "free space" (329), they express the desire for such a transformed and liberated version of everyday life.

At the conclusion of the first volume of his *Critique*, Lefebvre states that his future analyses of everyday life "will involve a methodical confrontation of so-called 'modern' life on the one hand, with the past, and on the other—and above all—with *the possible*" (I 251). The combination of past, present, and future elements that Lefebvre describes is evident in the community engagements with everyday life in *The Empire City*. The notion of the possible is central to the second volume of Lefebvre's project and is closely linked to a variety of issues. One such issue concerns the relation between the structure and "conjuncture" of everyday life (II 148). For Lefebvre, "The conjunctural [. . .] is the pressure of the process of becoming on structures"; it is a "virtual object" that represents the future possibilities of the transformation of everyday life (II 148, 114). Mynheer's fantastic adventures reflect the conjunctural element in Goodman's novel. Rather than reflecting a yearning for utopian escape, his desire to get "Out of This World" via "the hole in the midday" represents a wish for the conjunctural dimension of everyday life (406). His cosmic voyage into outer space fulfills this desire. In stating, "when I go out of this world, I do not get into *that* world, but again into *this* world" (466), Mynheer indicates that his adventures occur in a conjunction of everyday life and its transformation. When he lands on a "violet moon" (472), he encounters "thousands of regular objects" and seeks to flee the environment that he has encountered (473). However, he turns back to the "mobiles" that perturb him and is able to interact with them (481). A virtual object that intimates the future possibilities of everyday life, the "Uncarved Block" that Mynheer sees is associated with the lines from the *Tao Te Ching* that he reads:

> Yet Heaven and Earth and all between is a great bellows:
> it is empty, but its bounty never fails;
> work it, and more comes. (489)

Upon returning to the community with the Uncarved Block, Mynheer falls in love with "his Only World" (557). His travels through space are separated from his earthly experience, and he struggles to conjoin the two spheres. Nevertheless, these travels are oriented toward the conjunctural future and conclude with a happy return to everyday life and its possibilities.

The community in Goodman's novel also interacts with past and present aspects of everyday life. Goodman writes that the community accommodates itself to "the folkways of our society" (427). Such accommodation means that the narrative ceases to be an "Almanac of Alienation" and becomes a "Register of Reconciliation" (427). This narrative shift occurs in "Neolithic Rites," the first section of the part of the narrative that is subtitled "Modern Times." In the context of the present, the characters discover "a kind of neolithic faith, and they devote considerable time to rites and ritual games" (430). The neolithic interests of the characters do not constitute a utopian withdrawal from everyday life. Rather, they represent a return to historicizable elements of everyday life in the past that continue to exist in the present. For Lefebvre the critique of everyday life must study the interaction between "cyclic time" and "linear time" (II 49). Cylic time refers to the persistence of cultural rhythms and "symbols" of the past in the everyday life of the present (II 54). Often associated with medieval peasant culture, these symbols, for Lefebvre, "show through from the depths of the social spectacle" and "demand participation" (II 306). They are, therefore, integral to the shift from the alienation to the revolution of everyday life. In *The Empire City* Goodman emphasizes the synthesis of the symbols and rhythms of the past and "Modern Times." The chapter titles—"Conversing," "Dancing," "Concert," "Eating," Relaxing," "Welcoming"—suggest the characters' discovery of "neolithic" rituals in their accommodation to everyday life. In modern cities, according to Lefebvre, cyclic symbols are most evident in transitional spaces such as "the street" (II 309). Describing Manhattan as "Our Village," Goodman also portrays the street as the locus of both symbolic activity and the articulation of a localized and "archaic dialect" (553).[17] For example, children's games appropriate the space of the street and manifest symbolic play. In Lefebvre's analysis play is possibly "the starting point from which we could envisage the metamorphosis of the everyday" (II 139). Similarly, Goodman follows the descriptions of children's games with a portrayal of "Our Village Meeting" (587), which is designed "to move tentatively toward the next step" (587). Strengthened by Droyt's narrative of Lefty, who is able to live happily in the commonplace world of work, the characters make proposals for the transformation of everyday life.[18]

Unlike other characters in the novel, Horatio consistently negates utopian impulses and consequently undertakes a protracted engagement with everyday life. Horatio's narrative suggests that the best way to avoid dystopian experience is to negate utopianism. More so than any other aspect of *The Empire City*, Horatio's experiences also evoke the dialectical processes associated with the transformation of everyday life. The community generates plans for such transformation, but it is Horatio's sustained immersion in everyday life that leads to transformative actions. Horatio's disdain for utopianism is evident at the outset of "The Dead of Spring." While the other characters privately contemplate the possibilities of community, he joins the crowds on Broadway. Like the others, he is "frozen in dismay" (293), but he realizes that instead of "flying" he must "accept our total loss of paradise" (294). Horatio's experience differs from community withdrawal and fantastical flying, which characterize the disposition of other characters. For example, Mynheer's endeavors point to the transformation of everyday life, but they retain a distinction between reified materialism and otherworldly idealism. In Lefebvre's terms, Mynheer's narrative is informed by a disconnection between "superficial objectivism and illusively profound ontology" (II 195). Unlike Mynheer, Horatio strives for a form of conjunctural transformation that is firmly embedded in everyday life. His actions disclose the dialectic of the "lived" and the "living" that is described by Lefebvre (II 216, 217). The "living" refers to the horizon of possibilities associated with everyday life, and the "lived" denotes the actions and thoughts that are realized in everyday life. The continual transformation of the living into the lived and the lived into the living means that, for Lefebvre, the lived is "essentially dramatic" (II 218). Rather than being a static formation, the lived is the product of the dramatic judgments made from the virtual possibilities offered by the living. In the first two books of the novel, Horatio, as we have seen, makes the dramatic judgments that Lefebvre identifies with Brecht's plays. Such opposition to alienating circumstances becomes in the later books a transformation of everyday life and a confrontation with the Sociolatry. Horatio's actions take on these new qualities as a result of the emphasis on future possibilities that is apparent in Goodman's representation of the movement of the lived and the living.

Having departed from the community of human relations, Horatio takes a job drilling roads by the river. His occupation exemplifies his immersion in everyday life, but he leaves this job as soon as it becomes boring to him. Horatio's relation to work illustrates the movement of the lived and the living. While he makes the decisions that lead to the lived experience of labor, he remains open to other possibilities: "He was waiting almost confidently for objects and occasions of desire to present themselves. They would not have to be remarkable or very lucky, because in this mood he could have made golden things out of improbabilities" (327). Such openness is apparent in his relationship with Rosalind. To Horatio, Rosalind represents the possibilities of living. Preoccupied with observing the detritus of the city, he initially ignores Rosalind. However, under the tutelage of the youthful Eros, Horatio undergoes an emotional cycle that culminates in his affection for her. Together they walk the streets of the city. As usual, Horatio notes the variegated nature of the urban landscape: "[M]ost persons seem to think that the streets of our Empire City are irrevocably public, whereas it's not so bad as that; a complicated structure has many interstices" (362). However, Rosalind's knowledge of the city unnerves him and causes him to refashion his understanding of urban space. Rosalind therefore communicates new possibilities that Horatio must integrate into his lived experience of the city. When she states that she is attracted to "social and fantastic" clothing (362), Rosalind articulates a trope for such movement of the lived and the living: Horatio has a "social" understanding of the city, but he is open to the new and "fantastic" perspectives offered by Rosalind. The presence of Rosalind therefore enables Horatio to transform his experience of everyday life. Unlike the separation between everyday phenomena and fantastical travels that characterizes Mynheer's experience, Horatio enjoys a close and connected relation between lived experiences and new possibilities.

In Lefebvre's analysis, conjunctural transformation is based on the principles of "tactics" and "moments" (II 196, 340). The principle of tactics states that the critique of everyday life takes the form of "confrontation" (II 107). Rather than constituting a fixed mode of thought or behavior, critique is therefore an active opposition that is based on fluctuating circumstances and contingent opportunities. The purpose of tactics is to realize the moment, which Lefebvre defines as "the attempt to achieve the total realization of a possibility" (II 348). A festival, not a miracle, the moment emerges from the lived situations of everyday life; as Highmore states, Lefebvre's festival "doesn't suggest so much the end of history as the beginning" (124). In *The Empire City* Lefebvrean tactics and moments are evident in Horatio's confrontation with the Sociolatry. As part of the development of his relationship with Rosalind, Horatio is arrested and tried for evading the city's authorities. In jail, Horatio indulges in "childish sport" that enables him to alter and subvert the prison environment (378). Such endeavors further demonstrate his ability to transform the circumstances of everyday life. At the trial of "The Sociolatry vs. Horatio Alger" (383), Antonicelli, the prosecutor, accuses Horatio of "living in alienation" and "refus[ing] to recognize the existence of the Dilemma" (383, 387). Of course, this is the same dilemma noted by Mynheer: "If one conforms to our society, he [sic] becomes sick in certain ways. [. . .] But if he does *not* conform, he becomes demented, because ours is the only society that there is" (387). Horatio responds to these accusations by denying the validity of this dilemma. Instead, he claims that living in the city "has given me a long time to gather a little force of my own, to learn viable habits to make a little freedom around me, and to win an abeyance, an abeyance" (388). In other words, Horatio has succeeded in taking advantage of tactical circumstances to realize moments of festival in everyday life. Antonicelli retorts by stating that Horatio conflates "public evidence and arguments" with "private sentiment, hedged round with hints of miracles" (388). But of course Horatio is not concerned with miracles. As a result of Antonicelli's insistence on the distinction between public and private, he undergoes "asphyxiation" (388), the perennial disease caused by the Sociolatry. Horatio is acquitted, and his confrontation with the Sociolatry ends in success. By refusing to capitulate to Antonicelli's definition of social space, Horatio extends the transformation of everyday life into an effective challenge to forces of alienation.

In "The Holy Terror" the cycle of Horatio's alienation and disalienation continues. Horatio and Rosalind experience great difficulty in living without the sanction of a "socially shared insanity" (437). Such difficulties are exacerbated by Horatio's entrenchment in everyday life, and he becomes susceptible to extreme forms of alienation. His bitterness about the loss of utopia makes him want to be a part of the majority, and he supports "the General"—obviously Eisenhower—for president. That his belief in the General is associated with a love of the "folkways of the Americans" indicates the ease with which an appreciation of the folkways of everyday life can take a reactionary turn (501). Horatio overcomes his feelings for the General and his nostalgia for utopia, and he consistently disrupts the tendency toward fixity within the community of characters. Just as Lefebvre describes how "the moment reorganizes surrounding space" (II 353), Horatio seeks to negate alienation via the appropriation of the social space of everyday life. However, Goodman and Lefebvre offer precarious critiques of alienated society. By distancing themselves from historicist theories and political affiliations, they proffer representations that, as they acknowledge, can be reappropriated by the society that they critique. The differences between their positions and those of McCarthy and Arendt highlight the different versions of critical space that are apparent in midcentury culture. All of these writers reject dialectical models of history. Whereas McCarthy deploys critical space for primarily satirical ends, the other writers subject this concept to various forms of transformation. Like Dos Passos, Arendt strives to recover a political form of critical space that is associated with the decentralizing ideals of the early American republic. In contrast, Goodman and Lefebvre articulate dialectical critiques of social space and everyday life. Both writers struggle against utopianism and in consequence frequently turn to dystopian representations. Utopian elements remain evident in the work of Goodman and Lefebvre, but these either derive from historicizable forms of everyday life or manifest future possibilities for the transformation of everyday life. Because they expand and ultimately transcend the dialectics of social space described by these authors, subsequent treatments of critical space in critical theory and American fiction should be viewed as transformations of the positions articulated by Goodman and Lefebvre.

[4]

Realizing Abstract Space

Thomas Pynchon and William Gaddis

Among the texts that represent critical space in twentieth-century
American fiction, Thomas Pynchon's *Gravity's Rainbow* (1973) and
William Gaddis's *JR* (1975) occupy a decisive transitional position. In
these novels the localized spatial analytics of Goodman's *The Empire
City* are greatly expanded. Goodman portrays the effects of power in
spatial terms, and he attempts to imagine forms of community amid
the alienating aspects of midcentury American culture. In contrast,
Gaddis and Pynchon represent social power as inherently spatial in
nature. For them, power imposes itself on society through spatial
initiatives that reconfigure the entirety of social space. They are especially concerned with the imposition of spatial power through transformations of urban space. Of course, the urban domain dominates
Goodman's narrative as well, but for Gaddis and Pynchon this milieu is an agent of the social, economic, and political restructurings
of postmodernity. Much of *Gravity's Rainbow* takes place at the end
of the Second World War, but the novel is oriented toward urban
postmodernity in the United States. *JR* is obviously concerned with
the urban sphere of New York City and Long Island in the 1970s.
The emphasis on spatial power that is evident in *Gravity's Rainbow*
and *JR* is associated with different forms of spatial dialectics than
are articulated in *The Empire City*. Whereas Goodman's novel portrays the oscillating characteristics of everyday life, the narratives of
Pynchon and Gaddis identify the struggle between power and its
opposition in the larger domain of social space. The vast social vision
of *Gravity's Rainbow* and *JR*, more so than Goodman's exploration of
the possibilities of everyday life, represents a definitive replacement

of historical with spatial dialectics. At the same time, overt political commitments disappear in the narratives of Gaddis and Pynchon. While articulating some anarchist sentiments, *Gravity's Rainbow* criticizes anarchist utopianism in more stringent terms than are apparent in *The Empire City*. *JR* is wholly devoid of political attachments. The lure of the utopian past that recurs in Goodman's novel is nowhere to be found in either *Gravity's Rainbow* or *JR*. The perspectives on spatial dialectics that are articulated by Gaddis and Pynchon also mean that all forms of oppositional space are severely threatened.

Reading the novels of Pynchon and Gaddis in relation to the critical theory of Henri Lefebvre enables us to position them within twentieth-century spatial culture. In particular, Lefebvre's *The Production of Space* and *The Urban Revolution* posit theories of the spatial nature of power that illuminate the modes of critical analysis in these fictions of postmodernity.[1] In these texts Lefebvre reiterates many of the spatial concerns of the earlier-published first two volumes of *Critique of Everyday Life*. Chiefly, his theories remain deeply rooted in Marxist categories and continue to negate historical dialectics in favor of a model of dialectical struggle among different types of social space. However, in these texts Lefebvre emphasizes what Edward Soja calls "a socio-spatial dialectic" (*Postmodern* 77). Whereas in the *Critique* Lefebvre charts the dialectical interplay of alienated and unalienated aspects of everyday life, in *The Production of Space* and *The Urban Revolution* he polemically argues that spatiality is a fundamental determinant of all areas of society (social relations, class relations). The two texts are quite different in nature and scope. As its title implies, *The Urban Revolution* focuses on the social space of the city. In *The Production of Space*, Lefebvre offers a highly theoretical account of social space that is not limited to urban applications. Both texts represent a broadening of the *Critique*'s area of inquiry. Rather than being an empty or insignificant dimension, space in these texts influences the nature of society and is in turn influenced by society. This process of mutual influence defines the "socio-spatial dialectic" of Lefebvre's writing.

The Production of Space (hereafter *Production*) and *The Urban Revolution* (hereafter *Urban*) are also more historicist than the *Critique*.[2] In these later texts, Lefebvre narrates a sweeping history of social space in Western societies. In *Production*, he states that one of the most important events in the history of social space is the realization of "abstract space" (49). Lefebvre identifies abstract space with "conceived" maps of social space, or "the space of scientists, planners, urbanists, technocratic subdividers and social engineers." Abstract space entails the imposition of these "[r]epresentations of space" on social space and the violent eradication of all forms of social space that are not determined by its conceptualizations (38). In *Production*, Lefebvre states that abstract space has been realized in the transportational, financial, and military networks of late-twentieth-century neocapitalism. Similarly, in *Urban*, he argues that the principles of abstract space, which were generated by the industrial city, are manifested and disseminated in contemporary urban space. Despite the overwhelming power of abstract space, Lefebvre claims that it also gives rise to oppositional spaces. For example, in *Urban*, he argues that contemporary urban society is characterized by both the generalization of abstract space and the production of a "critical zone" in which the characteristics of oppositional space can thrive (14). His model of the dialectics of social space therefore has two components: the dialectic between space and society and the dialectic of abstract and oppositional space. Lefebvre hopes that the latter dialectic will produce a "differential" space, in which all the tendencies of abstract space are overthrown and reversed (*Urban* 52). As these comments exemplify, *Production* and *Urban* continue Lefebvre's interest in unalienated social space. While Gaddis and Pynchon differ in terms of their commitment to a dialectic of social space, both authors are concerned with exposing and analyzing the power of abstract space, investigating the possibility of its being opposed by alternative models of spatiality, and assessing its relation to contemporary urban society.

The urban context of the 1970s plays a very important role in *Gravity's Rainbow*. Much of the narrative portrays the formation of models of power that are realized in the abstract space of Los Angeles. The representation of Los Angeles occurs in just the last few pages of the text, but a postwar spatial orientation is evident in the most celebrated details of the novel. The theoretical and historical range of Lefebvre's *Production* provides an analytical framework that highlights the spatial attributes of *Gravity's Rainbow*. As Soja notes, *Production* is a "difficult" and "unruly" text that theorizes approximately seventy different types of space (*Thirdspace* 58, 59). Nevertheless, some dominant patterns emerge from Lefebvre's unsystematic writing. The basis of Lefebvre's theory is a triad of concepts that are presented in various forms and contexts. First, the concept of "perceived" space refers to the "spatial practice" that is evident through "the practical basis of the perception of the outside world" (40).[3] Second, the idea of "conceived" space designates the plans or "[r]epresentations of space" that are imposed upon social space (38). Third, "lived" or "representational" space is Lefebvre's term for the way space is used and appropriated through the creation of images and symbols (39).[4] For Lefebvre, any society is composed of these three elements, and at certain points in history, such as ancient Rome and Greece, these elements exist in a state of unity and harmony. However, the course of Western history is characterized by the fragmentation of these aspects of social space and the increasing dominance of conceived or abstract representations of space. In *Production*, Lefebvre describes abstract space as a homogenizing and fragmenting social force that seeks to destroy the potential for oppositional cultural space that lived space represents. Because it is constituted by three tendencies or "formants" that correspond with perceived, conceived, and lived space, abstract space appears as a continuation of this multifaceted model of social space (285). However, abstract space conflates and refashions these other types of space in accordance with its violent logic. Even though Lefebvre acknowledges the power of abstract space, he claims that its dominion is illusory because it contains many internal contradictions and does not wholly eradicate the oppositionality of lived space. Instead, Lefebvre claims that abstract space produces or gives rise to lived space, and he suggests that social space is characterized by a dialectical struggle between abstract space's logic of domination and the appropriating function of lived space.

The representation of critical space in *Gravity's Rainbow* shares Lefebvre's emphasis on the dialectic of abstract and lived space. Much of the distinctiveness of Pynchon's spatial dialectic is due to the ways in which *Gravity's Rainbow* reworks several key aspects of his earlier novel *The Crying of Lot 49*. In both novels, Pynchon, like Lefebvre, is interested in the late-twentieth-century manifestation of abstract space in the urban formations of advanced capitalist societies. He also shares Lefebvre's emphasis on the difficulty of perceiving the dialectics of social space. *The Crying of Lot 49* alludes to the power and range of abstract space, but an awareness of the meaning of social space is denied to Oedipa Maas, the novel's protagonist. Oedipa's attempts to execute the will of Pierce Inverarity lead her to discover the possible existence of a mysterious organization named Tristero, which appears to have been secretly involved in historical events during recent centuries. Early in the novel, Oedipa drives to San Narcisco in Southern California and observes the spatial distribution of the city, "census tracts, special purpose bond-issue districts, shopping nuclei, all overlaid with access roads to its own freeway" (24). Likening the city's spatial appearance to the printed circuit of a transistor radio, Oedipa becomes aware of "a hieroglyphic sense of concealed meaning, of an intent to communicate" and imagines that "a revelation also trembled just past the threshold of her understanding" (24). Along with her attempts to discover the truth about Tristero by hunting down clues from *The Courier's Tragedy*, Oedipa's belief that the space of the city might yield semiotic meaning reflects her conservative habits of mind.[5] Oedipa fails to understand the significance of the Berkeley campus of the University of California because her 1950s education has prepared her for the pursuit of meaning through the close attention to the details of literary texts rather than an awareness of the political activism of university campuses. Just as she awaits revelation when she encounters the urban environment, Oedipa does not attend to the university campus as a form of lived space that is meaningfully situated in a larger spatial dialectic.[6]

As she travels through Northern and Southern California, Oedipa comes across numerous different social and cultural zones, but each of them has meaning for her only as a symptom of Tristero. Oedipa's ultimately futile attempts both to trace back the phenomena that she observes to the original point of Pierce Inverarity and to reconstruct a continuous historical narrative of Tristero prevent her from regarding the distinct nature of such zones and considering the social relation between them and the space of the urban landscape. Oedipa learns that the Tristero story is one of power, but the binary code of historical dialectics in which the narrative of such power is presented to her is unstable and incoherent. Along with the political theory of the Peter Pinguid Society and other examples in the novel, Tristero's relation to the powerful postal network of Thurn und Taxis is characterized by indeterminate oppositions that undermine the credibility of dialectical history. Oedipa's "drift" through the city does enable her to encounter various autonomous spaces (110), such as the spontaneous order of the deaf-mutes' dance, but, as exemplified by the compassionate interaction with a drunken sailor that she witnesses, she is "so lost in the fantasy" of historical narrative that she cannot integrate her various spatial experiences into a social map of her world (127). Oedipa's semiotic and historicist preoccupations therefore work together to obscure the dialectics of social space.[7]

In *Gravity's Rainbow*, Pynchon overcomes the deficiencies of Oedipa's experience to present an analysis of the dialectics of social space. Whereas Oedipa never shakes free of the attempt to reconstruct a historical narrative, Pynchon's later novel offers a sustained critique of the attachment to historicity. This critique takes various forms. Throughout the novel Pynchon attacks Marxism's historical dialectics. Late in the novel the Soviet agent Vaslav Tchitcherine recalls a conversation he had with Wimpe, a representative of IG Farben. Wimpe states that the function of "Marxist dialectics" is to solve "[t]he basic problem" of "getting other people to die for you": "Die to help History grow to its predestined shape" (701). During a drug-induced "haunting" (703), Tchitcherine realizes that the fear of death caused him "to turn to a Theory of History—of all pathetic cold comforts" (704). In these scenes Pynchon evokes the dialectical history of Marxism as no more than a mechanism for killing and a salve for personal terror. Pynchon also associates dialectics with a belief in the power of "the Word" (705). In his haunting, Tchitcherine sees Galina, a woman he knew in Central Asia. She is described as coming "in from the chain-link fields of the Word" (705). Earlier, Tchitcherine thinks that he will remember Galina as "the shape of an alphabet" and as part of a "little dialectic" (339). As in *The Crying of Lot 49*, Pynchon here emphasizes the conjunction of semiotic and historicist preoccupations. Through the character of Ned Pointsman, Pynchon links dialectics with the power of language and death. Pointsman is one of the owners of "the Book" (47), a mysterious volume that seems to be about Pavlovian conditioning. When he realizes that other owners of the Book have died, he thinks that "the dialectic of the Book" will lead to his own death (142). While such incidents expand upon Pynchon's critique of history and semiotics, *Gravity's Rainbow* also includes alternative, spatial representations of dialectics. In one instance, Tyrone Slothrop visits the Odeon Café in Zurich. Slothrop wonders why Lenin, Trotsky, Joyce, and Einstein all frequented the Odeon: "[P]erhaps it had to do with the people somehow, with pedestrian mortality, restless crisscrossing of needs or desperations in one fateful piece of street . . . dialectics, matrices, archetypes all need to connect, once in a while, back to some of that proletarian blood, to body odors and senseless screaming across a table, to cheating and lasting hopes, or else all is dusty Dracularity, the West's ancient curse" (262–63).[8] In this passage Pynchon clearly articulates a dialectics of urban space that encompasses the lived space of "proletarian blood" and "lasting hopes." As in Lefebvre's writing, this spatial dialectic is opposed to the dialectics of history.

Gravity's Rainbow's critique of history is not restricted to attacks on dialectics. By repeatedly challenging the meaningfulness of terms associated with war, such as sides, fronts, and surrenders, the novel offers a critique of the notion of war as a legitimate agent of historical change. Also, the nonlinear textuality of the novel obviously disrupts chronological structures. In addition, as Steven Weisenburger describes, Pynchon's novel contains many instances of "hysteron proteron," or a reverse causality in which narrative events move from effects to their causes. Films that run backward, various aspects of the v-2 rocket, and "characters' fantasies" are all examples of the novel's use of this trope (92). According to Weisenburger, hysteron proteron is a violent form of modernist nostalgia that serves to underwrite conventional and linear narratives of history: "[R]eading the 'one, two . . .' (or *proteron, hysteron . . .*) orderings of plot will always be determined by the backward-glancing hysteron proteron of narrativization" (90). Yet, as Weisenburger notes, "[S]uch theories tend to deconstruct with their own tools" (97). In *Gravity's Rainbow*, the omnipresent foregrounding of hysteron proteron destabilizes the authority of linear history and reveals it to be an arbitrary imposition on disparate phenomena. "Contemporary physics," Weisenburger continues, has discredited the ideas of reversibility upon which hysteron proteron is based (100), and he suggests that the opposition between Franz Pökler's ideas of causality and the appeal of his wife, Leni, to "Parallel. Not series" thematizes this distinction between hysteron proteron and contemporary science (159). The distinction noted by Weisenburger also illustrates the novel's overall replacement of historicity with spatiality as a mode of critical analysis. Whereas Leni is part of a revolutionary group that discusses "street tactics" (158), Franz is afraid of "the street" and the political activities of his wife (158). In these passages Pynchon links theoretical concerns about causality and spatiality to social struggle. As in the case of Oedipa Maas, Franz's adherence to causality is accompanied by a lack of appreciation for the struggle for social space. In contrast, Leni's awareness of simultaneous connections between events is allied to a commitment to spatial politics.

By overcoming some of the limited perspectives that dominate *The Crying of Lot 49*, *Gravity's Rainbow* engages with the forms of social space that are evident in the earlier novel. The different facets of Oedipa's vague sense of the spatial nature of power are revealed as the components of Lefebvrean social space in the later novel. According to Lefebvre, a semiotic approach to the understanding of social space cannot succeed, because "power has no code" and thus "can in no wise be decoded" (162). *Gravity's Rainbow* frequently negates a semiotic reading of space and power. The narrative speaks disparagingly of "[s]hit, money, and the Word, the three American truths" and the Puritan obsession with textual interpretation (28). Slothrop comes from a family of "word-smitten Puritans" (207), and his "love for the Word" is associated with "his inertia of motion, his real helplessness" (207). Oberst Enzian and the Schwarzkommando are devoted to the rocket because they regard it as a "holy Text" (520), but in the Zone, Enzian wonders "if I'm riding through it, the Real Text, right now, if this is it . . . or if I passed it today somewhere in the devastation of Hamburg, breathing the ash-dust, missing it completely" (520). Here, Enzian has a dim awareness that the social space of his movements ought to be the object of his interests. While Enzian does not wholly forfeit his textual concerns, it does occur to him that the "distribution networks" and "routes of power" of social space are more significant than his perception of the rocket-as-text to be "annotated, explicated" (521). In negating Oedipa's semiotic preoccupations, the novel highlights the process by which social space is produced. In so doing, Pynchon subverts the notion of social space as a neutral, empty, or a priori dimension. At the novel's opening, Pirate Prentice dreams of the arrival of the v-2 rocket and the evacuation of the preterite from London. The evacuees move through a multileveled carriage, archways, a narrowing road, a hotel that is an extension of rail tracks, "warehouse aisles," an open elevator, and thousands of "invisible rooms" (4). That Prentice describes the city as a "coral-like and mysteriously vital growth" indicates that its space in the dream is *produced*. Similarly, Thomas Gwenhidwy's crazy ideas about the "City Paranoiac" expand Pirate's dream observations (172). Speaking to Pointsman in a halting Welsh brogue, Gwenhidwy describes the City Paranoiac as an "intelligent creature" that has grown over the centuries by "[c]ounter-feiting all the correct forces [. . .] the eco-nomic, the demographic" (172). Echoing Lefebvre's analysis of a sociospatial dialectic, Gwenhidwy describes the city, along with economics and demographics, as an active force in the production of society.

The space that is produced in the novel is that of the dialectic of abstract and lived space, which Oedipa fails to recognize. As the name suggests, abstract space is not reducible to localized perceptions of space. Instead, it is defined by the restructuring of broad conceptions of space according to abstract spatial models. A significant reference to abstract space in *Gravity's Rainbow* occurs as Katje Borgesius meets Enzian in the Zone. When Katje asks Enzian what Blicero means to him, he replies obliquely, "At this point, I would take you to a balcony. An observation deck. I would show you the Raketen-Stadt. Plexiglass maps of the webs we maintain across the Zone. Underground schools, systems for distributing food and medicine. . . . We would gaze down on staff-rooms, communications centers, laboratories, clinics" (660). Ostensibly an expression of Enzian as "[a]n estranged figure at a certain elevation and distance" (660), this response also equates Blicero with the realization of abstract space. Such representations of space are, for Lefebvre, simultaneously homogeneous and fragmented, and these two aspects form a contradiction that makes abstract space vulnerable to opposition. More specifically, abstract space initially appears homogeneous, but it actually consists of distinct aspects. In *Gravity's Rainbow*, Pynchon uses the abstract notion of "the War" to describe these general trends in the reshaping of social space. By describing the War as "a single damaged landscape" that Slothrop can only "begin to feel the leading edges of" (257), Pynchon suggests both the homogeneity of the War's space and the difficulty of comprehending it. Yet Pynchon also emphasizes the tension between claims of unity and division: "The War needs to divide this way, and to subdivide, though its propaganda will always stress unity, alliance, pulling together" (130). Such abstract designs of social space result in the eradication of areas of lived space: "[T]he Home Front is something of a fiction and lie, designed, not too subtly, to draw them apart, to subvert love in favor of work, abstraction, required pain, bitter death" (41).

The illusion of homogeneity belies the conflated presence of the different aspects or "formants" of abstract space (287). Pynchon's treatment of abstract space represents the different features of these formants, the means by which they are realized, and the manner in which they are coarticulated. According to Lefebvre, abstract space has a "geometric formant" that is based on the principle of conceived space and organizes social space as a homogeneous plane (285). While Oedipa is faced with this geometric formant of abstract space, which for Lefebvre is characterized by the integration of housing and industrial areas and transportation and communication networks, she cannot comprehend its nature. Since Lefebvre claims that the conceptual nature of abstract space derives from mathematics, his references to the geometricality of abstract space should be taken literally. In *Gravity's Rainbow*, Pynchon makes explicit the geometric formant of abstract space by emphasizing its mathematical nature. "Old Brigadier Pudding" has been "reactivated in 1940, set down in a new space, not only of battlefield [. . .] but also of the War-state itself, its very structure" (76). In order to express Pudding's disorientation in this unfamiliar social space, Pynchon writes, "The newer geometries confuse him" (77). The invocation of geometry suggests that the transformation of social space that occurs in the novel is predicated on developments in mathematics.

The calculus of the trajectory of the v-2 rocket is of course the primary form of mathematics in the novel. Pynchon's main concern with calculus is its evocation of a continuous arc of motion through the calculation of a vast number of points within this purported arc. Calculus is therefore a "pornograph[y] of flight" (567). Pynchon makes numerous analogies with the rocket's arc, such as the impression of continuous motion in film projection and Franz Pökler's construction of the unity of his daughter's life from sporadic encounters with her, and his overall purpose is to show how dominant forms of power create deceptive effects of holistic meaning. In particular, Pynchon highlights the illusion of unity generated by the fragmentation of abstract social space. As well as being based on calculus and realized in social networks, the geometric formant of abstract space is identified with the "rational structure" of corporate power that is imagined by Walter Rathenau—a structure in which unity and diversity among firms are equally stressed (165). Pynchon's equation of "Analysis and Death" encompasses the mathematical, infrastructural, and corporate components of abstract space, and his description of "American Death" as the "last phase" in the implementation of this structure evokes postwar American society as the location in which the geometric formant of abstract space is realized (722).

As well as its geometric formant, abstract space has "visual" and "phallic" formants (286). Just as the geometric formant engenders the conceived dimension of abstract space, so too the visual and phallic formants respectively produce abstract space's versions of perceived and lived space. For Lefebvre, abstract space is dominated by a visual relation that reduces tactile experience to a specular passivity based on semiotic interpretation. The objects of the visual formant of abstract space are symbolic presences that Lefebvre describes in terms of the "phallic brutality" and "masculine violence" of the phallic formant (287). The different formants of abstract space are frequently conjoined in *Gravity's Rainbow* to constitute various types of narrative structures.[9] When Pynchon describes the war as "spectacle," he highlights the visual formant in isolation (105), but it is more usual for him to evoke the visual in relation to these other formants. In particular, rocketry technology binds together the geometric and visual formants of abstract space. For example, in one of Franz Pökler's dreams, the rocket "would sometimes not be a literal rocket at all, but a street he knew was in a certain district of the city" (400). The dream suggests the continuity between technological geometries and visual architecture, a point that is underscored by the fact that the tunnels of the underground v-2 factory at Mittelweke are shaped like the double integrals of the calculus of the rocket. In a similar vein, Pynchon notes that Friedrich August Kekulé von Stradonitz—the chemist whose study of the benzene ring made possible the technology upon which the rocket was based—"brought the mind's eye of an architect over into chemistry" (411). The realization of the rocket and the science upon which it is based in the social space of the novel is similar to Enzian's identification of Blicero with the conceived map of abstract space because, in both cases, elements of Pynchon's narrative are metamorphosed into spatiality itself.

The many cities in *Gravity's Rainbow* constitute one of the most prevalent forms of the visual or perceived aspect of abstract space. Pynchon's evocation of the process of the production of space is often focused on cities. Vaska Tumir suggests that cities in *Gravity's Rainbow* are "inanimate and inorganic" (138), but, as we have seen, the City Paranoiac is described as "a growing neo-plasm" (173). Also, Pynchon depicts the Raketen-Stadt, "a giant factory-state here, a City of the Future," as "a system of buildings that move, by right angles, along the grooves of the Raketen-Stadt's street-grid" (674). With its "extrapolated 1930s swoop-façaded and balconied skyscrapers" (674), the Raketen-Stadt is an extension of the utopian modernist city, such as Le Corbusier's Radiant City. According to Lefebvre, the architecture of Le Corbusier, along with the entire project of the Bauhaus, was a crucial moment in the history of the production of space. Le Corbusier and the Bauhaus understood social space as a total system that comprised living and working units and the spatial links between them. For Lefebvre, such a project meant the realization of abstract space within the domain of perceived space and the creation of "the worldwide, homogeneous and monotonous architecture of the state" (26). Pynchon's evocation of "the City Dactylic" as a place where "there is no place to hide" reflects a critical stance toward the city's visuality that echoes the sentiments of Lefebvre (566). The modernist city is also a centralized space, and Lefebvre claims that the idea of the center is an essential component of the visual formant. Described as a "holy Center" (508), Peenemünde, the v-2 test and construction site, exemplifies the conjunction of the rocket and centrality in *Gravity's Rainbow*. Similarly, Slothrop describes the Nordhausen Mittelwerke as "a center he has been skirting" (312). In Lefebvre's analysis, the origination of the concept of the center in mathematics means that it is an especially important link between the geometric and visual formants of abstract space. Because the center defines that which occupies the visual dimension of abstract space, it also conjoins the phallic and the visual. Lefebvre states that the phallic formant annexes the symbolic meanings of lived space, and Pynchon often portrays cities as centers that function in this way. Zwölfkinder, the Nazi town for children that is built as "an official version of innocence" (419), is an example of the phallic appropriation of lived experience. The Schwarzkommando's occupation of Nordhausen, the town where the Mittelweke is situated, further illustrates how the novel's characters attach personal, symbolic meanings to the spaces of power. In moments such as these, Pynchon shows how the affinity with the phallic formant of abstract space enervates all other meaning and experience.

Along with the city, the rocket is of course the primary manifestation of the phallicism of abstract space. The rocket may not be the "Real Text" of power in the novel, but it is both the most prominent icon of power and the means by which it is realized. The brutal and masculinist attributes of the phallic formant are epitomized by the rocket. Because of its sexual associations, the rocket is an object of attraction and obsession for many characters. According to Lefebvre, abstract space engenders a relationship of fetishism. With reference to Marx's theory of commodity fetishism, Lefebvre states that abstract space is regarded fetishistically as a reified, alienating, isolated, and seemingly a priori dimension (351). [10] In *Gravity's Rainbow*, Pynchon represents this relationship as a sexual fetishism that is directed toward the phallic rocket. For example, the attraction of the rocket and that of fetishistic clothing are equated. More important, the "erectile" plastic of Imipolex G (699), which forms the S-Gerät that encases Gottfried in Rocket 00000, is the rocket material to which Slothrop has been conditioned to respond sexually. Pynchon makes more direct connections between fetishism and spatiality. He describes Enzian's desire for "the Center" as one of "the sexual fetishes Christianity knows how to flash" (321), and the "reconfigured" space of an IG Farben factory occurs via "an arrangement of fetishes" (520). The sexual function of the rocket extends beyond direct attraction to include structures of social behavior. Lefebvre states that abstract space reduces both sexuality and social encounters to the reproduction of "the family unit" (49). The rocket activities of Blicero combine the phallic presence of the rocket with the reproduction of a version of family life. Pynchon reiterates that Blicero produces "his own space" (486), "his native space" (487), within which Katje and Gottfried act out the roles of "the strayed children" (96). Centered upon the rocket, these deadly games culminate in both the firing of Rocket 00000 and the revelation of Blicero as "the father you will never quite manage to kill" (747). Lefebvre states that the Roman "Pater-Rex" served a crucial role in the historical development of abstract space. The principle of "The Father" made abstraction the basis of social life and "reconstituted the space around him as the *space of power*" (243). *Gravity's Rainbow* frequently identifies the phallic formant of the rocket with father conspiracies and paternal authority; for example, Enzian's obsessive pursuit of the rocket is described as an egotistical "holy-father routine" (525). As in Lefebvre's definition of the center of abstract space as the site of "sacrifice" (332), the phallic and fetishistic formant of the rocket, in conjunction with paternal, familial, and spatial elements, leads to the death and sacrifice of Gottfried in the visual center.

Despite the dominance of the modernist city and the rocket, their function is ultimately superseded in *Gravity's Rainbow*. Pynchon's novel is primarily concerned with the war as a moment of significant transformation in the nature of abstract social space. References to the culture and society of the United States reflect Pynchon's concern with the impact of this transformation on American social space. *Gravity's Rainbow* suggests that aspects of contemporary American society are extensions of the economic, military, and technological attributes of Nazi Germany, and as the section on Lyle Bland and the Great Pinball Difficulty illustrates, Pynchon is primarily interested in the "*real* work" of an "American synthesis" of industrial cartelization, psychological research, and political manipulation (581). Because of Géza Rószavölgyi's Weberian comments about the need for "a concentrated point of light, some leader or program powerful enough to last them across who knows how many years of Postwar" (80–81), it is tempting to regard a single technological initiative, such as the Apollo space program, as the form in which the power structures forged by the Nazis' v-2 rocketry program and the industrial cartel of IG Farben are maintained.[11] But as John Hamill comments, *Gravity's Rainbow* is also *"about* the formation of the Cold War in its techno-bureaucratic context" (417). Yet even Hamill's comments do not encompass the entirety of the novel's postwar concerns. The novel's continual emphasis on spatiality suggests that Pynchon envisions a form of power that extends beyond any single program or "System" to impact and reconstruct vast reaches of social space (Hamill 417).

For Lefebvre, abstract space is fully realized in the transportation, financial, and communication networks of contemporary neocapitalism, and the interrelation of different formants is the means by which this type of social space is brought into being. In *Gravity's Rainbow*, the transportation networks of the decentralized postmodern city extend the attributes of the modernist city and the rocket to become the site of the final manifestation of abstract space. Pynchon's concern to portray the network city as the realization of abstract space accounts for his portrayal of the freeway system of Southern California in the novel's concluding pages.[12] Richard M. Zhlubb, a fictional version of Richard Nixon, drives on the Los Angeles freeways. His journey conjoins geometric and visual formants because the abstract system of the transportation network produces the kind of visual experience of space that Lefebvre describes: "[T]he driver is concerned only with steering himself to his destination, and in looking about sees only what he needs to see for that purpose; he thus perceives only his route, which has been materialized, mechanized and technicized" (313). The final sentences of *Gravity's Rainbow* allude to the phallic formant because the rocket is about to descend upon the Orpheus Theatre, which is managed by Zhlubb. By literalizing Enzian's claim that "the Rocket can penetrate, from the sky, at any given point" (728), this final section suggests that the rocket's violent threat has permeated abstract space to become virtual and omnipresent. As is suggested in an earlier scene in the novel, the rocket has been transformed from a localized and phallic form into the general configuration of abstract social space itself: "The moving vehicle is frozen, in space, to become architecture, and timeless" (300). Whereas *The Crying of Lot 49* offers just a glimpse of the abstract space of Southern California, *Gravity's Rainbow* depicts such space as the culmination of a shift in the nature of social power.

In *Thirdspace*, Soja discusses Lefebvre's critique of the "double illusion" of spatiality (62). Lefebvre warns against understanding space as either an objective, empirical domain or a subjective, mental representation. Soja defines these two perspectives on space as, respectively, "the realistic illusion" and "the illusion of transparency" (*Thirdspace* 64, 63). For Soja, Lefebvre theorizes social space as a third term that encompasses and yet is distinct from these two versions of spatiality. Referring to *Gravity's Rainbow*, Hanjo Berressem argues, "Pynchon understands Europe not so much as a mere grouping of geopolitical units but more as both a real and a mental territory, a 'state of mind' in which psychic and geographic space are conflated" (121). One of the primary effects of the shifting and groundless ontology of *Gravity's Rainbow* is the negation of stable distinctions between subjective and objective space. As in Soja's reading of Lefebvre, the conflation of mental and physical space noted by Berressem gives rise in Pynchon's novel to the representation of social space. Soja recasts Lefebvre's sociospatial dialectic, in which society and spatiality are mutually determining, as a "trialectics" of mental, empirical, and social space. He then posits that *Production* is generally characterized by a process of "thirding-as-Othering," and he explicates Lefebvre's "thematic trialectics" (spatial practice, representations of space, spaces of representation) in terms of this process (*Thirdspace* 64, 65). Specifically, lived space (spaces of representation) is a form of spatial "Othering" that ruptures the binary of material spatial practices and abstract representations of space. Soja's definition of lived space as a form of "radical openness" resonates with *Gravity's Rainbow*, which is obviously a text that is ontologically "open" at numerous points. Along with Pynchon's representation of social space, the textuality of *Gravity's Rainbow* is a form of spatial "thirding-as-Othering" that overcomes the binary of mental and physical space.

While Lefebvre discusses three terms of social space, his analysis is often reduced to an opposition between abstract and lived space.

The spatial dialectics of *Gravity's Rainbow* are also characterized by such an opposition. As well as a textualized third space, Pynchon represents various forms of lived space in the narrative. In *Production*, abstract space may seem to dominate the entirety of social space, but it dialectically gives rise to and thus cannot wholly eradicate lived space. Whereas abstract space is rooted in conceived representations of space, lived space is identified with the symbolic uses and meanings of space that are associated with the body and "lived experience" (203). Unlike the ordering principles of abstract space, the representational spaces of lived space "need obey no rules of consistency or cohesiveness," are "[r]edolent with imaginary and symbolic elements," often derive from "childhood memories" and dreams, emerge from "lived situations," and are "essentially qualitative, fluid and dynamic" (41, 42). Opposed to the property principle of abstract space, lived space generates everyday art objects from "the clandestine or underground side of social life" (33). Also, lived space counters the homogenized fragmentation of abstract space with differential unity. At the same time, lived space is the realm of artists "who *describe* and aspire to do no more than describe" (39). Soja refers to lived space as "the space of social struggle" (*Thirdspace* 68), but, as he concedes, Lefebvre's theory of lived space is informed by a sense of passivity and impotence. In *Gravity's Rainbow*, Pynchon shares Lefebvre's dialectic of abstract and lived space. Abstract space engenders lived spaces that are celebrated in terms that are as enthusiastic as those of Lefebvre. Yet Pynchon also represents the limits of spatial dialectics. Lived spaces often remain dialectically trapped in the logic of abstract space. They are therefore undercut by the process that enables them.

The celebration of lived space in *Gravity's Rainbow* exhibits many of the features noted by Lefebvre. The sanctuaries of "love-in-idleness" that characters such as Slothrop and Roger Mexico experience exemplify the lived spaces that lie beyond the formants of abstract space (22). While there are many examples of pockets of lived space in the novel, the production of lived space from the contradictions of abstract space is epitomized by Pynchon's description of the Zone. As it attempts to achieve a quantitative expansiveness over the social field, abstract space generates a qualitative shift in the nature of social space. More specifically, the homogenized fragmentation of abstract space is transformed into a new space of differential unity. On several occasions Pynchon notes how groupings of autonomous differences result in social unity. Slothrop's realization that there are "[n]o zones but the Zone" and Geli Tripping's comment on the "arrangements" of the Zone emphasize the unity and order that spontaneously emerges in the Zone (333, 290). One such example, "Der Platz," a tenement occupied by friends of Säure Bummer, illustrates the symbolic creativity of lived space. Der Platz is described as "an ingenious system" that includes "a system of rivers and waterfalls" and "an anti-police *moat*." As well as exhibiting these innovative symbolic qualities, Der Platz is a site of refuge for "isolates, fetishists, lost stumblers-in," and others whose difference drives them from the normativity of abstract space (686). For Lefebvre, the symbolic dimension of lived space is produced by subjective experiences such as dreams and childhood memories. Similarly, Pynchon suggests that the realization of the meaning of both lived and abstract space is derived from the experience of "dreams, psychic flashes, omens, cryptographies, drug-epistemologies, all dancing on a ground of terror, contradiction, absurdity" (582). In Lefebvre's account, "Differences endure or arise on the margins of the homogenized realm, either in the form of resistances or in the form of externalities" (373). Pynchon's reference to the possibility of "a Revolution-in-exile-in-residence, a continuity, surviving at the bleak edge over these Weimar years" also denotes the emergence of lived space at the margins of power (155). At other points, Pynchon emphasizes the opposition to abstract space that emerges from these sites of lived space. For example, the opening scene, in which Pirate Prentice cooks his famous banana breakfast, typifies Pynchon's use of everyday symbolic life as a means of resistance against the power that he describes.

However, the spatial dialectics of the novel also work against the production of lived space. For Lefebvre, abstract space seeks to dominate and reappropriate lived space. Lefebvre's analysis of "absolute space" offers an illustration of this process (234). Usually associated with sacred or profane characteristics, absolute spaces are natural locations with reference to which nomadic and seminomadic societies are organized. Even though absolute space often exhibits the attributes of lived space, it can become conceptualized as a representation of space and thus be appropriated as part of abstract space. Lefebvre's analysis of spatial appropriation is linked to his discussion of induced, produced, and reduced spatial differences. For Lefebvre, "*induced* differences—differences internal to a whole and brought into being by that whole as a system aiming to establish itself and then to close (for example, the suburban 'world of villas')—are hard to distinguish either from *produced* differences, which escape the system's rule, or from *reduced* differences, forced back into the system by constraint and violence" (382). As in Lefebvre's comments, the induced differences of abstract space, the produced differences of lived space, and the reduced differences of reappropriated space are often difficult to separate in *Gravity's Rainbow*. The case of Enzian and the Schwarzkommando reflects the process of spatial appropriation. Enzian's dream of "mythical return" is evoked as a desire for a natural space of alterity: "Somewhere, among the wastes of the World, is the key that will bring us back, restore us to our Earth and to our freedom" (519, 525). Enzian appears to seek an absolute space that would represent a produced difference within the terrain of abstract space. Yet Enzian's devotion to the rocket as a means of attaining this dream reflects a reduced difference that is reappropriated within the framework of abstract space's phallic formant.

The spatial dialectics of reappropriation is integral to Pynchon's representation of Squalidozzi and the Argentinean anarchists. As Graham Benton argues, "[T]he shape and scope of the novel, in all its complexity, are informed by anarchist thought" (152). Therefore, Pynchon's treatment of anarchism represents spatial dynamics that resonate throughout the text. Voicing a spatial theory of anarchism to Slothrop, Squalidozzi claims that social struggle is defined in terms of the conflict between repressive centralization and liberatory decentralization. In the Argentinean context, centralization is associated with the urban network of Buenos Aires, and decentralization is identified with "the anarchic oneness of pampas and sky" (264). Squalidozzi explains that centralization is ordinarily dominant, but that the war is an exceptional time in which the fragmentation of social space has been replaced by the openness of the Zone. However, he believes that such openness represents both "hope" and "danger" to his anarchist cause (265). Squalidozzi's ideas are played out as Gerhardt von Göll offers to film the Argentinean anarchists in a version of the epic poem *Martín Fierro*. The poem, which is in two parts, is regarded as an allegory of the distinction between centralization and decentralization to which the anarchists subscribe. In the first part, Martín is enlisted in General Roca's campaign to annex the pampas and kill its indigenous inhabitants. Martín refuses to participate in such atrocities, deserts Roca's army, and "flee[s] across the frontier, to live in the wilderness, to live with the Indians" (387). In the second part, Martín rejoins Buenos Airean society and betrays all the values that he upheld in the first part. Von Göll persuades the anarchists that the film will enable them to recapture in the Zone the open and unified space of which they dream. Yet he also argues that they should film both parts of the poem because "even the freest of Gauchos end up selling out" (387). By capitulating to von Göll's "madness" (388), the anarchists, like the Schwarzkommando, identify their desire for an oppositional space with a return to absolute space. Such a strategy signals the reappropriation of lived space within the abstract space of von Göll's filmic project. As a result, the anarchists become just another one of the many reduced differences of the Zone.

Toward the end of the novel, Pynchon offers three variations on the dialectics of abstract and lived space. Despite evading the attractions of absolute space, these variations do not guarantee the viability of lived space. Formed in London among characters who are opposed to the alleged "They-system" (638), the Counterforce is a form of oppositional lived space that exists in a dialectical relation with abstract space. "Dialectically," thinks Katje, "sooner or later, some counterforce would have to arise" (536). These thoughts are reiterated by Prentice: "For every They there ought to be a We. In our case there is. Creative paranoia means developing at least as thorough a We-system as a They-system" (638). As many critics note, Pynchon satirizes the Counterforce.[13] In stating that the members of the Counterforce are unable "to disarm, de-penis and dismantle the Man" (712), Pynchon suggests that they cannot break free of the phallic formant of abstract space. Also, Mexico's realization that the Counterforce is "playing Their game" qualifies Osbie Feel's belief that they act in opposition to the abstract space of "Their rational arrangements" (639). Nevertheless, the Counterforce highlights the dialectics of social space and thus negates abstract space's claim to totality.[14] The problem with the Counterforce is not its dialectical production but its status, in Lefebvre's terms, as a reduced difference that does not escape the logic of abstract space. In contrast, Slothrop represents a produced difference within the social space of the novel. His conditioned responses to the rocket mean that his subjectivity is dialectically bound up with the formants of abstract space. Yet he becomes "Slothropian space" (238), a mobile version of lived space. As Rocketman, he regards the German Autobahn as "a deadly barrier" and "[l]eaps broad highways in a single bound" (380). He therefore understands the nature of the formants of abstract space and is able to escape them. Just as Blicero and the rocket become the formations of abstract space, Slothrop realizes lived space when he lies down on the earth and becomes a "crossroad" in the Zone (626). By undoing "the Man" (712), the egotistical subjectivity that Pynchon and Lefebvre associate with phallicism, Slothrop's infamous dissipation represents the further negation of the formants of abstract space.

In his representation of Los Angeles, Pynchon offers a third variation on the dialectics of social space. Driving on the Los Angeles freeways, Zhlubb observes people by the roadside who play harmonicas and kazoos. To Zhlubb, these are subversive individuals who disturb the queues at the Orpheus Theatre, but Pynchon evokes them as the preterite constituents of lived space. Since Slothrop may have appeared as a kazoo player on the cover of a rock album by a band called The Fool, he is identified with the kazoo players. The scenes outline a direct confrontation between abstract and lived space. Speaking of the kazoo-playing protestors, Zhlubb is confident that "[t]here'll be a nice secure home for them all, down in Orange County. Right next to Disneyland" (756). Zhlubb therefore states that lived space, such as that embodied in Slothrop, will be incorporated into abstract space. As we have seen, Lefebvre states that "reduced differences" are "forced back into the system by constraint and violence" (382). If the redistribution of the preterite is a form of constraint, the threat of the v-2 rocket that hangs over the heads of the preterite audience at the Orpheus Theatre is a form of violence. Despite the impending presence of the visual-phallic formant of abstract space, the preterite song that the audience sings suggests that the autonomous culture of lived space is not yet annihilated. For Lefebvre, the lived spaces that are dialectically produced by abstract space reintroduce the force of history and class struggle into its static expanse. In the preterite song, the reference to "a Hand to turn the time" similarly suggests that lived space might renew history in its opposition to abstract space (760). *Gravity's Rainbow* therefore concludes on an ambiguous note. The status of lived space is precarious, and the preterite are about to become reappropriated as a reduced difference in abstract space. However, Pynchon insists that abstract space is not a totality because it dialectically produces lived spaces. These lived spaces do not have a utopian function in *Gravity's Rainbow*. They are not idealized models of social space, and they are not the source of effective political resistance. Rather, Pynchon exchanges spatial utopianism for spatial analytics.[15] He is not primarily concerned with representing the resolution of a dialectical struggle in favor of either abstract space or its opposition, but he is interested in depicting the formation of abstract space, the emergence of lived space, and the confrontation between these two forms of social space in contemporary urban society.

The emphasis on postwar urban space that is evident at the conclusion of *Gravity's Rainbow* informs the entirety of William Gaddis's *JR*. Through the narrative of J. R. Vansant, a sixth-grade boy who builds a financial empire from devalued stocks, speculative real estate deals, and other business transactions, Gaddis's novel criticizes the practices of finance capital in the early 1970s. Set amid the social landscapes of Long Island and New York City, *JR* portrays how such business practices engender abstract space in contemporary urban society. Unlike *Gravity's Rainbow* and *Production*, *JR* does not contextualize the realization of abstract space in terms of a long historical assessment of the conjunction of its formants. Instead, *JR*'s narrow narrative time frame represents the moment of the manifestation of abstract space in urban society. In so doing, Gaddis's novel resonates most strongly with Lefebvre's *Urban* and, to a lesser extent, "Right to the City."[16] In these texts, which represent an earlier moment in Lefebvre's thought than *Production*, Lefebvre describes post–World War II urban society as a distinct phase in the history of capitalist modes of production (14). For Lefebvre, urban space manifests "abstract space" because it is "occupied by interrelated networks" and characterized by the coexistence of "homogeneity (quantitative, geometric and logical space)" and "differences" or fragmentation (167). As Gottdiener comments, urban planning realizes abstract space through "state intervention" (146), and these various factors lead Lefebvre to define the process that he criticizes as "[t]he politics of space" (48). For Lefebvre, the realization of abstract space is a "crisis" in which "the urban problematic becomes a global phenomenon" (18, 15). He is committed to the sociospatial dialectic and articulates a "spectral analysis" of the dialectical interplay of different "levels" of society ("Right" 142, 113). *Urban* also suggests that urban society will give rise to "generalized self-management" and the "right to the city" (150). But Lefebvre's emphasis on urban developments causes these utopian gestures to seem at times more like prophetic visions than dialectical convictions. Similarly, Gaddis's critique of the extensive presence of abstract space in urban society results in more limited and more compromised representations of oppositional space than are evident in *Gravity's Rainbow*.

In *Urban*, one of the most important components of Lefebvre's analysis of the abstract tendencies in contemporary society is his discussion of the relation between industrial and urban space. For Lefebvre, urban society represents a distinct phase beyond that of industrialization in the history of capitalist modes of production. His polemic in *Urban* is directed against those Marxists who regard the urban sphere as either an empty and neutral phenomenon or simply the superstructure of a more fundamental economic base. He claims that such a "blind field" is due to the perception of the city as the locus of industrialization (30). In contrast to this view, Lefebvre posits that industrialization is "a step toward urbanization, a moment, an intermediary, an instrument" (139). Most significantly, urban space usurps industry's role as a determinant of social structures. Lefebvre's postindustrial perspective on the city is therefore central to his articulation of a sociospatial dialectic.[17] Urban space is distinctive because it is the site of the production of surplus value through commerce and banking: "There is nothing but offices, one after the other" (128). In "Right to the City," Lefebvre reiterates that urban centrality is reduced to "the centre of decision-making" (81). As stated in *Urban*, urban society is continuous with the abstractions, "will to homogeneity," and "quantitative rationality" of industrial organization (125), and Lefebvre denies that "the phenomena associated with industrialization [. . .] have been completely supplanted by urban phenomena" (138). However, the fragmenting principle of abstract urban space ruptures the social fabric and thus differs from the unified rationality of the industrial era. Because of their commitment to "the rationality of business" (145), writes Lefebvre, the urban spheres in the United States epitomize these abstract tendencies. Moreover, Lefebvre's logic also suggests that American cities are especially vulnerable to the "accentuated" financial crises that he identifies with urban space (169).

In *JR*, Gaddis evokes the abstract nature of urban space through his portrayal of business activities and their relation to industrialization. Gaddis's representation of the office space of Manhattan shows how centers of financial decision making dominate urban society.[18] Many of the scenes in Manhattan occur at the Wall Street offices of Crawley and Brothers and the headquarters of Typhon International. The locus of many of JR's financial activities, these stockbroking and corporate locations dominate the narrative of the city. The dominance of urban space by business interests engenders the dystopian homogenization that characterizes abstract space. During the course of the narrative, Manhattan locations such as the Automat cafeteria, the 96th Street apartment, the Metropolitan Museum of Art, and a hospital all become the sites of business activity.[19] Trains, taxis, and limousines are also transformed into urban zones of financial dealing. Through references to the conquest of Manhattan by European settlers, Gaddis identifies business activities with the entirety of the island. During the school trip to Manhattan made by JR and his class, Davidoff, the public relations official at Typhon, "found himself standing alone—on the northernmost line of defense of this tiny Dutch settlement" (82). Also, the price of the share in Diamond Cable that the class buys, twenty-four dollars, is the same as the amount for which Manhattan was originally purchased. Referring to the Federal Reserve Bank, Davidoff proclaims, "[T]here are millions of dollars right under your feet, in vaults five stories down in bed rock" (82). In these moments Gaddis identifies the materiality of urban space with business activity. At other points in the novel, Gaddis emphasizes the process by which urban space and financial decision making produce each other. When Crawley suggests that JR's financial empire is "having a little space problem" and thus should be moved to the Waldorf Hotel (444), he alludes to the takeover of urban space caused by the growth of JR's corporation. Similarly, Davidoff tells Amy Joubert, the daughter of a Typhon executive, that "the new parent world headquarters building up the street" will be part of the "new corporate restructuring" (195). By identifying the transformation of urban space with the reorganization of business practices, Davidoff describes the sociospatial dialectic that is the context for the events of the novel.

In *Urban*, Lefebvre insists that urban space should be viewed as a "form" or set of tendencies in social space rather than a material object (171). Gaddis shares this view and portrays tendencies that encompass the dialectics of urban space and industrial production. Through JR's self-perpetuating financial pursuits, Gaddis represents business practices that not only marginalize the importance of production but also thrive on the declining fortunes of industrial concerns. JR's practices represent the moment at which, in Lefebvre's terms, "the urban interven[es] as such in production" ("Right" 110). In other words, JR's colonization of urban space displaces an interest in industrial production. Instead of investing in production, JR undertakes a continual process of investment that itself becomes the source of value. For example, the only reason he sets up JR Shipping Company is to receive government contributions, and his book and matchbook concerns serve primarily as advertising media for his other acquisitions. His actions fragment industrial space and subordinate industrial production. When he sees a picture of the plant of Eagle Mills, a concern that he takes over, JR notices that the mill, offices, garage, and softball field are spread out over terrain that is connected by railroad tracks. JR's plan to bring the offices into the mill and sell off the other assets destroys the existing integration of the plant. Such activities illustrate the point made by Lefebvre regarding the manner in which the concentration of business in urban space fragments the unified structure of industrial space. At the same time JR hopes to homogenize and consolidate the space into "one parcel" (295). Later in the novel JR plans to turn the plant into "a park and a speedway" (525). The promise of the transformation of the plant into a space of leisure pursuits further represents the eradication of industrial production. JR is excited to read the newspaper report of the visit to Eagle made by Edward Bast, his reluctant business associate, because it repeatedly refers to his business practice in terms of "downtown financial interests headquartered in the New York area" (293). JR's gleeful response to the newspaper report shows that the urban centralization of financial power and the dismantling of areas of industrial production form the crux of his endeavors.

The tendencies of JR constitute a dialectic that leads to the realization of abstract space and the displacement of industrial production. Along with JR's corporation, Typhon and General Roll participate in a sociospatial dialectic of urban space and industrial production. In addition, there is a dialectical interaction among the different companies in the novel, which usually results in takeovers by JR's corporation. Differences between the companies can also be considered in terms of an archeology of relations between urban form and industrial production. The dialectical archeology of the novel reiterates Gaddis's interest in the process of postindustrial transformation. The strongest distinction in the novel's archeology of production is between JR's corporation and General Roll, a company based in Astoria, New York. As we have noted, JR transforms all areas of Manhattan into business zones and undermines industrial production. In contrast, General Roll is located away from the urban centers of decision making and upholds the values of production. Inside the factory, Norman Angel, the boss of General Roll, speaks above "the clatter of machinery" about the need to integrate production: "This problem we been having over there with number three, if we just go get this wall knocked out right there and move this whole setup right over around this way we've got the line running right through with nothing to hinder, you see what I mean?" (149). In other words, Angel remains committed to the unified production structure that JR seeks to fragment. Angel also considers reviving "an old Welte-Mignon" piano and placing it in the company offices, he lives by the motto of "produce or get out" (150, 151), and he speaks affectionately of the "quality product" made by Nathan Wise (355), a manufacturer of condoms. Yet General Roll is being left behind by the investment practices represented by

JR's corporation. For example, Angel does not fully understand the implications of the distribution of General Roll's shares. However, he does realize that the shoddy quality of the "new production layout" is continuous with the fragmentation that the company will undergo if it goes public and becomes the prey of investors and stockbrokers (354).[20] As a result of the dialectical processes in which General Roll participates, JR ultimately takes control of the company and Angel ends up in a coma following a suicide attempt. Described as a "desolate place" that is "next to nowhere" (147, 358), the Astoria location of General Roll exemplifies the urban peripheries that are run down by the concentration of abstract principles of value in the business centers of Manhattan.

The dialectical relation between JR's corporation and the practices of Typhon is another component of Gaddis's archaeology of urban tendencies and industrial production. Archaeologically, Typhon represents a business tier that exists between General Roll and JR's corporation. There are therefore both similarities and differences between Typhon and JR's practices. Like JR's company, Typhon is associated with the concentrated centers of decision making in Manhattan and the primacy of investment over production. In his discussion with Amy, Davidoff evokes the nature of the urban production of value. By informing Amy that on the site of the new building there is "[n]othing but a big hole there now" (195), Davidoff describes a situation in which the absence of industrial production is a sign of the urban expansion of business. Yet Typhon does not penetrate the urban space of Manhattan as thoroughly as does the flux of JR's financial transactions.[21] Also, Typhon retains a corollary commitment to dispersed industrial production. Typhon is engaged in building a cobalt processing plant in the African nation of Gandia. The company plans to stimulate a civil war in Gandia that will lead to the secession of the province of Uaso, exploit Uaso as a "company town" for their industrial plant (523), and bring laborers in from the nearby nation of Malwi. Typhon's focus on the details of industrial production and extensive ties to military and political groups result in a careful and widely unified corporate policy that differs greatly from JR's single-minded pursuit of new companies. Also, Typhon's manipulation of the social space of Gandia differs from JR's total disregard of the social space of the town in which Eagle Mills is situated. Governor John Cates would like to conduct business in the manner of JR, but when he informs Monty Moncrieff that "I know a plant can't be declared surplus and sold until it's built," he indicates an awareness that the business structure of Typhon precludes the implementation of JR's code of abstract value (427). Typhon's planned construction of a pipeline also highlights an approach to business that is not shared by JR. In purchasing the Ace Development Company, JR acquires land through which Typhon intends to build the pipeline. After making this transaction, JR is disappointed to learn that even though he has obtained drilling rights to land that might contain valuable minerals, he has miscalculated Ace Development's stock value. The reason for this response, of course, is that he only desires companies as the basis upon which to garner more concerns. When Typhon hears of this purchase, Beaton, the company's legal adviser, refers to JR's "obvious intention" to obtain mining rights (431), and Cates thinks that JR's decision to buy Ace Development must have been based on information about Typhon's proposed pipeline. Both statements are wrong because they assume that JR shares Typhon's commitment to industry.

As JR's Family of Companies buys into interests controlled by Typhon, Gaddis portrays the dialectical interaction of the two corporations. The progress of such interactions is accompanied by a turn toward an interest in "operational" industry on JR's part (657). Specifically, the projects undertaken by Ray-X, a company acquired by JR, are described in terms of their industrial basis. They also share key attributes with the Typhon pipeline. Along with its investments in the communications industry through Diamond Cable, Typhon's pipeline is a manifestation of the homogenizing networks of abstract space. Frigicom and Teletravel, the two Ray-X projects, also promise the realization of abstract space.[22] As a system of noise elimination by "the placement of absorbent screens" in "our major cities" (527), Frigicom creates urban homogeneity through the physical spatialization of sound; Teletravel, a method of instantaneous transportation, altogether eliminates the contingencies of spatial difference. JR's enthusiasm for the Ray-X projects indicates that he has not fully abandoned the industrial base. According to Lefebvre, abstract space is realized in the material infrastructure of neocapitalist societies. Therefore, industrial production is essential to the production of abstract space. Yet the larger reaches of abstract space are brought about by a transformation in the dynamic between urban space and industrial production. In Lefebvre's analysis, the dominance of the urban form over industrial production ensures the realization of abstract space. It is precisely this conjunction of elements that Gaddis portrays through JR's business activities. As JR's business practices colonize urban space, the urban becomes the agent, not simply the site, of financial power. The effect of such colonization is the realization of abstract space within and beyond urban social space.

As we have seen, Gaddis shares Lefebvre's emphasis on the tendencies of urban space. The representation of the urban center of Manhattan is a crucial aspect of Gaddis's portrayal of urban space, but the spatial tendencies associated with General Roll, the Gandia project, and the Typhon pipeline are equally important in *JR*. Moreover, Gaddis's archaeology of industry and business highlights the dialectical interplay of urban and industrial space. In contrast, Lefebvre argues, the identification of urban space with the empirical details of urban locations and empty geometrical plans tends to mask the dialectic of urban and industrial space. For Lefebvre, "urbanism" comprehends urban space in these empty and empirical terms. As a result, urbanism hides the true nature of urban space and promotes the abstract principles associated with "the application of industrial rationality" (41). In *Production*, Lefebvre writes that in abstract space "the town [. . .] has disintegrated" (53), but it is in *Urban* that he offers a detailed account of urbanism as the mechanism by which abstract space is realized and "the town" is destroyed.

Caught between private and political interests, the "state utopia" of urbanism is, for Lefebvre, a fragmented amalgam of several different discourses (for example, environment, infrastructure, art, technology, and science), branches of knowledge (for example, sociology, geography, architecture, and demography), and institutions (163). The various aspects of urbanism exist in a state of "confusion" because they are separate from each other and yet each one claims to represent the totality of social space (60). Real estate speculation is an important component of urbanism because it engenders the form of surplus value associated with urban space. By generating the concept of "Culture," urbanism makes knowledge subservient to the market and uses the exigencies of "the technical division of labor" to foster "the social division of intellectual labor" (61, 60).[23] In other words, seemingly objective distinctions in occupation are used to justify the unequal distribution of power in society. The functionalist basis of urbanism is also complicit with "ideological naturalization" (27), or the transformation of nature into signs of nature; urbanism's "fetishism of satisfaction" (159), for example, is evident in advertising's use of nature to suggest that commodities fulfill particular needs. For Lefebvre, "public squares" epitomize this process of transformation because they constitute "a poor substitute for nature" that is defined by the "function of passive observation" (27). Worst of all, urbanism's abstract homogeneity replaces "habiting," the creative lived experience of domestic urban space, with the reified functionality of "habitat" (81).

JR shares Lefebvre's critique of urbanism. Just as Gaddis's representation of the dialectic of industrial production and urban space is centered on Manhattan and financial speculation, his treatment of urbanism is articulated through his descriptions of the urban space of Long Island. Gaddis states that *JR* was initially inspired by "the postwar desecration of the Long Island village of Massapequa" (Kuehl and Moore 5), and, as illustrated by the many references to "a little space problem" in the Long Island sections of the novel (175), much of the published version of the novel evokes urban change as a process of deterioration. In particular, Gaddis's representation of Massapequa is dominated by the urbanist realization of abstract space.

In his analysis of urbanism, Lefebvre discusses the spatial dialectics that take place among different levels of society. He identifies a global level of urban planning in which public and private interests intersect. Similarly, the realization of abstract urban space in *JR* is driven by the complicity between public and private interests. Such complicity is presented most clearly through the character of Whiteback, who is both the principal of JR's school and the president of the local bank, and who brings together local politicians and corporate representatives. Gaddis also suggests that the dynamic between public and private institutions undergoes transformations that alter the urban space of Massapequa. A major aspect of this dynamic is the infiltration of public institutions by private interests. In JR's school, Major Hyde encourages the placement of the products of Endo Appliances. The introduction of these appliances reshapes the physical space of the school and in so doing displaces the school kindergarten and marginalizes academic subjects. As Hyde puts it, the school could "fit a whole washing machine in the space the Great Books take" (176). In addition, he claims that Dan DiCephalis's Responsive Environments testing equipment is unnecessary because "a washing machine's a responsive envirement [sic]" (224). Hyde's comments reiterate the sociospatial dialectic because, in this example, the reorganization of physical space has social and educational consequences. Hyde also advocates placing Stye, the African American insurance agent, on the school board. If Stye's election to the school board is successful, Hyde will reward him with a position in his company. The role of Stye therefore shows how a nominally public body, the school board, is controlled by private concerns.

The dynamic between public and private forces in the school is replicated on the larger level of urban planning in Massapequa. Congressman Pecci, who is also a lawyer, conducts negotiations between the Flo-Jan Corporation and Catania Paving regarding development contracts in the town. As these negotiations reveal, local government works on behalf of private corporations. Yet private interests do not completely take over public institutions. Referring to his roles as bank president and school principal, Whiteback states that he "keep[s] the fish and the fowl separate" (175), and he is described as having "a grandstand view of both sides of the coin" (175). The example of Whiteback illustrates how private concerns are invested in maintaining the appearance of the autonomy and credibility of public bodies.

Lefebvre identifies not only a global level of urban space but also an "intermediary" urban level, which is made up of "streets, squares, avenues, public buildings such as city halls, parish churches, schools, and so on" (79, 80). Lefebvre suggests that urbanism implements abstract space on this intermediary level by regarding urban space in empirical terms. The empirical treatment of urban space is prevalent in Gaddis's novel. When, for example, Hyde discusses a possible television special on his Civil Defense Shelters, he refers to "what

America's all about, wall thickness, food storage, waste, what we have to protect" (179). Also, DiCephalis's request for mortgage refinancing is turned down by Whiteback because of the empirical facts of "the spacing of wall studs" in his home (227). In *JR*, the focus on empiricism denies the validity of understanding urban space in terms of the social, economic, and political "forms" or tendencies that Lefebvre seeks to bring to light.

The intermediate realization of abstract space also requires the perception of urban space as an empty site. In the descriptive sections that link the conversations of *JR*, Gaddis describes the town's "empty walk," "empty pavement," and "the empty concrete shell of the Marine memorial where a disabled French machinegun and a vacant flagpole held off the sky" (31, 132–33). As well as being a by-product of the urban decay wrought by the transformations that the novel describes, such emptiness is a central goal of urbanist development. The production of empty space is associated with the suburban homogeneity that Hyde attributes to the houses and streets where he lives. The "reek of asphalt" permeates the novel (188), and the process of blacktopping empties, levels, and homogenizes urban space. The blacktopping of parking lots exemplifies the encroachment of empty space that we see throughout the novel. The paving company's blacktopping of not only Vern Teakell's "small driveway" but also his lawn emphasizes how such space also displaces nature (325). That this emptiness is a goal of urbanist development is suggested by Congressman Pecci's defense of Catania's actions: "Two-inch pressed blacktop the best, indestructible, no grass to mow, nine thousand square feet no grass to mow, no leaves to rake all the time, he parks the car anywhere, no trees to smash the fenders, no birds shitting the Simoniz . . ." (325).

The increasing homogenization and emptiness of the town fragments urban space. New highways and widened roads eliminate pedestrian space and reflect the imposition of abstract space's fragmented geometry. The garbage that increasingly dominates the urban landscape is just one way in which Gaddis links emptiness and highway fragmentation. In a single sentence, Gaddis describes both "the immediate prospect of open acres flowered in funereal abundance" and "candy wrappers and beer cans nestled along the hedge line

up the highway" (17). Through references to characters' manipulation of "certain amendments to the state law relating to highway
construction standards" (27), Gaddis further indicates that the highways exemplify the manner in which the global conjunction of public
and private interests impacts the urban infrastructure. The highways
also serve as demarcation points between the different districts of
the town. Whiteback and the others at the school discuss the area
where highways cross near Bast's house as the "border with district
thirteen" (178). This location is significant because it divides very
different urban areas.

   In *Urban*, Lefebvre states that urbanism engenders "the segregation
of moments of life and activities" (140). For Lefebvre, segregation
refers both to the fracturing of urban experience and a spatial plan
that inhibits the formation of "assemblies and encounters" (124), and
he states that the experience of African Americans in the "urban ghet-
toes" of North America represents a "powerful" form of "social segregation" (145). Gaddis also emphasizes the relation between race
and segregation. By facilitating his objectification of the insurance
agent Stye, the notion of the "border with district thirteen" reinforces
Hyde's racism. Hyde's comparisons between the town and Watts and
Newark further indicate that his ideas of urban segregation bolster
paranoid and racist views. At the same time, Whiteback attempts
to exploit urban segregation for the benefit of business. In order to
suggest that both the school and Hyde's corporation are sensitive
to the "inner city concept," he "airbrushe[s]" a photograph of JR's
class so that it seems that a group of African American children took
the field trip to Wall Street (255). While this cynical endeavor seems
to advocate racial integration, it actually furthers racial division and
urban segregation.

   The incident of the airbrushed photograph should not be viewed
as tangential to the project of urbanism. Rather, issues of culture are
central to the reshaping of urban space in *JR*. In "Right to the City,"
Lefebvre suggests that culture plays an important role in bringing together the different aspects of urbanism.[24] As we have seen, he states
that urbanism is made up of numerous and seemingly autonomous
discourses. Because each of these discourses claims to be independent, the overall logic of urbanism is obscured. In *JR*, the discourse of

culture is an important contributor to the confused image of urbanism that Lefebvre describes. The same individuals who promote urban homogeneity and fragmentation in *JR* also advocate various cultural projects. As in the case of the airbrushed photograph, these cultural projects often appear to be separate from and even antithetical to other aspects of urbanism. However, in reality urbanism cynically appropriates the idea of cultural autonomy and critique within its own logic. At the same time, the discourse of culture provides a common reference point for the different components of urbanism and thus serves to integrate them. In portraying culture as both a unifying and a seemingly independent discourse, Gaddis, like Lefebvre, attaches negative connotations to the notion of culture. For Gaddis, the concept of culture reflects the redefinition of art and knowledge in ways that are consistent with the goals of urbanism. That the novel's cultural projects are located in spaces that play a significant role in the other aspects of Gaddis's portrayal of urban change underscores the connection between the colonization of intermediary urban space and culture in *JR*.

The sections of the novel dealing with the school offer significant representations of culture. As both a key element of the conjunction of private and public interests and the site of many discussions concerning the development of the town, the school is one of the most important sites associated with urbanism in *JR*. Numerous changes occur in the school that are consonant with the goals of urbanism. As exemplified by the creation of a "new home ec center" that will include products from Hyde's Endo Appliances company (454), the school's curriculum is changed in order to further corporate interests. The "space problem" that the new appliances cause refers not only to the physical limitations of the school buildings but also to the conceptual space of the curriculum (453). Many incidents in *JR* represent the confused map of academic disciplines in the school. One of the most significant aspects of the novel's "straying from the curriculum" (346), as Gibbs calls it, is the redefinition of curriculum according to a new language of efficiency and productivity. For Gaddis, the redesignation of "English" as "Communication Skills" reflects the manner in which intellectual activities are defined in terms of the technocratic logic of urbanism (34). The most significant of the new appellations in the school is the discourse of culture. Miss Flesch's production of Wagner's *Ring* is described by Whiteback as part of a "cultural drive" aimed at impressing the school's financial sponsors. Whiteback also describes the production as "preparation" for a "cultural festival" that will "pay off like never before in mass consumers, mass distribution, mass publicity, just like automobiles and bathing suits" (19). Elsewhere described as a "Spring Arts Festival" (27), this anticipated event represents the commodification of art through its redesignation as culture. The insistence of Whiteback's reference to "the cultural aspect of the arts" explicitly discloses the act of cultural designation as a unifying force among the discourses of urbanism (39).

The discourse of culture also encompasses other areas of the town and is closely related to urbanism's treatment of nature. The building of the new Cultural Plaza is connected to the culture drive in the school. Referring to the Spring Arts Festival, which is, as we have seen, conjoined with the Wagner production, Whiteback hopes to "[t]ie it in with this Culture Center" (27). The various cultural initiatives in the novel are therefore unified through urbanist interests. The most prominent of the cultural forms that occupy the plaza is the sculpture entitled Cyclone Seven. Described as "one of the most outstanding contemporary sculptural comments on mass space" (672), Cyclone Seven appears to be a critical form of art. However, a young boy is trapped in the sculpture for five days, and the local authorities threaten to break it apart. The imprisoning effects of the sculpture suggest that its abstract and "arbitrary arrangement of force and line" lacks critical force. Rather, Cyclone Seven is a form of culture that is wholly complicit with the project of urbanism and that can only simulate a spatial critique.

The simulatory nature of the sculpture suggests links to Lefebvre's discussion of nature and urbanism. In Lefebvre's analysis, urbanism involves the eradication of nature, the promotion of the commodified signs of nature, and the transformation of the expanse of nature into its open and empty simulation, as epitomized by the plaza. Since the building of the Cultural Plaza entails the destruction of trees and hedges in the locale of Bast's house, it can be regarded, as in Lefebvre's discussion, as a simulation of nature. The location of the Cultural

Plaza at the border with district thirteen suggests that it also enhances the fragmentation of abstract urban space, and the blacktopping of the plaza by Parentucelli indicates its role in the homogenization of the town. Along with motifs such as Dan DiCephalis's umbrella of "simulated birch" and the prohibition against real flowers in the private cemetery (52), the replacement of nature with its sign or simulation is further illustrated by the blacktopping of Burgoyne Street and its renaming as Summer Street. In this context, the remnants of nature that do still exist can be viewed only as a "hostile spectacle of growth" (57).

In addition to the promotion of culture and the simulation of nature, the homogenization and fragmentation of intermediary urban space relies upon the commodification of space as real estate. Since the consideration of the profitability of space is the mechanism by which urban homogenization and fragmentation are realized in *JR*, real estate speculation is an integral feature of the impact of urbanism on intermediate space in the novel. "Today," writes Lefebvre, "space as a whole enters into production as a product, through the buying, selling, and exchange of parts of space" (155). "What is new," he continues, "is the global and total production of social space" (155). Moreover, Lefebvre claims that as industrial production declines, the "second circuit" of real estate speculation becomes an important and even dominant aspect of the production of surplus value (160). In *JR*, Gaddis represents the rising significance of the economic production of space that Lefebvre describes. Most notably, the buying and selling of real estate is indistinguishable from urbanism's transformation of Massapequa. In his televised presentation at the school, Gibbs refers to the "shy little church squatting on millions of tax-free dollars' worth of real estate" (180). Hyde is incensed with Gibbs's use of the term "squatting" because it implies the existence of urban space that has not been incorporated into the "second circuit" of real estate. As exemplified by the billboards that advertise "unfinished apartments, Now Renting" (247), the novel also suggests that the transformation of space into surplus value precedes and thus marginalizes its utility. Yet it is of course the character of JR who articulates the transformational role of real estate most directly and opportunistically. He tells Bast that a "zoning change" will create "improved property" and lead to the building of a "new shopping center" opposite his house (58, 59). Along with the fact that the first of JR's mail order catalogs that Bast sees is for the Gem School of Real Estate, this discussion intimates that the production of spatial value represents the paradigmatic core of all JR's financial dealings.

As we have seen, Gaddis's novel shares many of the perspectives of Lefebvre's theory of urbanism. The consideration of Lefebvre's ideas enables us to identify the different components of Gaddis's representation of urban space and the manner in which they are related. There are, however, significant differences between *Urban* and *JR*. For Lefebvre, the third level of urban space is that of "privately owned buildings" (80), or housing. The most contested domain of urban space, this private level is the site of struggle between principles of "habiting" and "habitat" (81). Habiting refers to the realm of everyday lived experience and the "grandeur and spontaneous poetry" that emerge from creative domesticity (83). It is therefore equivalent to the lived space that Lefebvre describes in *Production*. In contrast, Lefebvre designates the reduction of domesticity to elementary functions as habitat. He also writes that habitat usurps habiting and furthers the principles of abstract urban space: "Habitat was imposed from above as the application of a homogeneous global and quantitative space, a requirement that 'lived experience' allow itself to be enclosed in boxes, cages, or 'dwelling machines'" (81). In the project of urbanism, the private level is regarded as the least important. For Lefebvre, the rising importance of the urban experience over industrial production brings with it a reversal of urbanism's hierarchy of levels. In the "critical zone" of the urban revolution (14), the private level of urban space becomes the most significant. Lefebvre insists that the urban form is retained during this critical phase, and he is highly critical of "nomadism" and other attempts to replace the "intense mobility" of "urban centrality" with "displacement" (98, 97). For Lefebvre, the dominance of the private level constitutes the realization of the urban "as a place where differences know one another" (96). While Lefebvre acknowledges the varying effects of the critical phase, he does believe that the new role of private space represents the utopian and liberatory quality of the urban revolution.[25]

JR shares many features of Lefebvre's analysis of the third level of urban space. Gaddis is critical of urbanism's destruction of domestic habiting. Early in the novel, he evokes "the graveled vacancy of a parking lot where a house [. . .] had held out till scarcely a week before" (18). After observing a "broken fence enclosing a fleet of rusting hulks," Bast concludes that it is impossible to live a "comfortable" life amid such debris (243). Many of Gaddis's descriptions of the eradication of nature are also elegies for the demise of lived space. In particular, the building of the Cultural Plaza and the new shopping center entails both the destruction of nature and the removal of Bast's home. Following the realization that his home has been lost, Bast becomes delirious and is admitted to a hospital. His cry of "Where are the trees" indicates that the loss of nature and home are entwined in his mind (669). According to his hospital roommate, Duncan, Bast "says let's improve this orange place by chopping everything down like the olden times" (671). In Bast's case, the loss of domestic space leads to the use of *JR*'s language of property improvement and real estate speculation. The discourse of urbanism therefore supplants the experience of habiting. The importance of this process of supplanting is suggested by its recurrence in the novel. Early in the novel, Bast's studio is described as a sanctuary for the creative domesticity of Lefebvrean habiting. As Bast states, "[I]t's the one place an idea can be left here you can walk out and close the door and leave it here unfinished the most, the wildest secret fantasy and it stays on here by itself" (69). The vandalization of the studio exemplifies the fragility of creative habiting in *JR*. Following the attack, Bast takes seriously JR's suggestion to "have your own import export business right from your own home" (133). The experience of habiting is therefore supplanted by the domestication of the economic activities that Gaddis criticizes. At other times Gaddis suggests that the functionality of Lefebvrean habitat has replaced habiting. In particular, the DiCephalis home is portrayed in terms of banal domestic functions. Yet, unlike Lefebvre, Gaddis does not counter the demise of habiting with a representation of the triumph of private space. In *JR*, the dialectic of industrial and urban space engenders the total domination of urbanism. Gaddis values habiting as highly as Lefebvre does, and the presence of many homeless people in the novel suggests that he shares Lefebvre's critique of nomadism and homeless wandering. However, he does not suggest

that the urban revolution is accompanied by the positive transformations that Lefebvre anticipates. *JR* is replete with representations of
the dialectics of social space. For example, the Long Island sections
of the novel portray the dialectical interplay of the levels of urban
space. But lived space is unable to offer any dialectical resistance to
the dominion of abstract urban space.[26]

Through representations of the dialectics of social space, the critical
space of *Gravity's Rainbow* and *JR* transforms prominent characteristics of early-twentieth-century radical American fiction. Specifically,
the subordinate utopian space of the earlier fiction is expanded in
these novels to the point where it fully displaces the historicist tendencies of the texts of London and Sinclair. Primarily geared toward
analyses of the spatial nature of power in postwar American society, the versions of spatial dialectics in *Gravity's Rainbow* and *JR* are
more capacious and far-reaching than the spatiality of *The Empire City*.
Pynchon and Gaddis share Lefebvre's critique of abstract space as a
dominant form of power that produces the contradictory tendencies
of homogenization and fragmentation in social space. In pursuing a
critique of abstract space, these novels articulate more varied models
of spatial dialectics than are evident in *The Empire City*. Both novels
portray a general sociospatial dialectic in which space not only is the
location of events but rather determines aspects of society. In *Gravity's
Rainbow*, Pynchon suggests that the three formants of abstract space
are fully conjoined in the decentralized neocapitalist city. Yet Pynchon
also evokes the production of lived space within the contradictions
of abstract space, and he gestures toward the oppositional politics
of anarchism. The novel's oppositional spaces are reappropriated by
abstract space, but Pynchon's narrative evokes an incessant process
of spatial production that negates the idea of abstract space as totality.
The embers of utopian and anarchist space in *Gravity's Rainbow* look
backward to the spatial aspects of early-twentieth-century radical
American fictional texts, which frequently invoke anarchism in their
representations of utopian space. In contrast, the spatial dialectics of
JR emphasize the dialectic of urban space and industrial production
and the interplay of the different levels of abstract urban space. By
abandoning the dialectic of abstract and lived space, *JR* is further
removed from the utopianism of the early-twentieth-century texts

discussed in this book than *Gravity's Rainbow*. In Gaddis's novel, capacious spatial dialectics are wholly shorn of the possibility of utopian space and the semblance of political identity. *JR* therefore looks forward to the novels of Joan Didion and Don DeLillo, in which the issue of spatial difference is raised without reference to the dialectic of abstract and lived space.

[5]

Territoriality and the Lost Dimension

Joan Didion and Don DeLillo

The fiction of Joan Didion and Don DeLillo shares Pynchon's and Gaddis's emphasis on the centrality of critical space as a mode of social analysis. However, the representations of critical space that we find in the texts of Didion and DeLillo are not predicated on models of dialectical opposition. Like Pynchon and Gaddis, these authors are concerned with spatial analyses of the cultural, technological, and political power that emanates from the United States. However, the spatial distribution of power in Didion's and DeLillo's fiction lacks the monolithic and contradictory qualities of abstract space. These novels are also devoid of the oppositional space that is alternately celebrated and negated in *Gravity's Rainbow* and quashed in *JR*. Rather than reflecting the dialectical victory of abstract space, the absence of distinct oppositional space is due to the nature of spatiality in these texts. In *A Book of Common Prayer* (1977), *Democracy* (1984), and *The Last Thing He Wanted* (1996), Didion portrays the territoriality of state power in terms of both political demarcations and covert movements. In *Underworld* (1997), DeLillo evokes connections between the shrinking of global space, the intersection of media and military technologies, and the decimation of social space. The main impetus of the critical space of both Didion and DeLillo is to expose the spatial nature of power. Critical tendencies are evident in these novels, but they do not constitute a separate form of spatiality that dialectically interacts with geographical formations of power. The absence of spatial dialectics in the fiction of Didion and DeLillo represents a renunciation of the textual methodology that informs much of the fiction studied in this book and thus a further transformation of critical space than is evident in the writing of Pynchon and Gaddis.

In order to chart the spatial dynamics of Didion's and DeLillo's fiction, I refer to the critical theory of Gilles Deleuze and Félix Guattari and Paul Virilio. Specifically, I discuss Didion's fiction in relation to Deleuze and Guattari's *A Thousand Plateaus*, the celebrated second volume of *Capitalism and Schizophrenia*. I then assess the novels of DeLillo in the context of various writings by Virilio. Like Lefebvre, Deleuze and Guattari prioritize the spatial analysis of power, but they abandon the architecture of dialectics in favor of fluid and "rhizomatic" articulations of spatial processes (6). Whereas Lefebvrean dialectics refers to a circumscribed system of opposed and distinct dualities, Deleuze and Guattari's rhizome denotes an open-ended lattice of interconnected concepts. Fredric Jameson argues that Deleuze and Guattari's writing is characterized by "dualism" ("Marxism" 17). However, as Alain Badiou notes, Deleuze's writing is "essentially antidialectical" because dualisms constantly undergo "nomadic subversion" (32, 34). Also, Deleuze and Guattari's dualisms are interwoven with each other and other conceptual sets in ways that are irreducible to dialectics.[1] Virilio also departs from Lefebvre's dialectics of space, and he shares the anarchist sentiments of Deleuze and Guattari.[2] For Virilio, social space is subject to dramatic transformations that are driven by technological innovations. By describing genealogies of media and military technologies, Virilio claims that the omnipresence of media images and the sophistication of military systems have turned social space into a lost dimension. He is interested in modes of perception that might recover the dimension of social space, but he does not identify untainted oppositional space. Just as the numerous spatial processes described by Deleuze and Guattari share key features with the novels of Didion, so too DeLillo's writing engages with the same interplay of space and technology that animates much of Virilio's discourse.

An important figure in the New Journalism of the 1960s, Joan Didion is well known as both a political essayist and a writer of fiction. Also, her journalistic perspective deeply informs her novels. The narratives of *A Book of Common Prayer*, *Democracy*, and *The Last Thing He Wanted* exhibit a similar journalistic structure. In each case a female narrator conducts investigative reporting in an attempt to reconstruct the life of a female protagonist. The conjunction of the protagonist's experiences and political events results in complex narratives. Through representations of political struggles within and between the United States and regions such as Southeast Asia and Central America, Didion portrays a political world that is dominated by obscure affiliations, covert operations, incidental contacts, and unspoken arrangements. Just as major political decisions and events lack prominence, personal attributes, such as motive, are indeterminate. Instead, seemingly ephemeral details become the centerpieces of personal and political life. Nevertheless, the consequences of events are dramatic and usually tragic. All these characteristics of Didion's fiction result in the foregrounding of critical space. The political dimension of Didion's novels, especially the influence of the United States on other regions, is portrayed in terms of the flow of information, military hardware, and strategic alliances. Similarly, the most stable traits of Didion's protagonists are transience and mobility. The interrelation of political and personal movements creates variegated and differing treatments of spatial processes in Didion's fiction. From *A Book of Common Prayer* to *Democracy* to *The Last Thing He Wanted*, the substantiality of the narrator's identity and the overtness of military and political scenarios are equally in decline, and such developments are integral to the representations of critical space that are apparent in these novels.

Reading Didion's fiction in relation to Deleuze and Guattari's *A Thousand Plateaus* highlights the patterns of spatiality in these novels. In this text, Deleuze and Guattari develop a vast range of spatial concepts and state the priority of geography over history on many occasions. Speaking of Deleuze and Guattari's geographical terminology, Marcus Doel states, "It would be better to approach space as a verb rather than as a noun" (125). As Doel's comments suggest, the authors of *A Thousand Plateaus* do not traffic in utopian or dystopian nouns. Of the numerous geographical terms developed by Deleuze and Guattari, the concept of territoriality, or "the T factor" (316), is one of the most significant. Territorialized space is controlled, segmented, and embodied in modern state power. The process of territorialization is accompanied by a countertendency toward deterritorialization. Deterritorialization undoes the codes and structures of territorialized space but does not necessarily lead to a weakening of state power. It is regularly followed by acts of reterritorialization, and the "line of flight" of "absolute deterritorialization" definitively breaks with segmentarity (14, 197). However, Deleuze and Guattari insist that these processes should not be viewed in terms of a temporal sequence or dialectic. Another central geographical term discussed by these authors is the line of flight of the nomadic war machine. For Deleuze and Guattari, nomadic life is characterized by speed, flow, and the occupation of space beyond that of the territoriality of the state. Nomads occupy a "smooth" space that differs from the territories of "striated" space (353). Also, nomadism is a war machine that only engages in war once it has been appropriated by the state. Along with the war machine, the state can also appropriate the attributes of smooth space. Such considerations are significant because they suggest that smooth space, like the movement of deterritorialization, is not inherently liberatory. There are some similarities between Deleuze and Guattari's multifaceted description of territorialized space and Lefebvre's discussion of abstract space. Resolutely anarchist, Deleuze and Guattari prioritize the opposition to state power that also informs Lefebvre's writing. However, *A Thousand Plateaus* does not share Lefebvre's interest in principles of dystopian state power and utopian oppositional space. Throughout *A Thousand Plateaus*, Deleuze and Guattari criticize the notion of "evolution" as applied to the concepts that they discuss (69). Rather than viewing the spatial characteristics of the state and the war machine as subsequent to one another, Deleuze and Guattari describe them as existing in various forms of interaction. As William Bogard argues, Deleuze and Guattari focus on conjunctions of smooth and striated space. For Bogard, "the more interesting problems about the constitution of society involve smoothing, and specifically the *re-smoothing* of striated, societalized forms" (271). In Didion's fiction, spatial tendencies akin to those described by Deleuze and Guattari interact in a variety of ways. Didion emphasizes the lines of flight of her characters, but she also shares Bogard's interest in the manifestation of the smooth space of the war machine within state power's logic of striated space.

In *A Book of Common Prayer*, the dynamic between the state and the war machine is rooted in the society of the fictional Central American country of Boca Grande. The narrator, Grace Strasser-Mendana, is the widow of Edgar Strasser-Mendana, a member of the country's most powerful family. As Grace administers the family business, Edgar's brothers, Victor and Antonio, struggle to dominate politics in Boca Grande. Interactions between the state and the war machine occur via a perpetual cycle of revolution in which the brothers participate. Grace's narrative focuses on these political events and the character of Charlotte Douglas, an American woman who leaves her family and arrives in Boca Grande. While the novel is permeated by a dissonance between Charlotte's personal reactions and the politics of Boca Grande, the spatial emphases of Grace's commentary suggest the connectedness of these narrative lines. Insisting that Boca Grande has no history, Grace characterizes the nation in terms of the striation of space by state power. A city of boulevards and pyramids built on a landfill in the country's "big bay" (16), El Progreso *primero* is imposed on what Deleuze and Guattari describe as the smooth space of the sea. Another city, El Progreso *otro*, has a corollary function in that it annexes the "interior" via a striating road that appears from the air as "a straight line of paler vegetation" (18). Grace states that Charlotte misunderstands the striated spatiality of Boca Grande. Charlotte adheres to "the teleological view of human settlement" that Deleuze and Guattari repeatedly discredit (18). In her "Letters from Central America," Charlotte also claims that Boca Grande is a "land of contrasts" (13). Grace invalidates Charlotte's dialectical view by stating that apparently geographical and political contrasts are illusory. In particular, the opposition between "*guerrileros*" and "colonels" is false (13). Also, Charlotte erroneously describes Boca Grande as "the economic fulcrum of the Americas" (14). Stating that the country is just a refueling point for flights between cities in other countries, Grace insists that Boca Grande is a transitional zone, not an arrival point.

Charlotte's misunderstandings of spatiality prevent her from comprehending the country's politics and their connections to her own life. According to Deleuze and Guattari, "guerilla warfare" exemplifies a "reviv[al]" of the war machine against state power (386). In *A Book of Common Prayer*, the war machine of guerilla insurrections is wholly appropriated within the state. The guerillas "spend their time theorizing in the interior" and are separated from the concerns of the nation's working class (28). Ironically, the smooth space of the interior therefore facilitates the appropriation of the nomadic guerillas. Cryptically, Grace states that revolutions in Boca Grande are made not by the guerillas but by "people we know" (29). Whenever political forces seek to take power, they deploy the revolutionary tactics and principles of the guerillas for their own ends. As a consequence of constant revolution, the state becomes little other than an institutionalized form of the insurrectionary force of the guerilla war machine, and Didion refers to unfinished and dilapidated public works as a means of suggesting the absence of governmental activity in Boca Grande. The nature of power in Boca Grande relates to Deleuze and Guattari's distinction between the "emperor" and the "jurist" in their discussion of state power (424). For Deleuze and Guattari, the emperor is associated with the "despot" who takes control of agricultural communities and subjects the war machine to "magic capture" (427). In Boca Grande, the Strasser-Mendana family serves as a despotic emperor, and the legislative aspects of power are of little concern. As illustrated by the revolution that occurs toward the conclusion of the novel, outsiders perceive events in Boca Grande as popular democratic uprisings. However, the revolution is fabricated by Gerardo, Grace's son. Motivated by little more than boredom, Gerardo encourages Antonio to seize power from his brother.

The conjunction of the power of the emperor and the war machine is seemingly unstable. The revolution in the novel does not go according to plan because the guerillas have more weaponry than usual, and they are able to hold on to their autonomy for longer than expected. Leonard Douglas, Charlotte's husband, repeatedly states that the transition from Victor's rule to that of Antonio will not be "smooth" because of the new conditions pertaining to the guerillas (243). Because he associates the autonomy of the guerilla war machine with a disruption of "smoothness," Leonard's terminology appears to be antithetical to that of Deleuze and Guattari. However, the actions of the guerillas remain geared toward the realization of the striated space of state power and thus do not become autonomously smooth in the sense used by Deleuze and Guattari. Along with the suggestion that Rasindorf and Kiley, two agents of the American government, are the source of the guerillas' newfound power, the use in the melee of Armalite rifles adopted by the U.S. military raises the possibility of American involvement in the revolution. Didion therefore accords with Deleuze and Guattari's theorization of the appropriation of the war machine by intimating that the guerillas serve the larger striation imposed by the state power of the United States.

While American state power is restricted to the background of *A Book of Common Prayer*, the American war machine is prominent. Two close family relatives of Charlotte are types of the war machine: Leonard and her daughter, Marin. Both Leonard and Marin are portrayed in terms of their involvement with insurrectionary groups and are usually associated with air travel. In this and other novels by Didion, airports and air travel are powerful tropes for the line of flight and the experience of both smooth and striated space. Leonard is a legal representative for revolutionary and insurgent groups throughout the world. As exemplified by the meeting between Leonard and an Israeli general that could only be arranged "between planes" (35), his work is defined by constant movement through global air space. We hear about this meeting from Charlotte, who speaks of Leonard at a Boca Grande party as someone who "runs guns" (38). "I don't mean he literally buys and sells the hardware" (38), Charlotte quickly explains, but her comments identify Leonard with the military disposition of the war machine. On other occasions, Leonard flies on Air Force One and facilitates arms deals between Caribbean states. These incidents suggest that Leonard's air travel is also identified with the striated space of state power. Deleuze and Guattari describe a "punctual" system as one in which the line of flight is "subordinated to the point" (295). Leonard's movements are characterized by both the line of flight and the point. As a representative of various liberation movements, he moves through the smooth space of the war machine. However, his association with different governments highlights the role of state destination points in his work. Like the guerillas on Boca Grande, Leonard represents the appropriation of the war machine by the state. However, the groups that Leonard represents are appropriated to a lesser degree than the guerillas. Whereas the former seem to espouse nationalist causes and thus are committed to the transformation of the war machine into the state, the latter are cynically deployed by the state in an "empty revolution" (249). The ineffectuality of the guerillas is due to the despotic power of the emperor that captures them. As a lawyer, Leonard can be identified with the legislative pole of Deleuze and Guattari's two-part model of state power. The relative autonomy of these revolutionary groups suggests that the legislator appropriates the war machine less fully than does the emperor.

Marin exemplifies a war machine that is wholly exterior to state power. Described by the FBI as a "pitiless revolutionist" (58), Marin is a member of a terrorist group that bombs the Transamerica Building in San Francisco, hijacks and then burns a plane, and goes into nomadic hiding. In conducting these actions, the group appropriates the mechanism of striated space and turns it toward the ends of smooth space. Marin is allegedly in Hanoi and lots of other places, but there are no definite location points for her, and Charlotte worries that her daughter is now "loose in the world" (146). On a cassette tape released to the media, Marin describes the group's flight and mobility in smooth space: "When the fascist police think we are near we will be far away. When the fascist police think we are far away we will be near" (79). Prior to her terrorist actions, Marin visited her mother's home and removed photos of herself from it. But Marin's plans for visual anonymity are foiled, and a two-year-old newspaper photograph of her is broadcast on the television news. In this photograph, "Marin was almost indistinguishable, clearly a complaisant young girl in a pinafore but enigmatically expressionless, her eyes only smudges on the gravure screen" (76). In their identification of "faciality" with reterritorialization, Deleuze and Guattari write that deterritorialization occurs "when the face is effaced, when the faciality traits disappear" (115). The absence of all but a distorted facial image of Marin reinforces the sense that she exists outside the territories of striated space. However, Marin's comments on the cassette tape are simply repetitions of another guerilla's tautologies. Also, when Grace goes to visit her at the novel's conclusion, Marin seems unthinkingly to mouth revolutionary rhetoric. She despises her mother as a member of the bourgeoisie and assumes that she spent all her time in Boca Grande playing tennis. Marin may have escaped the striated space of state power, but her views are reterritorialized as a version of "class analysis" that rests on dialectical opposition (259). To varying degrees and differing forms, these three examples of the war machine—the guerillas, Leonard, and Marin—are all appropriated and reterritorialized. Rather than condoning or condemning the war machine as either utopian or dystopian, these representations suggest the differing ways in which nomadic space limns and constitutes the territoriality of state power.

Throughout *A Book of Common Prayer*, Charlotte is portrayed as someone without political concerns who is nevertheless caught up in the consequences of the intersection between the state and the war machine. Such an intersection of personal and political elements is typical of Didion's female protagonists, who are usually the wives, lovers, and daughters of men who are directly associated with politics.[3] At the same time, there are integral connections between Charlotte's behavior and the events that pertain to the war machine. In *A Thousand Plateaus*, Deleuze and Guattari describe jewelry as a nomadic art that is "related to pure mobility" (401). Similarly, in Didion's novel, references to Charlotte's jewelry, especially her emerald ring, link her to the smooth space of the war machine. The ring is initially given to Leonard by Edgar Strasser-Mendana, Grace's husband, for assistance in revolutionary activities similar to those involving the guerillas in Boca Grande; Leonard then gives the ring to Charlotte, who asks Grace to pass it on to Marin. The ring is therefore both an example of the spoils of the war machine and the personal item most strongly identified with Charlotte. The narrative of the emerald ring identifies Charlotte's actions with those of individuals who are overtly involved in political struggle. Two other references to jewelry address the relation between Charlotte and members of her family. When Marin visits her mother to remove the photographs, she finds her great-grandmother's gold bracelet in her drawer. She calls it "dead metal" (64), but Charlotte insists that she take it with her as a form of protection. Later, Charlotte removes a gold pin that belonged to her grandmother from a bank safe-deposit box. She imagines that the pin is attached to a bomb, and then the pin reminds her of being a child at her grandmother's house in Hollister, California. While Marin's rejection of the gold bracelet reflects her idea of a dialectical opposition to her mother, Charlotte's insistence that she take the bracelet evokes the congruity of their pursuits. When she hears of Marin's disappearance, Charlotte becomes preoccupied with personal memories. She then undertakes a line of flight that includes leaving Leonard, traveling with Warren Bogart, her first husband, around the southern United States, visiting Antigua, Mérida, and Guadeloupe, and finally arriving at Boca Grande. The gold pin represents the importance of memory in this line of flight, and the association between the gold pin and the bomb indicates that Charlotte's movements constitute a version of the war machine.

As her peregrinations commence, Charlotte leaves San Francisco for the Hollister ranch of her childhood. Like many other moments in Didion's writing, references to the ranch evoke rural California in utopian terms and echo sentiments expressed by authors such as Jack London and Upton Sinclair. According to Grace, Charlotte is "a child of the western United States" who was raised to believe in "the virtue of cleared and irrigated land" and "the generally upward spiral of history" (59, 60). As with Marin, who is "lost [. . .] to 'history'" (11), Charlotte remains attached to the dialectical oppositions that are central both to models of historical struggle and the distinction between utopian and nonutopian space. As symbolized by Leonard's installation of eight telephone lines, the Hollister ranch has been incorporated into the networks of striated space. Charlotte's utopian impulse is consequently thwarted, and she is then able to undertake the line of flight. However, her behaviors continue to exhibit territorializing, dialectic, and utopian elements. When she eventually arrives on Boca Grande, Charlotte indulges in repetitious actions. She goes to the airport on a daily basis, and at a piano in the Hotel Caribe she continually plays a melody from a song entitled "Mountain Greenery." As in Deleuze and Guattari's discussion of "the Refrain" (323), Charlotte's behavior "draws a territory and develops into territorial motifs and landscapes" (323). Boca Grande reminds her of "the matchbox model village" that she and her brother built at the Hollister ranch (195). While Boca Grande is located at the equator, she thinks of it in terms of "[t]he illusion of the tropics" (218). In these examples, notions of circumscribed utopian space and the exoticism of the tropics arrest Charlotte's line of flight. When the insurrection occurs in Boca Grande, Grace urges Charlotte to leave. However, she stays because she hopes that Marin's line of flight will also lead her to Boca Grande. Of course, no such reunion occurs, and Charlotte is killed during the insurrection. According to Deleuze and Guattari, the line of flight is accompanied by the danger of despair and the feeling of the "[t]ime to die" (200). While in some senses Charlotte attains the smooth space of the war machine, her adherence to territorialized space ensures the realization of the danger noted by Deleuze and Guattari.

In *Democracy*, Didion focuses her attention on the nature of American power. The primary character is Inez Christian, a member of a wealthy and powerful Hawaiian family. Inez marries a prominent politician named Harry Victor. The most dramatic events of the novel take place in 1975. As Saigon falls and American personnel are evacuated from Vietnam, Inez leaves her husband and goes to Hong Kong with her former lover, Jack Lovett. Soon after these events, Jack dies. Inez then moves to Kuala Lumpur and spends her time helping refugees. The narrative is framed by references to territoriality. We learn that Inez was born in the "Territory of Hawaii" (44), and Didion describes Kuala Lumpur as "the flotsam of some territorial imperative" (228). Such references to spatial territorialization exemplify Didion's representation of colonial influence in the geographical area portrayed in the novel. While it shares *A Book of Common Prayer*'s evocation of the interplay of spatial territorialization and tendencies toward smooth space, *Democracy*'s coarticulation of these spatial elements differs from that of the earlier novel. In order to create this spatial tale, Didion, a fictionalized version of whom is the narrator of *Democracy*, struggles against certain narrative conventions. Contrasting her narrative with others, Didion states that she has "[n]o Tropical Belt Company" to trigger the events of her island tragedy (18).[4] As in *A Book of Common Prayer*, the tropics are associated with an exoticism that obscures the spatial attributes that Didion describes. The reference to other narratives also reflects Didion's abandonment of the *primum mobile* and linear chronology. In her role as character-narrator, Didion states, "In 1975 time was no longer just quickening but collapsing, falling in on itself" (72), and this experience of the disintegration of a sense of history suggests the larger context of her rejection of chronology. By describing her warning to the reader about her impatience with linear narrative as a "travel advisory" (164),

Didion suggests that the needs of spatial narrative must supplant temporal conventions.

One of the strongest dualisms in *A Thousand Plateaus* is of course that of arborescence and the rhizome. Unlike hierarchical treelike structures, the rhizome is a lateral root system of multiple and non-hierarchical connections. Didion's narrative concerns are closely related to this dualism. The family tree of the Christians is a paradigm of arborescence. In declining to write "a study in provincial manners, in the acute tyrannies of class and privilege by which people assert themselves against the tropics" (22), Didion distances herself from arborescent family narrative and forecloses the possibility of regarding the Christians' exploits in reified terms. Instead, she presents a critique of the Christians' territorialization of colonial space. In Deleuze and Guattari's terms, the Christians are the emperors of state power. Every family member is tainted by "the colonial impulse" (26). Through corporate development schemes, they capture and striate the environment of Hawaii, Guam, Hong Kong, and Dubai. Didion criticizes such colonial striation by contrasting it with the more fundamental processes of geological space. Whereas the other narratives that Didion cites include an "unequivocal lone figure on the crest of the immutable hill" (18), Didion as character-narrator writes, "[A]s the granddaughter of a geologist I learned early to anticipate the absolute mutability of hills and waterfalls and even islands" (18). In *A Thousand Plateaus*, Deleuze and Guattari state that the movement of territorialization and deterritorialization that they describe occurs in geological "strata" (40). As Manuel DeLanda states, "[T]hese geologic structures represent a local *slowing-down* in this flowing reality, a temporary *hardening* in those lava flows" (129). Similarly, Didion's description of the island of Oahu, the location of the family home, as a "temporary feature" that is subject to physical deterritorialization indicates her interest in fluid transformations that apply equally to geology, social and political formations, and the behavior of her characters (18). Didion uses two strategies to deterritorialize the apparent fixity of the Christians' striation of space. First, Janet, Inez's sister and wife of property developer Dick Ziegler, expresses inaccurate memories about growing up on Hawaii and thus exposes the delusional nature of the family's "marvelous simple way of life" (67).

Second, the character of Paul Christian shows how a deterritorialized line of flight is produced within territorialized space. Paul becomes disillusioned with the family's business dealings and leaves Honolulu for Tunis. Upon his return he murders both his daughter, Janet, and Congressman Wendell Omura because he is angered by their property activities on the island.

As the novel's title suggests, Didion offers a critique of political power in the United States.[5] If, in Deleuze and Guattari's terms, the Christian family is the emperor of the novel, Harry Victor is its legislator. Harry worked for two years in the Justice Department and organized the Neighborhood Legal Coalition in East Harlem. He was a member of the United States Senate, ran unsuccessfully for the presidential nomination of the Democratic Party in 1972, and was involved in various committees and fact-finding missions. He is described as an abstraction. His latest project is the Alliance for Democratic Institutions, which is designed "to keep current the particular framework of ideas, the particular political dynamic, that Harry Victor had come to represent" (110). A comment made by Harry to the narrator makes apparent the spatial claim of his abstract political persona; the narrator observes, "I was struck by the extent to which he seemed to perceive the Indian Ocean, the carrier, and even himself as abstracts, incorporeal extensions of policy" (83). As Alan Nadel states, Harry's abstract view of space "attempts simultaneously to extend distance and diminish it" (112). In many respects, Harry is akin to the "abstract machine" of "the State apparatus" that Deleuze and Guattari describe (223). By imposing itself on "social space," this particular abstract machine "brings about a dualist organization of segments," "generalized overcoding," and "a divisible, homogeneous space striated in all directions" (222, 223). Harry overcodes social space in dualist terms because he reduces all political conflict to an opposition between democratic and nondemocratic forces. When Harry and Inez visit Indonesia, they encounter political unrest and attacks on American citizens, but Harry repeatedly states that that the events "reflected the normal turbulence of a nascent democracy" (99). Inez feels the effects of Harry's homogenization of social space most acutely. At Harry's political appearances, she repeats the same statement "[i]n twenty-eight states and at least four languages" (106). Along with such refrains, she cannot escape the incessant faciality of being constantly photographed. Inez feels as though she is losing her personal memories in the repetitive construction of social and political space that Harry creates. In the language of Deleuze and Guattari, Harry only perceives large-scale "molar" segments and does not register the seemingly irrelevant "molecular" details that Inez treasures (59). The distinction between molar and molecular space is also apparent in Harry's relationship with Jessie, his and Inez's daughter. As Americans are evacuating Vietnam in 1975, Jessie decides to look for work in Saigon. Jack Lovett states that a radar specialist has seen Jessie, but Harry dismisses such information as trivial and unreliable. Of course, Jack is correct, and he successfully tracks down Jessie. As in her representation of the Christian family, Didion uses incidents such as these to suggest both the substantiality and the limitations of state power's models of social and political space.

In *Democracy*, state power relies on the war machine. Of all the war machines portrayed by Didion, Jack Lovett is the most complex and ambiguous. In Deleuze and Guattari's analysis, the war machine is appropriated by the state and mediates between the two poles of state power. Such appropriation is unstable because the nomadic war machine is associated with a form of enumeration that has more to do with the movable logistical quantities of smooth space than striated measurements. In these and other respects, Jack typifies the war machine. His profession is obscure. An expert in logistics, he turns up at global sites of political insurrection and facilitates the supply of aircraft and other forms of military hardware. To Jack, "Asia was ten thousand tanks here, three hundred Phantoms there" (37). He is wholly identified with constant movement through smooth space. He is introduced to the reader as someone who "just got off a plane" (33), and he is "comfortable" in the transient environments of airplanes and hotels (35). As illustrated by his intermittent appearances in the milieus of both the Christians and Harry Victor, Jack connects corporate and political interests in the covert operations that he undertakes. His antipathy toward Harry illustrates the tension between state power and the war machine that it appropriates. Also, Jack sees little difference between state and nonstate actors, and he does not identify with the perspective or interests of any single nationality.

Despite these qualifications of Jack's attachment to state authority, he is a fully militarized war machine and thus remains tethered to state machinations.

Jack's role in the novel is complicated by his relationship with Inez. In *A Thousand Plateaus*, Deleuze and Guattari distinguish between "near-seers and far-seers" in fiction (200). Whereas the near-seers notice only the binary segments of striated space, the far-seers perceive "a whole microsegmentarity, details of details, 'a roller coaster of possibilities,' tiny movements that have not reached the edge, lines or vibrations that start to form long before there are outlined shapes" (201). If Harry and the Christians are near-seers, Jack is a far-seer. As exemplified by his establishment of "lines of access" for "the insurgency problem" in Saigon in 1955 (90), Jack observes the deterritorialized details and patterns of emergence that escape the gaze of the near-seers. As Deleuze and Guattari note, the situation of the far-seer is ambiguous. The far-seers serve the interests of state power but also participate in deterritorializing lines of flight: "Although they are collaborators with the most rigid and cruelest project of control, how could they not feel a vague sympathy for the subterranean activity revealed to them?" (202). Certain conditions put further pressure on the far-seer. As Deleuze and Guattari suggest, "[A] far-seer will abandon his or her segment [. . .] and depart on a line of flight to meet a blind Double approaching from the other side" (202). In *Democracy*, Inez is the double that Jack meets. They are each other's double because both are characterized by "temperamental secretiveness" (41). Also, Didion notes that the personalities of Inez and Jack never seem fully defined: "They were equally evanescent [. . .] and finally elusive. They seemed not to belong anywhere at all, except, oddly, together" (84). Jack's relationship with Inez enhances his frustration with state power, but it does not enable him to wholly break free of segmentarity. As we have seen, Jack diverts his deterritorializing impulse toward finding Jessie and returning her to the United States. However, during his flights to and from Honolulu, Saigon, and Hong Kong, Jack continues to pursue the business of covert insurrection. When Jack describes the South China Sea as "down there" (196), it seems to the narrator that the entirety of the sea is made visible and "telescoped by the pressure of his obsession" (196). As Jack views the sea in the same molar terms as Harry gestures toward the Indian Ocean, the telescope of the far-seer serves the purposes of the near-seer. Ultimately, Jack's tendencies toward smooth space that are accelerated by Inez's presence are reterritorialized into the workings of state power.

In *Democracy*, Inez undertakes the line of flight that Jack is unable to pursue. She is a type of war machine that becomes wholly detached from state power. According to Deleuze and Guattari, secrecy and betrayal are the signifying practices of the nomadic war machine. While Jack and Inez share the characteristics of secrecy and betrayal, these traits propel Inez beyond the milieus within which Jack remains. Deleuze and Guattari associate the nomadic signifying regime with the erasure of faciality and the movement toward the "imperceptible" (115).[6] As in the case of Inez, these factors initiate in *A Thousand Plateaus* the absolute territorialization of the line of flight. As Harry's wife, Inez is frequently photographed, and she cannot imagine "[l]ife beyond camera range" (66). She wishes to work with refugees and is described as a refugee by the narrator, but instead she is encouraged to become "a consultant for the collection of paintings that hung in American embassies and residences around the world" (56). The references to refugees indicate Inez's tendency toward deterritorialized smooth space, and painting and photography exemplify the faciality that inhibits the line of flight. Just as Inez's affair with Jack illustrates her secretive nature, her wish to remove both personal information from *Who's Who* and the photograph of her deceased sister from a prominent place in her uncle's home shows how Inez shifts away from faciality and toward imperceptibility. The decisive initiation of Inez's line of flight occurs when she leaves Dwight and Ruthie Christian's home with Jack in the aftermath of the murder. It is an overt act of betrayal that leads to her departure for Hong Kong and then Kuala Lumpur. By stating that Inez "just left" (166), the narrator denies any motive for her actions and thus evokes Inez's flight as a dramatic irruption within the world of Harry Victor and the Christians.

In Kuala Lumpur, Inez tells the narrator that she has lost interest in family arborescence and renounced the molar segmentarity of "the American exemption" (211). The fact that Inez assists refugees in Kuala Lumpur underscores her identification with the line of flight. The letter that she sends to Billy Dillon from Malaysia articulates the experience of her line of flight: "Colors, moisture, heat, enough blue in the air. Four fucking reasons. Love, Inez" (232). Designed to explain why she stays in Kuala Lumpur, these comments suggest that Inez has attained what Deleuze and Guattari describe as "the haptic, smooth space of close vision" (493). In these "local spaces of pure connection," Inez's experiences are also equivalent to Deleuze and Guattari's "haecceities," "relations of movement and rest," and "capacities to affect and be affected" (493, 261).[7] Detached from Jack and the militarization that he represents, Inez becomes the disappropriated war machine of smooth space. Unlike Charlotte Douglas in *A Book of Common Prayer*, Inez succeeds in pursuing the line of flight without falling victim to the dangers of reterritorialization. Inez achieves absolute deterritorialization not by inhabiting an alternative spatiality to that associated with the Christians, Harry, and Jack. Rather, she follows deterritorializing tendencies that are at work throughout *Democracy* to the point where perceptual intensities materialize and reterritorialization fails to occur.

In *The Last Thing He Wanted*, Didion returns to key narrative elements of both *A Book of Common Prayer* and *Democracy*. In so doing, she presents a version of the deterritorializing line of flight that differs from those portrayed in the earlier novels. The protagonist of *The Last Thing He Wanted* is Elena McMahon, a news reporter on the 1984 presidential campaign who suddenly and inexplicably leaves her position. Elena's decision initiates her line of flight. Rather than returning home to Washington DC, she visits her father, Dick McMahon, in Florida. An aged version of Jack Lovett, Dick facilitates the covert movement of military equipment to volatile regions of the world. When Elena arrives, Dick is involved in a deal to send a large cache of military hardware to Costa Rica. Dick believes that this deal will make him rich, but he is too ill to complete it. He therefore asks Elena to conduct the deal. Working with various contacts, Elena delivers the equipment to Costa Rica but does not receive payment. She is then instructed to travel to an unnamed Caribbean island on a false passport. On the island she learns that her father is dead, and she begins to suspect a plot against her. Through the comments of Didion's unnamed narrator, we learn that this plot is part of a covert operation to weaken the Sandinista government in Nicaragua. On the island, various operatives hope to place Elena at the site of the assassination of Alex Brokaw, the American ambassador. At a late date, the object of the assassination attempt is switched from Brokaw to Treat Morrison, "America's man-on-the-spot in the world's hotspots, ambassador-at-large with a top-secret portfolio" (137). The goal of the plot is to make Elena seem like the assassin, associate her with the Sandinista, and therefore provide justification for the United States' support of the Nicaraguan contras. Identified as the assassin, Elena is killed by FBI agents. She is also posthumously linked to the Sandinista government. However, Morrison survives the assassination attempt, and the intended political fallout from the plot does not come into being.

As suggested by the presence of an unnamed island and unnamed narrator, Didion's novel lacks striated textual markers. Also, the narrative's conspiratorial focus means that state power does not have a strong and overt role in *The Last Thing He Wanted*. Rather than initiating events, the House of Congress, along with the Rand Corporation, commissions an investigation to determine the context of the events of the narrative. The origin of the assassination plot is linked to Mark Berquist, a Washington aide who becomes a senator, but Berquist is a marginal representative of state power. Persistent rumors suggest that Brokaw has facilitated the assassination plot and thus has "play[ed] the Reichstag card" (174). However, Brokaw is referred to as a "career" not a "political appointee" (92), and he is devoid of agency. Instead of political legislators and corporate emperors, Didion's novel is peopled with numerous logistical fixers. Dick McMahon, Max Epperson (also known as Bob Weir), Barry Sedlow, Paul Schuster, Colonel Álvaro García Steiner, and other characters conduct covert business in political subversion and military hardware. By stating that such characters "exclusively" make history (33), Didion places the war machine at the center of her novel. Described as a "transit passenger" who travels without needing to show a visa (67), Steiner mysteriously appears at key locations in the novel and epitomizes the smooth movements of the war machine. The prominence of smooth space occurs at the expense of the striated space of state power. Speaking to the narrator in his corporate office, Wynn Janklow, Elena's former husband, refers to an electronic Mercator map on the wall and states that, even though the map tells you where there is daylight in the world, "it doesn't tell you shit about what's happening there" (122). Janklow's comments indicate the limitations of the striated maps of corporate power. When she transports the military equipment, Elena notices a map of Costa Rica that does not include the location in which she has arrived. The scene proves the validity of Janklow's observations because events occur in the smooth space of the mobile war machine and not within the map's striated coordinates.

The striated space of state power lacks an overt presence, but it remains a factor in narrative events. Also, the prominence of the war machine does not mean that it has broken free of state appropriation. Rather, the war machine remains oriented toward military conflict and takes on the functions of state power. In *A Thousand Plateaus*, Deleuze and Guattari suggest that the state's appropriation of the war machine can be reversed: "We could say that the appropriation has changed direction, or rather that States tend to unleash, reconstitute, an immense war machine of which they are no longer anything more than the opposable or apposed parts" (421). Crucially, the war machine implements a "neonomadism" of smooth space "for the purpose of controlling striated space more completely" (480). In other words, the war machine becomes the vehicle for state power. As in Deleuze and Guattari's analysis, smooth space and striated space converge in *The Last Thing He Wanted*. The war machine's "alternative infrastructure" of secret runways is described as "a regular little piece of U.S.A." (69, 70). Also, the man who assists Elena in transporting the weapons wears a T-shirt that is "printed with an American flag and the legend THESE COLORS DON'T RUN" (104). Both these examples show that the war machine is identified with American state power. As Deleuze and Guattari repeatedly note, the homogenization of striated space means that it always takes on the appearance of smooth space. In Didion's novel the homogenization of smooth space underscores its convergence with striated space. The sameness of the houses that Dick McMahon rents exemplifies the homogenized war machine. However, the war machine also splinters into internecine elements. Rather than struggles between smooth and striated space, Didion's novel represents conflicts between different incarnations of the war machine. Dick attempts to create a "safe zone" (53), a smooth space in which Elena can carry out the arms deal. However, Dick is caught in the plot of other war machines, and his safe zone is destroyed. Treat Morrison also gets caught in the battle of the war machines. His perception of the Caribbean Sea as "our lake" indicates his promotion of striated state authority (69). By suggesting that, in the words of Hart Crane, Morrison also exhibits a "wide spindrift gaze toward paradise" (47), Elena associates him with nomadic smooth space. Yet Morrison's sphere of influence is limited, and he falls victim to a more powerful war machine. As an expression of American foreign policy that has seemingly unrestricted access to covert movement, the version of the war machine that attacks Dick, Elena, and Morrison is also the smoothest and most striated in the novel.

The convergence of smooth and striated space also affects Elena's line of flight. According to Deleuze and Guattari, nomad science involves a "hydraulic model" (361), and striated space includes "conduits or channels" (371). In Didion's novel the two sets of images mentioned by Deleuze and Guattari are combined to suggest the melding of smooth and striated space. The narrator observes that official documentation of the events of the story contains much "hydraulic imagery" and that Elena "got caught in the pipeline, swept into the conduits" (10, 12). In Deleuze and Guattari's terms, her hydraulic disposition toward nomadic space makes her vulnerable to the effects of striated conduits. On several occasions, Didion evokes Elena's actions as a nomadic line of flight. As well as leaving her job, she abandons her home with Wynn Janklow and contemplates "walking away" from her father and daughter (43). When she realizes that there is a plot against her, she "go[es] feral" and tries to "stay alert in the wild" (117, 118). As indicated by these comments, Elena undergoes the deterritorializing process of "becoming-animal" that Deleuze and Guattari describe (233). Also, she relishes the island's view of the smooth space of the sea. Because she lacks the "firm, calm lines" that the narrator describes as effective orientation mechanisms (74), Elena turns to her father's plot as a source of order and meaning. Elena furthers the goals of the striated war machine of the state, but she does so by utilizing her nomadic qualities. Of course, these nomadic tendencies have striated effects because they undergo a degree of reterritorialization. Deleuze and Guattari state that the deterritorialized line of flight is "repudiat[ed]" by "passional subjectification" (133, 125). Elena's loyalty to her father and clandestine relationship with Treat Morrison are both manifestations of her passional subjectification. Unlike Morrison, "Elena inserted herself in a certain kind of situation and went all the way with it" (158). In other words, Elena's lines of flight become fixed and restricted. As a result of her passionate involvement with Morrison, she is "lined up" by the striated war machine (168). Such language suggests that the smooth line has become the agent of striation. The various tendencies associated with Elena also relate to what Deleuze and Guattari describe as "holey space" (413). These authors describe "ambulant" blacksmiths who "[t]ranspierce the mountains instead of scaling them, excavate the land instead of striating it, bore holes in space instead of keeping it smooth, turn the earth into swiss cheese" (413). Holey space is rhizomatic, but it also "plugs the lines of flight" (415). Elena's secret meetings with Morrison at the Aero Sands Beach Resort create a holey space within the island's increasingly militarized environment. As the location of Elena's death, the motel also curtails her line of flight.

As is well known, Deleuze and Guattari state that the deterritorializing line of flight is widely evident in Anglo-American literature. The novels of Joan Didion exemplify Deleuze and Guattari's observation because they are centered on protagonists' lines of flight. The critical space of Didion's fiction also involves representations of the interplay between the smooth space of the nomadic war machine and the striated space of state power. In Marcus Doel's terms, Didion is more interested in representations of the verb, "[t]o space" (125), than in fixed models of utopia or dystopia. Each of the three novels discussed in this chapter offers a distinct portrayal of these spatial elements. In *A Book of Common Prayer*, Didion represents the war machine in seemingly autonomous modes. However, the guerillas, Leonard, and Marin all exhibit striated characteristics that reflect the merging of the war machine into state activity. Charlotte is unrelated to state power, but her line of flight is informed by key elements of territorialization. *Democracy* depicts the full incorporation of the war machine into state power. Jack exemplifies the restlessness of the appropriated war machine, and Inez is a war machine that attains absolute deterritorialization. Through the character of Elena, *The Last Thing He Wanted* depicts the reappropriation of the war machine. In this novel, overt military conflicts decline in significance and the spatiality of power becomes increasingly smooth. In *A Thousand Plateaus*, Deleuze and Guattari describe a "worldwide war machine" that displaces state power and engenders "a form of peace more terrifying" than total war (421). The realm of high-speed travel and electronic communication that is depicted at the opening of the narrative also hints at the total smoothness of Deleuze and Guattari's worldwide war machine. Despite the differences between these novels, Didion consistently negates the dialectics of social space and evokes the presence of smooth space in power's striated domain.

Joan Didion's fiction offers a critique of the appropriated smoothness of social space. In *Underworld*, Don DeLillo extends Didion's concerns and suggests that extreme smoothness transforms space into a lost dimension. In Régis Debray's terms, *Underworld* exchanges the "semiological" emphasis of DeLillo's previous fiction for a "mediological" discourse that represents the technological erosion of social space (49). In the tradition of influential media theorists such as Marshall McLuhan and Hans Magnus Enzensberger, Debray defines media according to how they organize human behavior through networks of technological material rather than in terms of linguistic models of their content. As in McLuhan, media are significant to the extent that they transform the "scale or pace or pattern" of human activity (24). Just as semiotics overturned structuralism, so Debray proposes a mediology that would abandon the poststructuralist emphasis on the semiotic code and involve a further "going to the object" than is evident in semiotics (51). Mediology would not study "media," a term that implies discrete and autonomous media forms (print, television, film, radio, and so on), but instead the "mediasphere, or middle ground, setting or environment of the transmission and carrying of messages and people" (Debray 12, 26). In *Underworld*, media significance breaks from the problematic of referentiality to become spatial and material, and thus DeLillo undertakes the "going to the object" that Debray advocates. Billboards, for example, are more monumental than semiotic. The power of billboard advertisements to generate their surrounding reality that is felt by Brian Glassic, a colleague of Nick Shay (the novel's major protagonist-narrator), is a function of the "neurotic tightness" and "inescapability" of their spatial extent rather than their rhetorical suasion (183). Also, what the crowds that attend the miraculous appearance of the image of the murdered girl Esmeralda on the Minute Maid billboard actually witness and are drawn to is the spatial mediasphere of subway train and billboard advertisement. The billboard reads "Space Available" once the Minute Maid advertisement is removed (824), which underscores the fact that the vision of Esmeralda is a spatial rather than semiotic event.

Paul Virilio's writing shares many aspects of DeLillo's representation of space. Both writers are concerned with the impact of technology on social space. Instead of proffering dystopian representations of social space, DeLillo and Virilio chart the processes that cause it to disappear. DeLillo does not simply critique particular technological forms, nor does he underestimate the importance of technology. Like Virilio, DeLillo evaluates technological trends rather than specific technologies, and he acknowledges that social space is organized and defined by media and military technologies.[8] As Tim Luke and Gearóid Ó Tuathail argue, Virilio believes "all human geography is ultimately a product of warfare" (365). Citing countless examples from Thucydides to the Internet as evidence, Virilio argues that media technologies represent the civilian implementation of military technologies and that their increasing range and sophistication reflects an equally substantial militarization or "endo-colonization" of civilian society (*Pure* 98). In *Underworld*, the description of Nick's mother's home as a military fortification and the conversion of military bases into landfills denotes the endo-colonization of social geography. In *The Lost Dimension*, Virilio describes a "Critical Space" that comes into being "by virtue of the instantaneity of mass *communication* as much as through the performances of delivery vectors of massive *destruction*" (130). The conjunction of media information and military delivery systems erodes the significance of spatial distinctions, geographical locations, and sensory perceptions: "The imbalance between the direct information of our senses and the mediated information of the advanced technologies is so great that we have ended up transferring our value judgments and our measure of things from the object to its figure, from the form to its image, from reading episodes of our history to noting their statistical tendencies." As a result of the intense "movement and acceleration" of the lost dimension, "substance" is viewed as illusory and insignificant (*Lost* 52, 48). For Virilio, the declining significance of direct perception causes the human body to be disregarded and made the object of violence. Through depictions of the mutations of the atomic bomb, military imaging systems, television, and computer networks, DeLillo maps the spatial concerns that animate Virilio's discourse. Like Virilio, DeLillo also seeks to renew bodily perception and recover the lost dimension of social space.

In the prologue to *Underworld*, J. Edgar Hoover learns of the Soviet Union's second atomic bomb detonation while attending the famous 1951 baseball game between the Brooklyn Dodgers and the New York Giants at the Polo Grounds. Known as "the shot heard 'round the world," Bobby Thompson's game-winning home run is associated by DeLillo with the Soviet detonation. Just as the media transmit news of the home run, American atomic sensors pick up evidence of the bomb's explosion. By beginning the novel with such associations, DeLillo emphasizes the role of media and military technologies in the shrinking of social space. Given the fact that during the Cold War no exchanges of nuclear weapons took place, it might seem strange that DeLillo's prologue, which evokes the news heard by Hoover as a sinister presence within the festive game atmosphere, is entitled "The Triumph of Death." However, it is the deathly militarization of space that triumphs. Hoover approves of Harry Truman's intention to make an immediate statement on the subject of the Soviet bomb because this will demonstrate that "we've maintained control of the news if not of the bomb" (28). In this instance, the media's control of societal space is defined as a surrogate explosion. For Virilio, news media are as explosive as a bomb.[9] Similarly, DeLillo attributes to the media an explosiveness that obliterates social space. Magazine advertisements may be "easier to identify than the names of battlefields" (39), but since many instances of media advertisements are "sublimated forms of destruction" (529), these exchanges do not mean an end to military influence. Elsewhere in *Underworld*, Jell-O is described as "a push-button word" (517), and a Bronx street preacher insists that "[t]he business of the generals" remains active in civilian society (352). Like the abstraction of the bomb into news, these incidents suggest that the military function colonizes social space despite or even because of the loss of its referential grounding in the business of armed conflict.

Much of *Underworld* traces the technological genealogies that engender the destruction of space. One strain within these genealogies concerns the relation between media and military technologies of light. In *The Lost Dimension*, Virilio states that the eradication of space is "an effect of celerity, understood not as 'acceleration' so much as 'illumination'—less speed than subliminal light, the light of the velocity of light that illuminates the world, in the instant in which it offers up its representation" (62). According to Virilio, "the bombs dropped on Hiroshima and Nagasaki were *light-weapons*," by which he means not only that the light from these explosions penetrated dark areas and bleached buildings but also that, like photography, the bomb was a method of "engraving with light," which imprinted clothing designs on victims' bodies (*War* 81). DeLillo also associates the bomb with lighting effects, which confirms the media-military relation in *Underworld*. When Hoover hears of the Soviet explosion, the foreboding it brings colors Hoover's memory of the news of Pearl Harbor, in which the light associated with the news flash, photojournalism, and the Japanese attack converges: "[T]he news seemed to shimmer in the air, everything in photoflash, plain objects hot and charged" (24). Later in the novel, Louis Bakey, a crew member of a B-52 bomber during the Vietnam War, tells the story of how, earlier in his military experience, he participated in a simulation of a nuclear bomb drop during a B-52 run. The drop is a simulation but the explosion is not, and for Louis the detonation reveals an x-ray vision of himself and his fellow crew members as skeletons: "Then the world lights up. A glow enters the body that's like the touch of God. And Louis can see the bones in his hands through his closed eyes, through the thick pillow he's got jammed in his face" (613). For both Hoover and Bakey, the effect of military technology is not one of material destruction but of an illumination that overrides even the sightlessness of closed eyes. As in Virilio's writing, the authority of human perception is exceeded by the space of technological illumination. Also, DeLillo's emphasis on the power of military weapons to make things visible suggests their equivalence to media technologies, such as film and television, which use light to observe, record, and project.

Through the character of Matt, Nick's brother, DeLillo articulates key aspects of the novel's technological genealogies. "All technology refers to the bomb" (467), thinks Matt, but in the post–Cold War phase of *Underworld*, DeLillo is more concerned with how the bomb mutates into other technologies than with the bomb as a culmination of technological vectors. This emphasis is evident in DeLillo's portrayal of Matt's work for the army on military technologies in Vietnam and "the Pocket," a secret installation in the New Mexico desert, where various aspects of nuclear weapons systems are developed. The consistent aspect of Matt's work is the fact he is not a "weaponeer" (461). With Matt, we are one step removed from the bombs dropped during the Vietnam War and those being prepared in the Pocket and one step closer to media technologies. In Vietnam, Matt studied aerial reconnaissance footage, "an endless series of images sucked up by the belly cameras of surveillance planes" (462). As Virilio argues in *War and Cinema*, in reviving the significance of "aerial observation" in war (18), the Vietnam conflict marked the moment in military history when "[d]irect vision [became] a thing of the past" and "the target area [became] a cinema 'location'" (11). Virilio writes at length about how the development of cinema technologies was coterminous with their military applications, and the cinema-military mutation that DeLillo fictionalizes through Matt's work represents what Virilio considers to be a decisive heightening of the dominance of the media image in war. Virilio writes that, in this new dispensation, "what is perceived is already lost" (*War* 4) and that, as a result, military weapons become the "vision machine[s]" of imaging technologies and invisible-to-detection stealth technologies (*Vision* 59). As we have seen, the images that Matt studies are effects of both these technological trends.[10] According to Virilio, the United States was incited to develop Matt's imaging and other stealth technologies by the Soviet Union's detonation of the hydrogen bomb (*War* 81). Similarly, DeLillo evokes news of the Soviet detonation as a version of the light technologies with which Matt works.

By harnessing the illumination associated with the bomb, stealth imaging technologies represent an important phase in the mediatization of the military conquest of social space. Such technologies mutate into media technologies in *Underworld* in terms of the power of the image, which in Virilio's terminology represents the replacement of reality by a visual "reality effect" (*Art* 20). For Virilio, the reality effect is the means by which the authority of the social space of human perception is undermined. As he tries to interpret the ground images from Vietnam, Matt experiences the incommensurability of the reality perceived by human senses and the reality effect of images processed by technology. Matt's job involves "cranking rolls of film across a light box. [. . .] It was all about lost information, how to recover the minutest unit of data and identify it as a truck driven by a man smoking a French cigarette, going down the Ho Chi Minh trail" (462). Matt is to mark the dots that appear to represent significant objects, but a dot was "an object that had no properties except location" (464), and he is disturbed to realize that he cannot identify the objects represented by the dots. The value of perception is further eroded in the Pocket, where Matt manipulates abstract symbols on a computer screen. Like his co-workers, Matt is unable to comprehend the electronic space in which the "weapons work" of the Pocket is integrated and made meaningful (402). The real-time network communication of the Pocket eliminates both the need for physical proximity among network nodes and, in what is probably Virilio's most insistent point, the time for reflection upon which democratic processes depend. The relation between this military work and the erosion of social space is suggested by the visit Matt takes to "a wildlife preserve and gunnery range" in the desert (449). Described as "remote Sonoran waste" (451), this civilian tourist area is also an uninhabited military zone. In a sedentary bunker beneath a topographical wasteland, Matt reacts to real-time screen images that connect in ways he literally has no time to understand. As such, he embodies Virilio's vision of the lost dimension.

Much of Matt's experience in Vietnam and the Pocket is generally extended through nonmilitary media images that claim semiological rather than mediological significance. In other words, the displacement of the space of human perception persists through the practice of media interpretation. Marvin Lundy is on a quest to find the home run baseball that was hit by Bobby Thompson of the New York Giants in the famous pennant-winning baseball game. Marvin procures "original film" and photographs of the game to try to see where the ball landed in the crowd (175). Marvin spends his time studying "the photographic detailwork, the fineness of image, the what-do-you-call-it into littler units" because he subscribes to "the dot theory of reality, that all knowledge is available if you analyze the dots" (175). In other words, he is interested in the media image as a means of referring to and revealing the real human subject in question, not as a component of the impact of media technology upon social space. Marvin's faith in dots is misplaced, and his attempt to see the person who got the ball fails because he "could not find a way, for all his mastery of the dots, to rotate the heads of the people on the ramp so he could see the face of the individual in question" (177). Virilio informs us that *ligne de foi*, or "faith line," is the French term for the military line of aim. However, for Virilio the fact that the word "faith" is no longer used in this way indicates that "the ideal line appears thoroughly objective, and the semantic loss involves a new obliviousness to the element of interpretative subjectivity that is always in play in the act of looking" (*War 2*, 3). Marvin's faith in the image cannot produce the presence of Cotter Martin, the African American youth who gets the ball, yet, as in Virilio's analysis, he does not question the ability of the image to produce its referential content, and as a result he remains allied to a failed notion of technological meaning. This continued faith in a reality effect that fails is central to the mutation of media and military technologies, because what for Matt had been simply a matter of following orders within massive command networks has become normalized as a general faith in media's representational power. Therefore, this example illustrates not only that media imaging technologies are derived from their military predecessors but also that a mediaspheric relation between humans and technologies involving obedience to the faith line has also been maintained.

Through the sequences involving the Texas Highway Killer, DeLillo shows how television and video also continue the effects of military imaging technologies. A twelve-year-old girl captures home video footage of a random highway murder by this serial killer, and the images are repeated incessantly on television. As in Matt's experience, these technologies are described in terms of their impact on social space and the faith line of media content. In *The Lost Dimension*, Virilio states that television was initially designed to be part of rocketry apparatus (117). The fusion of military and media promised in this anecdote is fulfilled in Virilio's description of Howard Hughes. For Virilio, the history of military technology has been one of increasing speed, and "the automation of war" implied by electronic networks that react more quickly than human reflection represents the culmination of this ancient trend (*Pure* 72). In terms of social space, the attainment of instantaneous communication quickly translates into cultural standardization and homogenization and personal immobility, or what Virilio calls "polar inertia" (*Pure* 74). As someone who greatly indulged in speed and movement only to end up immobilized in a hotel room for years, Hughes prefigures this spatial trend. The fact that, according to Virilio, Hughes spent his time watching the same film, *Ice Station Zebra*, 164 times indicates that the societal destiny that attends upon the tendency toward increasing speed in military technology is to be sat before the media screen observing the same images again and again. And just in case we might have forgotten that such a destiny is a military situation, Virilio posits that "the ordinary penetration" of television into the lives of the domestic masses marks a new form of "lightning warfare" that makes the old-style weaponry of tanks and planes obsolete (*Popular* 70).

The broadcasting of the images of the Texas Highway Killer produces effects similar to those described by Virilio. The killer lives in the solitude of Howard Hughes, and actual social space, especially the "open space" of the supermarket (272), is frightening. The conjunction of television and video engenders immobile social space because of the temporal nature of their images. Real-time potentialities have caused an explosion in audiovisual devices that Virilio describes as a "panic anticipation" of the recordable event (*Vision* 66). For Virilio, such technological developments are military in nature because real-time technologies are the outcome of military vectors of technological speed and also engender a culture of public surveillance that furthers the process of the militarization of civilian life. Since in *Underworld* "this kind of crime became more possible when the means of taping an event and playing it immediately, without a neutral interval, a balancing space and time, became widely available" (159), the compelling and numbing effects of the footage of the serial killer are a function of the temporality of its images. The "unrelenting footage that rolls on and on" is characterized by "noneventness" (156), and Albert Bronzini, a friend of Nick's from his Bronx childhood of the 1950s, resigns himself to the fact that the footage will be repeated "to the ends of the earth" (233). Characters in *Underworld* succumb to spatial immobility before these images because of their faith in them. For DeLillo's characters these images are "more real, truer-to-life than anything around you" (157). For example, a hypothetical male character wants his wife to watch the footage with him because "it is real this time, not fancy movie violence—the realness beneath the layers of cosmetic perception" (158). Combined with such referential faith, the spatiotemporal effects of such technologies contribute to the production of a social experience that is characterized by violence and a concern with security, two obvious aspects of combat experience.

Matt's technical work is yet further extended through the electronic computer networks of *Underworld*. In *Open Sky*, Virilio claims that real-time computer networks cause the spatial interval of geographical separation and the temporal interval of past, present, and future to be replaced by the "real instant" of the interval of light-speed (18). By creating a megasuburb or "world city" (*Open* 71), a virtual community existing in the time interval of light-speed communications, such media technologies transform citizens into contemporaries, and "transpolitical intensity" replaces "geographical extensivity" (*Lost* 92). Since, for the purposes of such media technologies, the world can never be sufficiently "desertified" (*Open* 81), these developments cause the ghettoization of social space and the decline of urban centers that, for Virilio, are the best means of resisting endo-colonization (*Pure* 114). As a result, our communities exist in electronic time and we come to loathe our spatial neighbors as enemies (*Politics* 41–42). Virilio defines this situation as one of "dromospheric contamination" or "grey ecology" (*Open* 40, 41), where "the sudden pollution of distances and lengths of time [degrades] the expanse of our habitat" (*Open* 58). In order to emphasize the literality of such pollution, Virilio argues that it is related to the ecological degradation of nature, and he cites the example of the Atlantic Ocean, which "is just a big garbage can now"

(*Politics* 60), to show that the pollution of distances caused first by transport and now by electronic media results in actual ecological pollution. In the area of work, Virilio writes that "hyperconcentrated real-time computer systems are taking over from the traditional administration office" (76), which means that employees are constantly traveling to other corporate nodes as part of a "business tourism" that Virilio fears because private time and space are collapsed into a permanent work mode (*Open* 76). These consequences are reminiscent of Virilio's earlier writings on military proletarianization, and, once again, Virilio affirms the military basis of the societal operationality he describes by noting how "man-the-target [sic] is assailed on all sides" by the information blitz of media technologies (*Art* 132).

DeLillo addresses many of the concerns voiced by Virilio through his treatment of Nick. Like Virilio, Nick is concerned about targets. He thinks that the name and packaging of Lucky Strike cigarettes must refer to "a penetrating hit from a weapon" (90). However, Nick, who "rushed inside" (95) literally and psychologically when the Giants beat the Dodgers (and, for Glassic, such psychological inwardness is associated with the Cold War reaction to Kennedy's assassination), thinks that the Lucky Strike target explains the disappearance of his father and does not associate it with the external mediasphere of electronic communication. Instead, Nick is blithe about electronic connectivity and unaware of the military implications of the language of his own thoughts: "You feel the contact points around you, the caress of linked grids that give you a sense of order and command. It's there in the warbling banks of phones, in the fax machines and photocopiers and all the oceanic logic stored in your computer" (89). Elsewhere, Nick feels similarly comforted by security systems based on "the smart new world of microprocessors" (303), and at the novel's conclusion he still has fond regards for the "order and command" of the networked office (806). Nick's sentiments should be taken in the context of his life in Phoenix, where he feels comfortable because he is able to keep all his "isolated feelings" inside himself (341). The consistent association of Nick with both inward psychic life and computer enthusiasm reiterates the perspective of Marvin, where an appetite for technology is linked to a belief in the representation of inner meaning.

Nick's experience epitomizes the Virilioan combination of an integrated electronic domain and a de-urbanized environs, and his numerous visits to various landfills suggest a connection between the world of intensive electronic time and the transformation of the landscape into garbage dump. Further, as a business traveler working on multinational projects, Nick exemplifies Virilio's point regarding how extensive work-related movement exists in tandem with network euphoria. On his trip to Kazakhstan to learn about how the company Tchaika uses former-Soviet nuclear weapons to detonate waste, Nick contemplates the decline in the significance of space, but he is unable to fathom what, in the post–Cold War scenario, has replaced the "dream of vast land empires" that leaders formerly sought (787). This inability to recognize contemporary spatial significance is a function of Nick's inwardness. Like Marvin, Nick prefers sexual information to be withheld and unspoken, but whereas Marvin realizes that "words unprintable through history" are now emblazoned on T-shirts (188), Nick's inability to attain an equivalent insight prevents him from unifying his thoughts and attaining the Virilioan point of acknowledging how his own computer fascination and landfill projects participate in the technological trend that erodes social space in favor of intensive time.

Occasionally, Nick does counter this tendency with realizations of an external significance that is often hidden by a preoccupation with inner meaning. For example, he believes that waste, the answer that is "staring us in the face," solves "those romantic desert mysteries" of inexplicably abandoned communities (343). The contradictory and ambivalent nature of Nick's character is further expressed in his attitudes toward cyberspace. On the one hand Nick regards his son's activities on the Web with equanimity, but on the other he criticizes cyberculture in Virilioan terms for promoting cultural homogenization and decline: "[T]he force of converging markets produces an instantaneous capital that shoots across horizons at the speed of light, making for a furtive sameness, a planning away of particulars that affects everything from architecture to leisure time to the way people eat and sleep and dream" (786). By focusing on the contrast between the character of Sister Edgar and other elements of the novel, several critics argue that the ambivalence toward cyberspace that we observe in Nick's character is applicable to the novel as a whole.[11] From this perspective, Sister Edgar embodies a desire for "salvation" (Begley, "Don" 502), "faith" (Green 596), and "grace" that acts as a counterweight to DeLillo's critical remarks on cyberspace (Parrish 718). However, it is also in keeping with *Underworld*'s discourse of materiality to say that the desire to find transcendent content in media technology prevents us from comprehending its spatial effects. Rather than acting as a contrary force, devotion to cyberspace actually serves to further the effects DeLillo criticizes, which result from the fact that cyberculture intensifies and accelerates the effects that other media have derived from military technology.

James Wolcott regards *Underworld* as "unwieldy and disjointed" and argues that the focus on cyberspace at the novel's conclusion represents a forced attempt "to position some of the themes and characters into some sort of harmonic convergence" (69). However, such passages clearly extend the attributes of the other technological mutations in the novel. In a passage that has already become canonical in DeLillo studies, Sister Edgar visits a Web site devoted to H-bomb explosions. The description of this Web site as the culmination of technological trajectories extending from the atomic bomb to cyberspace obviously alludes to the origins of the Internet in nuclear defense networks, but DeLillo, like Virilio, is primarily concerned with the spatial effects of this culmination. Virilio is fond of noting Einstein's prediction that a "computer bomb, the bomb of totalitarian information" would succeed the atomic bomb (*Politics* 36). Cyberspace represents the realization of the computer bomb's "interactivity" (*Politics* 80), which develops the threat to human activity presented by the radioactivity of the atomic bomb. The post–Cold War era of cyberspace marks the abandonment of the "nuclear standard" and the advent of "the permanent disequilibrium of a strategy of tension, where global logistics supplants intercontinental ballistics" (*Virilio* 81). Rather than analogy, Virilio's formulations deal in a form of technological mutation that identifies the real-time interactivity of decentralized computer networks not only as the outcome of initiatives in military technology but as the agent of a military surveillance that immobilizes and isolates people into a state of terminal siege (*Open* 86). Just as Virilio argues that the "fusion" of object and image in image technologies creates human social "confusion" (*War* 83), so too Sister Edgar regards the cyber-representation of atomic "fusion bombs," with their "atoms forcibly combined," as having the operationally standardizing effect of ironing out any difference between herself and J. Edgar Hoover: "[A]ll argument, all conflict [is] programmed out" (826). For DeLillo, it is the intensive time of media technologies that continues the military-technological elimination of spatial "horizons" and engenders the effects feared by Sister Edgar and Nick (786).

Cyberspace is complicit with the deterioration of social space associated with the mutations of media and military technologies. "All terror is local" (816), thinks Sister Edgar, and her fears, which are also those of Virilio, are proved correct when Esmeralda is murdered. Virilio is critical of the myth of rapprochement or communication that accompanies cyberspace (*Politics* 18). For Virilio, such rhetoric expresses the "cybercult" of "technical essentialism" that exemplifies the foundationalism of modernity's worship of progress (*Virilio* 20). In accordance with this view, cyberspace tends to deteriorate rather than salvage human communicativity and social space. The inclusion of the interactive commands "Keystroke" and "Searching" in the paragraph that describes the murderer suggests that this is a cyberkiller (817), who updates the deadly media fetish of the Texas Highway Killer and whose actions confirm the localized ghettoization created by technologies of intensive time. The conflict between technological vectors and their surrounding reality is highlighted in the discrepancy between the self-referentiality of the former and the extension of the latter. Sister Edgar tries to imagine "the word on the screen becoming a thing in the world [. . .] a word extending itself ever outward [. . .] but it's only a sequence of pulses on a dullish screen and all it can do is make you pensive" (827). DeLillo's rhetoric suggests that "Peace" (827), the word on the screen, fails to produce the harmony it promises, which intimates that the post–Cold War is no peace at all, but rather stands in the same relation to the Cold War as the Cold War does to World War II—a lessening of the possibility of combat, but a greater penetration of military uniformity and degradation into everyday life.

The critical space of *Underworld* uses various means to counter the effects of media and military technologies. As well as denouncing the appeal of the content of media images, DeLillo strives to recover the social space that these technologies eradicate. Rather than seeking out oppositional or untainted spaces, DeLillo evokes technologies that intensify the perceptual and interpretive encounter with spatiality and thus restore the meaningfulness of social space. In pursuing these ends, DeLillo undertakes what Virilio calls "divergence" (*Politics* 23). Divergence refers to the process by which dangerous technologies spawn critical versions of themselves. For Virilio, modernist painting and sculpture articulate orders of speed and movement in matter that differ from those realized by photography and cinema. Such art is therefore a divergence of photography and cinema that is inseparable from these new media technologies (*Politics* 23). Virilio advocates that the resistance to technological militarization take the form not of an opposition to technology but of a technological mutation that subverts the "ocular drilling" (*Politics* 86), or standardization of perception, to which such militarization tends. DeLillo attempts to imagine cultural forms that achieve such subversion while articulating alternative perceptions of the human body's spatial dimension.

DeLillo provides many instances of the attempted divergence or further mutation of media-military technologies, and much of the significance of these attempts is apparent in the experiences of Klara Sax. If Nick embodies the ambivalence of the novel toward the effects of technology, then Klara represents the possibility of transforming the media-military conjunction into technologies that promote different conceptions of human materiality. The progression from Klara's attendance at a film showing in the summer of 1974 to the land art project she creates in the spring of 1992 reflects a movement from the observation to the creation of divergence. Klara and Miles Lightman attend a showing of Eisenstein's fictional film, *Unterwelt,* at Radio City Music Hall. According to Virilio, the divergence effected by Eisenstein's films is a "paradox" because "the art of montage" that Eisenstein developed and that represents a critical intensification of militarized perception is itself a product of the perceptual exigencies of war (*Politics* 29). The effects of *Unterwelt* are equally complex and paradoxical. The showing is a "cross-referenced event" (423), and *Unterwelt*'s "ambivalence" and "contradictions" are reiterated (425). Such references ostensibly designate the juxtapositions of film and theater, comedy and seriousness, which are apparent during the film's showing. However, the fact that *Unterwelt* deals with the same issues as *Underworld*, notably the impact of military technologies upon civilian populations, suggests that the film is a microcosm or allegory of the novel. Prior to the showing, the Rockettes perform a mechanized dance routine while clad in military attire, and real-time video footage of them is projected onto a screen in the theater. Virilio would condemn the combination of the militarization of theater and cybernetic projection as a dire expression of the extensions of military observation. Yet in *Underworld* the projection of the dancers enables Klara to understand "how a crowd is reconfigured, teased into methodical geometry, into slipknots and serpentines" (428). In other words, the military aspects of the performance are diverged or intensified into Klara's perception of the spatial contours of the crowd. However, the successful divergence that Klara experiences becomes less certain as the film's narrative progresses.

The film is in two halves. In the first half, the prisoners of a mad scientist struggle to escape their underground domain. By comparing the fact that some of these prisoners are transformed by atomic rays into mutants to 1950s science fiction films, in which "creatures not only come from the bomb but displace it" (430), DeLillo raises the question of whether the displacement of the bomb by these prisoners represents a further mutation of military power or a critical divergence of it. In the second half of the film, the prisoners escape to the surface of the earth. Now the landscape is presented with "formalist excess," which displaces the earlier "themes of atomic radiation or irresponsible science and [. . .] state terror." The prisoners remove their hoods to reveal their "external features," which reveal nothing about "nationality and strict historical context" (443). The replacement of underground themes by surface externalities at this point in the film resonates with *Underworld*'s material and spatial emphasis. Yet the conclusion to *Unterwelt* is ambiguous. When the prisoners are recaptured, Klara realizes that this fate was foreshadowed by the Rockettes' militarized movements. In other words, her earlier divergence of the Rockettes into affirmative crowd materiality has been rediverged into militarized control. Like a military battalion, the prisoners are marched to the music of Prokofiev, which Klara and her associates recall was used by a radio show that featured the catch phrase "The FBI in Peace and War" (442). Just as the reference to the continuum between peace and war echoes how the society of *Underworld* is permeated by media that have mutated from military technologies, so too the recapturing of the prisoners designates how the displacement of the bomb represents a continuation of military power.

Nevertheless, Klara's appreciation of the material spatiality of *Unterwelt* contributes to her own artistic divergence. Klara's land art project, Long Tall Sally, in which she and volunteers paint in vivid colors two hundred and thirty ex–Cold War planes of the United States military, exemplifies the attempt to produce such divergence. The divergence embodied in Long Tall Sally differs from that expressed by *Unterwelt*. Communicated through a visual medium that is linked to military technology, the critical divergence of militarization enacted by *Unterwelt* remains mired in narrative content and its ambiguities. In contrast, Long Tall Sally goes directly to the source of military technology and attempts a form of divergence that bypasses issues of inner meaning. Yet both *Unterwelt* and Klara's art project attempt to recover the social space of the human body. Of her project, Klara says, "[W]e're trying to unrepeat, to find an element of felt life" (77). The reference to "felt life" indicates that the purpose of this material divergence is to facilitate a material perception that is otherwise obscure. For Klara, the image of Long Tall Sally, a pin-up woman on the nose of a B-52, represents the quiditas of "individual life" that she tries to reclaim for all the planes (78). Long Tall Sally appears to be a successful form of material divergence because it is able to present an image of human corporeality within the same military materiality that it transforms. However, the television image of Klara that Nick contemplates suggests how Klara's work might be rediverged by media technology. Elsewhere, DeLillo claims that such pin-up images serve the same mass social function as repetitious video footage, such as that of the Challenger disaster or Rodney King (Begley, "Art" 301–02). Given his critique of the effects of the Texas Highway Killer footage, this association casts doubt upon the efficacy of Long Tall Sally's divergence. While DeLillo's condemnation of land and nose art is not as categorical as Virilio's, the perception of human spatiality that Long Tall Sally articulates remains trapped within the logic of media-military technologies that it seeks to diverge.[12] As Timothy L. Parrish argues, Klara, like Nick, expresses nostalgia for the very Cold War militarism that her art project diverges (718), which, along with the recuperative dangers involved in seeking to establish a critical art out of the same material as that which one criticizes, reflects the failure of the attempt to create a wholly effective subversion of the media-military relation by subjecting that relation to further mutation.

As if in response to the limitations of media divergence, *Underworld* portrays other means of countering the lost dimension. DeLillo's most sustained departure from the effects of media and military technologies occurs in his representation of the baseball game. Here, DeLillo's attempted recovery of social space forfeits the emphasis on technological mutation. His portrayal of the body does not rely on either the inwardness of the subject or the representational function of technology. DeLillo thematizes the difference between the body and the ghost of inner being by saying of the baseball game, "[T]his midcentury moment enters the skin more lastingly than the vast shaping strategies of eminent leaders, generals steely in their sunglasses—the mapped visions that pierce our dreams" (60). As in the case of the B-52s that represent "a force in the world that comes into people's sleep" and Nick's dream of the gun that he inadvertently uses to shoot George the Waiter (76), military forces are associated with the interior realm of the subject, but the baseball game becomes part of the external body. The baseball game also facilitates a perception of the body that negates the effects of the lost dimension: "There are things that apply unrepeatably, muscle-memory and pumping blood and jots of dust, the narrative that lives in the spaces of the official play-by-play" (27). Moreover, DeLillo suggests that the recovery of spatial perception can extend beyond the domain of the baseball game. Whereas Marvin thought that Cotter Martin could be represented by the dots of media images, DeLillo describes the bodily motion that escapes the dots (points) of formal occurrences and the statistics they become. As Cotter sneaks into the game and evades the police, "[h]e is just a running boy, a half-seen figure from the streets, but the way running reveals some clue to being, the way a runner bares himself to consciousness, this is how the dark-skinned kid seems to open to the world, how the bloodrush of a dozen strides brings him into eloquence" (13). Such extensions indicate that it is not the distinct spatiality of the baseball game that interests DeLillo. Rather, he evokes a spatial perception that is associated with baseball but is more widely applicable. In other words, he is uninterested in utopian or oppositional space. As in Virilio's writing, DeLillo suggests that the mode of perceiving space that he evokes is the best means of undoing the lost dimension. Scott McQuire argues that Virilio's theory reintroduces "a phenomenological notion of immediate presence" and "the ideal of the unified humanist subject" (153). Similarly, it is tempting to read DeLillo's novel as a nostalgic appeal to humanist subjectivity. However, both DeLillo's and Virilio's interest in the movement of the human body in social space disposes with phenomenology and humanism.

There are many continuities between the fiction of Didion and DeLillo and that of Goodman, Pynchon, and Gaddis. All these authors abandon models of history, prioritize analytical representations of social space, and narrate the grave and expansive reach of power. But Didion and DeLillo abandon the representation of the dialectical struggle between distinct forms of social space that is evident the novels of Goodman, Pynchon, and Gaddis. Most notably, the possibility of oppositional space that haunts the spatial dialectics of these authors is absent in the writing of Didion and DeLillo. By repudiating the spatial dialectics that, in the fiction of Goodman, Pynchon, and Gaddis, rework the historical dialectics of early-twentieth-century writers, the novels of Didion and DeLillo represent a further mutation of the critical space of American fiction. Rather than portraying oppositional space, Didion depicts forms of spatial difference that are interwoven with each other. Her novels portray forms of power that are anchored in the territoriality of the state and the smooth space that is appropriated from the war machine. In *Democracy*, Didion portrays the escape of the war machine and the attainment of a line of flight that is not bound by state power. DeLillo's *Underworld* depicts an accelerated version of smooth space. Here, the mutation of the war machine into media technologies overrides the power of the state and causes space to become a lost dimension. Media technologies offer semiotic invitations that obscure the eradication of social space that they engender. The lost dimension leaves no room for a line of flight, but the intensification of technologies of interpretation into technologies of bodily perception recovers social spatiality. The texts of Didion and DeLillo are related to important tendencies in critical theory. For Deleuze and Guattari and Virilio, the assessment of the dynamics of social space necessitates an abandonment of Lefebvre's dialectical perspective. Just as Didion shares Deleuze and Guattari's emphasis on the interplay of territoriality and the line of flight, DeLillo's representation of social space echoes Paul Virilio's depiction of a "Critical Space" that is eroded by light-speed technologies and military logistics. The spatial discourses of Deleuze and Guattari and Virilio articulate an anarchist sensibility that shares Lefebvre's hostility to the state. In the narratives of Didion and DeLillo, personal and technological elements respectively signal the absence of any political position. As we have seen, these novels lack even the remnant of a politics of oppositional space that is evident in Gaddis's *JR*. For much of the twentieth century, representations of critical space in American fiction were linked to political concerns, especially those having to do with the relation between socialism and anarchism. The novels studied in this chapter reflect both the resilience of critical space and its unmooring from such political issues.

Conclusion

Scholarly considerations of developments in twentieth-century American fiction often do not prioritize connections between the radical fiction of the early twentieth century and narratives of the era of postmodernity. It is as if, in the scholarly imagination, the writings of authors such as Upton Sinclair and Josephine Herbst are wholly unrelated to novels by Thomas Pynchon and Don DeLillo. In this book I have sought to overcome this division and suggest, first, that the late-twentieth-century fiction that I discuss is strongly indebted to the radical fiction of the earlier period and, second, that midcentury fiction, such as that of Mary McCarthy and Paul Goodman, serves as the relay or transformation point between these two major areas of American fiction. Through a genealogy of critical space, I argue in the preceding chapters that late-twentieth-century American fiction's preoccupation with power relations in social space derives from the inverted utopianism of radical fiction in the pre-1939 period. As well as highlighting the spatial elements of the fiction under consideration, the theoretical readings that I undertake suggest that the rise of critical space is central to developments in both Marxist and post-Marxist critical theory and American fiction. The overall goal of *After Utopia* is to highlight unity and differentiation among the fictional and theoretical cultures that I discuss. While there are broad and powerful correlations among these areas of fiction and theory, each manifestation of critical space that is addressed in this book constitutes a singular textualization. By emphasizing textual singularities, I hope to avoid the suggestion that the fiction I discuss can represent or stand in for other tendencies in twentieth-century American fiction.

Clearly, a study that is as selective as *After Utopia* cannot and indeed does not seek to offer definitive or comprehensive analyses. Rather, I intend that the preceding readings in critical space, which strive to undo the dichotomization of politics and aesthetics and connect texts with varying allegiances to prominent political identities, might lead to analyses of other forms of American fiction and, in the process, undergo transformation.

In chapter 1 I unite the fiction of Jack London and Upton Sinclair under the rubric of utopian naturalism. The concept of utopian naturalism designates the ratio of historical to spatial priorities in the writings of these authors. The primary interest of both London and Sinclair is the representation of naturalistic processes of history. Derived from their socialist commitments, the models of history in the fiction of London and Sinclair imagine the means by which capitalist power in the United States might be overturned. Because these authors traffic in dualistic oppositions between subjectivity and objectivity and models of class antagonism, it is appropriate, I think, to discuss their ideas of history as examples of dialectical transformation. However, the textualizations of history that we see in these novels are restless and varied. In order to tease out distinctions among ideas of history, I read these novels in relation to Georg Lukács's theoretical writings. Lukács's texts are especially helpful in highlighting the relationship between revolutionary subjectivity and the determinism of Second International social democracy in these novels. In the writing of London and Sinclair, we see a persistent utopian and spatial modification of naturalist history. This conjunction of spatial and historical factors is best understood in relation to Ernst Bloch's notion of "concrete utopia" (*Principle* 1: 146). Unlike the abstract utopias of fully imagined societies that Bloch derides, concrete utopias are spatial representations that offer glimpses of a utopian future and, harnessed to a model of historical change, inspire human subjects to struggle for that utopian vision. Concrete utopian spaces abound in the fiction of London and Sinclair and serve the same purpose as that described by Bloch. Yet the combinations that define the utopian naturalism of London and Sinclair are characterized by conflict. Ambivalent about working-class narrative representations and increasingly unable to imagine valid forms of socialist history, London turns, in *The Valley of the Moon*, to a conservative version of utopian naturalism. Sinclair's adherence to social democratic ideas of history never wavered, but the fusion of this model of social transformation with other radical theories, such as anarchism, and representations of concrete utopian spatiality that we see in *The Jungle* becomes more untenable as his literary career progresses. As a result of these conflicts, the novels of both authors are more certain about the ideals associated with concrete utopian spaces than the processes of history that these spaces are meant to support. The novels of London and Sinclair are therefore important texts in the rise of narrative spatiality in twentieth-century American fiction.

The trilogies of John Dos Passos and Josephine Herbst, which I discuss in chapter 2, retain the overall conjunction of historical and spatial elements that we see in the utopian naturalism of London and Sinclair. Dos Passos and Herbst adhere to the dominant principle of historical transformation, but their representations of models of history are more hesitant than those of the authors discussed in chapter 1. As in the Marxist theory of Antonio Gramsci, the notions of history that we see in *U.S.A.* and the Trexler trilogy are strongly informed by principles of cultural hegemony and mediation. The emphasis on cultural mediation qualifies models of dialectical transformation and negates the strong deterministic histories that feature in the writing of London and Sinclair. In *U.S.A.*, Dos Passos criticizes capitalist and communist versions of history because he believes that both are enmeshed in destructive forms of mediation. As in Gramsci's early writings on the Factory Councils in Turin, Dos Passos is sympathetic to syndicalist ideas of the transformation of history through the takeover of factories. Dos Passos evokes the beneficial forms of mediation associated with engineers and factory technicians, but the narrative depiction of syndicalist history in the trilogy remains insubstantial. Ultimately, the only form of history Dos Passos licenses is that of the incremental, technician-like mediation that the literary writer can accomplish. The ideas of history that Dos Passos promotes are supported by the concrete utopian principles of national and rural space. However, the negation of various types of spatiality in *U.S.A.*, especially those that are conceived in explicitly utopian terms, indicates that a shift from utopian to critical space occurs in Dos Passos's fiction. In the Trexler trilogy Herbst also pursues a credible form of radical history, but her conclusions on this topic are even more equivocal than those of Dos Passos. Both *U.S.A.* and the Trexler trilogy are informed by an awareness of the complexities of social space that is also apparent in Gramsci's writings. Herbst's awareness of the consequences of uneven social space, as exemplified by the tension between rural and urban workers, prevents her from allying with any particular model of radical history. The intertwined exploration of spatial and historical possibilities in Herbst's writing further enhances the critical as opposed to utopian function of space. Even though domesticity frequently reinforces capitalist power in the Trexler trilogy, Herbst consistently promotes domestic space as a means of enhancing radical oppositionality. Rather than a utopian refuge, domestic space is the place where the possibilities of hegemonic cultural mediation and radical history are born.

The midcentury fiction of Mary McCarthy and Paul Goodman represents the abandonment of the spatiotemporal paradigm of the fiction discussed in the first two chapters of this book. In chapter 3 I argue that McCarthy's *The Oasis* and Goodman's *The Empire City* dispense with the models of history that are so central to the radical American fiction of the early twentieth century. As suggested by their place-oriented titles, these midcentury novels treat social space with the emphasis and priority that London, Sinclair, Dos Passos, and Herbst impute to ideas of historical transformation. The focus on social space in these texts fully departs from utopian concerns and signifies the rise of critical space from a subordinate to a dominant position. Yet these are very different, in some senses opposed, novels. Since the spatial perspective of *The Oasis* is deployed to satirize the historical and spatial ambitions of leftist radical culture, McCarthy's narrative appears to close the two primary concerns of literary radicalism in the United States. During the course of the analysis of *The Oasis*, I refer to Hannah Arendt's theoretical writings on the relation between social and political space. As well as being long-term friends, McCarthy and Arendt both derided the pretentious manner in which the mores of social space annexed the sphere of political action and decision-making. McCarthy's conception of social space is therefore largely critical in nature: for McCarthy, critical space is a critique of the inflated self-image of social space. In contrast to the satirical intent of *The Oasis*, Goodman's *The Empire City* strives to renew radical critique via its negation of history and utopia. Rather than being utopian, the social space of Goodman's novel is critical, analytical, and dialectical. In other words, the characteristics that the fiction discussed in earlier chapters attributes to history are, in Goodman's text, assigned to spatiality. Just as London and Sinclair invert key aspects of nineteenth-century utopian fiction, so Goodman inverts the spatial dimension of early-twentieth-century radical fiction. But even though the narrative often wrestles with the utopian impulse, *The Empire City* does not return to utopianism. Instead, Goodman depicts the incessant interplay of alienated and unalienated elements of social space. The discussion of Goodman's treatment of spatiality is informed by a reading of Henri Lefebvre's *Critique of Everyday Life*. In many respects Lefebvre is the most significant critical theorist cited in *After Utopia*. His writing explicitly promotes spatial analysis as a necessary means of reinvigorating the Marxist critique of capitalist society. While Goodman, an anarchist, does not share some of Lefebvre's Marxist principles, he does share Lefebvre's view that the analysis of the localized social spaces of everyday life can offer a critique of capitalist society and highlight the zones of liberation that exist in its midst.

In chapter 4 I analyze the spatial dialectics of Thomas Pynchon's *Gravity's Rainbow* and William Gaddis's *JR*. Whereas *The Empire City* depicts the dialectical oscillations of specific urban spaces, the novels of Pynchon and Gaddis narrate various dialectical relations that are manifested throughout urban social space. These novels are centered upon the realization of, in Lefebvre's language, "abstract space" across the capitalist spaces of postmodernity (*Production* 49). For Lefebvre, abstract space denotes the homogenization and fragmentation of social space that expands and defines capitalist power in the period after World War II. Pynchon and Gaddis share Lefebvre's preoccupation with abstract space as the form and not simply the site of neocapitalist expansion. In *Gravity's Rainbow*, Pynchon revisits issues associated with social space that are raised in his earlier novel *The Crying of Lot 49*. The narrative of *The Crying of Lot 49* portrays the inability of Oedipa Maas to overcome her historical and semiotic attachments and perceive the dialectical aspects of the social space through which she travels. In contrast, *Gravity's Rainbow* counters dialectical history with a narrative analysis of the process by which abstract space is formed at the close of the war. As in Lefebvre's *The Production of Space*, Pynchon here isolates the geometric, visual, and phallic components of the realization of abstract space. These three formants of abstract space are crystallized in the v-2 rocket. The dialectical qualities of the novel concern the relation between abstract space and what Lefebvre terms oppositional or "lived space" (*Production* 39). By concluding with descriptions of Los Angeles in the 1970s, the narrative suggests that both urban and lived space are realized in the urban space of Southern California. Gaddis's *JR* is similarly committed to the fictionalization of abstract space. However, the spatial dialectics of Gaddis's novel differ from those of *Gravity's Rainbow*. To use Edward Soja's terminology, *JR* narrates interactions that constitute "a socio-spatial dialectic" (*Postmodern* 77). The dialectic of society and space involves the social effects of the transformation of urban space. Like Lefebvre, Gaddis suggests that the urban landscape of Manhattan displaces the realm of industrial production in favor of spaces of abstract financial investment. The activities of *JR* epitomize the devastation of industry and realization of abstract space that are associated with urban finance. Gaddis's portrayal of the town in Long Island extends the novel's depiction of abstract space and its treatment of spatial dialectics. In these sections, Gaddis narrates the decimation of the town by forces that Lefebvre describes as "urbanism" (*Urban* 41). Urbanism reshapes the spatial environment via the dialectical interaction of three social levels, which are manifestations of the three formants of abstract space noted above. The spatial dialectics of these three social levels—the conceived, the perceived, and the lived—segregates and homogenizes the town. As in *The Production of Space*, Lefebvre, in *The Urban Revolution*, states that the third level of urban space can take the form of the lived space of "habiting" as well as the "habitat" that promotes abstract space (81). The absence of lived space in *JR* means that Gaddis represents a failure of the dialectic that Lefebvre theorizes. Such failure suggests a negation of the dialectic of abstract and lived space and exemplifies a shift away from spatial dialectics in the critical space of American fiction.

The abandonment of spatial dialectics is wholly apparent in the fiction of Joan Didion and Don DeLillo, which I consider in chapter 5. These novels do not portray fixed oppositions between different forms of social space. Therefore, they embody a distinct moment in the rise of critical space beyond the apparent and failed dialectics of Pynchon and Gaddis. Yet the lack of dialectics does not entail the elimination of spatial difference and analysis. Rather, the texts of Didion and DeLillo redefine critical space in terms of fluctuations and irruptions that occur within the spaces of economic, political, and technological power. Didion's female protagonists are caught up in conspiracies that reach across multinational spheres of influence. The spatial narrations of these novels share concerns that are articulated in Gilles Deleuze and Félix Guattari's *A Thousand Plateaus*, which theorizes numerous and interconnected spatial principles. Within the general concept of territoriality, Deleuze and Guattari evoke processes of deterritorialization and reterritorialization that, respectively, perforate and reseal social and other types of spatial formations. These concepts are related to the distinction between the striated or regimented space of state power and the smooth spaces of flight and fluidity that evade the territoriality of the state and are traversed by the nomadic war machine. Crucially, the intermingling of different types of spatiality mean that these distinctions do not become oppositions; for example, the state appropriates smooth space as part of its own apparatus. The nomadic lines of flight undertaken by Didion's characters are usually appropriated with the territorializing impulse of state and corporate power. Yet in *Democracy*, Didion portrays a character, Inez Christian, who pursues a line of flight that attains the outside of striated space and thus reveals the existence of differentiality in the critical space of her novels. In *Underworld*, the last novel to be discussed in *After Utopia*, DeLillo regards the media of television and cyberspace as outgrowths of military technologies. By citing the critical theory of Paul Virilio, I suggest that, for DeLillo, light-speed media and military technologies undermine the diversity of spatial experience and induce what Virilio terms "polar inertia" (*Pure* 74). Underpinned by the threat of violence inherent in military capability, technological vectors transform social space into a lost dimension. Yet DeLillo, like Didion, discovers spatial differences that exist within and not in opposition to the spatialities of power that he subjects to critique.

Underworld's narrative mobilizes a form of perception that discloses social flows and bodily movements and consequently deviates from the representational assumptions imposed by media technologies. While DeLillo's novel succeeds in adhering to the notion of spatial difference, it is nevertheless dominated by the shadow of the lost dimension, a sense that the critical space of American fiction is in a state of crisis and impending demise.

Underworld embodies the termination of a particular trajectory of fictional spatiality that originates in late-nineteenth-century utopian fiction and courses through the various forms of American fiction studied in this book. It is a trajectory that closely parallels the transformations of Marxism and post-Marxism in critical theory in that it involves the gradual weakening of models of history and the refashioning and superseding of dialectics. Yet the continuation of this trajectory is much clearer in the area of critical theory than in that of American fiction. As well as being one of the most renowned theoretical texts of recent times, Antonio Negri and Michael Hardt's *Empire* is a nondialectical spatial critique of globalization that, among other things, puts concepts associated with theorists such as Deleuze and Guattari and Virilio in the service of an assertion of the global multitude and the overthrow of capitalism. In other words, *Empire* returns to some of the strongest anticapitalist viewpoints that are evident in the aforementioned trajectory of theories of critical space. In contrast, movements beyond the critical space of *Underworld* among contemporary American fictional texts are less easy to discern. DeLillo's own *Cosmopolis* is one example of a fictional narrative that incorporates the perspective of antiglobalization into a narrative of the impact of technological trajectories on the experience of urban space. But the position of a text such as *Cosmopolis* within the larger tendencies of contemporary American narratives is unclear. One of the tasks of current scholarship is to assess the tendencies that inform the depiction of social space in American fictional texts at the end of the twentieth and beginning of the twenty-first centuries. Such a project would be significant because it would map spatial critiques of capitalist authority and promote the existence of critical culture within the world's most powerful country. I hope that the analyses presented in *After Utopia* may be of some use in charting the critical space of

contemporary American fiction and establishing links between current narrative dispositions and treatments of economic and political
power from other moments in the genealogies of American fiction.
As I have attempted to show in this book, our understanding of the
spatial critiques that are articulated in American fiction is enhanced
by the interrelation of such critiques in the form of temporal narrative.

Notes

Introduction

1. Bruno Bosteels, for example, writes that spatial critique is "fast becoming tirelessly ubiquitous" (146). In contrast, Bill Brown's "The Dark Wood of Postmodernity (Space, Faith, Allegory)" demonstrates the health and vitality of new and ongoing spatial critiques.

2. In "The End of Temporality," Fredric Jameson regards the prevalence of spatial critique as evidence of the dominance of postmodern space: "[T]he dictum that time was the dominant of the modern (or of modernism) and space of the postmodern means something thematic and empirical at once: what we do [. . .] and what we call what we are doing" (696).

3. Engels's *Socialism: Utopian and Scientific* codified the prohibition against representations of utopian spatiality in Marxist theory, but as Vincent Geoghegan observes, Marx and Engels made numerous statements that reflect the ongoing influence of utopian thought in their work. Geoghegan's comments on Marx's writings on the Paris Commune are especially significant in this regard. In the initial draft of *The Civil War in France*, Marx writes, "[T]he last two ends of the movement proclaimed by the Utopians are the last ends proclaimed by the Paris Revolution and by the International." In these remarks, Marx identifies the spatial concepts of utopianism not only with the social space of the Paris Commune but also with that of the future communist society. In the published version of this text, as Geoghegan notes, these comments are replaced by one of Marx's celebrated attacks on utopianism: "The working class . . . have no ready-made utopias to introduce . . . They have no ideals to realize" (qtd. in Geoghegan 30). Taken together, these two statements exemplify the contradictory status of utopianism in the Marxist tradition. Instead of contradiction, Kristin Ross perceives in Marx's writings on the Commune a departure from the dialectical historicism of scientific so-

cialism. Marx's claim that the Commune discovered the "political form . . . under which to work out the economical emancipation of labor" is interpreted by Ross as an "autocritique" of the dialectical notion that the political form of the communist society cannot be imagined in the present and can only appear through the process of class struggle into the future (qtd. 21, 25). The comments of Geoghegan and Ross suggest the ongoing presence of utopian spatiality in Marx's work. The critical space of early-twentieth-century Western Marxist theory extends and refashions the spatial concerns that Geoghegan and Ross attribute to Marx.

4. As Kenneth M. Roemer notes, the decreasing production of utopian narratives from the late 1890s on was due in part to the failure of the political movements associated with utopian fiction (7). As Populism and Progressivism absorbed utopian demands into political reformism, the popularity of utopian political movements—such as the Nationalist movement, inspired by *Looking Backward*—rapidly dwindled. The failings of utopian politics are reflected in the ineffective representations of historical process in novels such as Bellamy's; as Jean Pfaelzer observes, utopian American novels "can hardly be understood as a serious prediction of historical process" (3). The isolation of the spatiality of utopian fiction from credible notions of historical transformation is also connected to political developments. The widespread popularity of fictions of utopian spatiality was partially attributable to nationalist sentiments. As Susan M. Materese argues, the utopian fictions of this period are often predicated on notions of the United States' "national greatness" and capacity for "world redemption" (13, 37). In *Utopia and Cosmopolis*, Thomas Peyser argues that utopian fiction reflects the mutual determination of "the universalizing forces of globalization" and "national particularism" in the late nineteenth century (16). The spatial preoccupations of utopian fiction are expressions of the fear that, in Peyser's terms, "national identity was yielding its primacy to a new, unprecedentedly intense form of cosmopolitanism" (19). Following the election of William McKinley as president in 1896, the United States embarked on a series of colonial endeavors in Cuba, Guam, Puerto Rico, and the Philippines. Utopian treatments of national and global issues, such as the socialism of *Looking Backward*, were superseded by imperialist versions of such concerns.

5. The study of spatial form in literature has proved remarkably resilient in twentieth-century criticism. Published in 1945, Joseph Frank's "Spatial Form in Modern Literature" was one of the earliest, most contentious, and most influential studies of the topic. Several other readings of spatial form have appeared since the debate surrounding Frank's essay. In *The Spatiality*

of the Novel, Joseph A. Kestner argues that novels employ "spatial secondary illusion" (9), a set of formal spatial qualities that supplement the temporality of fictional narrative. Similarly, Carl Darryl Malmgren discusses the progression from modernist to "paramodernist" to postmodern fiction in terms of transformations in the formal discontinuities of narrative space (115). Joseph Francese's *Narrating Postmodern Time and Space* is a more recent example of the critique of spatial form.

1. Utopian Naturalism in Conflict

1. For an assessment of the key biographical and theoretical connections between Bloch and Lukács, see Hudson 34–42.

2. In this chapter, all references to Bloch will cite *The Principle of Hope*. While Bloch wrote much of this text during the 1940s, it is highly relevant to the early-twentieth-century fiction of London and Sinclair. As Martin Jay notes, "Bloch's intellectual and political character seems to have matured at a specific moment in time and remained relatively unchanged for the remainder of his life. That moment was 1917, the year of the Russian Revolution, which Bloch observed with keen excitement from afar" (176). *The Principle of Hope* is an extended articulation of the position that Bloch arrived at in 1917.

3. Lukács does not directly take issue with Plekhanov's dialectical materialism in *History and Class Consciousness*, but as Michael Löwy observes, "Lukács's neo-Fichtean voluntarism had nothing in common with Plekhanov's or Kautsky's eighteenth-century materialism" (130). For a summary of Lukács's opposition to Plekhanov and Kautsky, see Kellner, *Critical* 11.

4. Concrete utopia combines spatial and historical principles. As Fredric Jameson posits, the spatiotemporal conjunction informs many of the conceptual sets devised by Bloch in *The Principle of Hope*. In Jameson's reading of Bloch, "tendency" and "allegory" are figures for history, and "latency" and "symbol" are tropes for "the more spatial notion of that adequation of object to subject which must characterize that moment's [the utopian future's] content" (*Marxism* 146). Jameson's comments demonstrate the central importance of the spatiotemporal conjunction in Bloch's work. For an excellent assessment of Bloch's ideas of history and Marxist dialectics, see Hudson 192–208.

5. As Philip E. Wegner discusses, the politics of *The Iron Heel* reflects London's disposition toward labor movements in the United States. For Wegner, "[t]he narrative's vision of the working class organizes itself around the two extremes of the iww and the afl" (138). Additionally, London's position in the American Socialist Party informs the narrative of *The Iron Heel*. In a

highly succinct account, Philip S. Foner describes London's attitude toward the splintering of the American socialist movement between 1897 and 1901 (43–45). The essence of this split was the secession of advocates of social democracy from Daniel DeLeon's Socialist Labor Party. In 1901 social democratic forces united as the Socialist Party under the leadership of Eugene W. Debs. While London is often associated with DeLeon's revolutionary zeal, he affiliated himself with the Socialist Party rather than the Socialist Labor Party. He must therefore be viewed as a revolutionary within social democracy who, in 1916, finally left the party because of its lack of revolutionary fervor. As Portelli observes, *The Iron Heel* is "a good example of how extreme forms of struggle are not incompatible with a reformist analysis of society" (184). London's position within American socialism accounts for the textual conjunction noted by Portelli and the novel's partial identifications with both social democracy and revolutionary activism.

6. Erica Briscoe observes that London's treatment of the Chicago Commune is highly expressionistic and "determinedly transcends" muckraking details (18). The "interminable excess" that Briscoe discusses engenders a metafictional or reflexive quality that asks the reader to approach the narrative in an ironic manner (18). Garthwaite's comments exemplify the Nietzschean irony that London directs toward his own fictionalized models of history.

7. As Ruth Levitas notes, the distinction between abstract utopia and concrete utopia is central to Bloch's theory (65). Levitas admirably states that concrete utopia differs from abstract utopia because it is more of a call to political commitment than a social vision. Interestingly, Levitas concludes her argument by stating that the need to create and choose the utopian future validates "the specification of the content of the good society" and ultimately means that the distinction between abstract and concrete utopia is "dubious" (78, 65). Levitas's conclusion reintroduces the utopianist bias that she initially criticizes.

8. Yung Min Kim identifies a paradoxical view of colonial space in *Martin Eden*. Kim notes that London criticizes colonial endeavors by identifying Martin "with the exploited native subject of colonized lands" (3). London's anticolonialism contributes to his critique of the false utopianism of the South Seas. However, Kim also suggests that *Martin Eden* articulates " 'imperialist nostalgia': a nostalgia for the thing one has destroyed" (3). The narrative is dogged by the sense that London is more attracted to imperialist than working-class space.

9. As Alex Kershaw notes, London was "dismayed" that contemporary reviewers of *Martin Eden*, "including those on the left, regarded the book as

proof that he had abandoned his belief in socialism" (211). Jonathan Auerbach addresses the issue of this critical response by noting that "in the case of *Martin Eden* it does little good to chide London, as did his daughter Joan, for misleading readers into thinking he was endorsing Eden's individualism instead of condemning it, when once such egomania is displayed in the open [. . .] then endorsement and condemnation can no longer remain very distinct, blurred by publicity itself" (230). Loren Glass also discusses the role of publicity in the interplay of author and character in *Martin Eden* (536–44). The analyses of Auerbach and Glass suggest that London's socialism had become simply a component of the public persona that his individualism led him to promote.

10. Jeanne Campbell Reesman describes London's representation of Saxon as a "feminist" endeavor that was influenced by "the 'New Woman' who appeared in popular fiction at the turn of the century." As "a living symbol of the American West," in Reesman's terms, Saxon differs greatly from Avis Cunningham and Ruth Morse ("Jack London's" 40, 43, 45). The varying depictions of critical space in *The Iron Heel*, *Martin Eden*, and *The Valley of the Moon* are reliant to a great degree on their portrayals of female characters. That London's "feminist" representation of a working-class woman should be accompanied by a rejection of socialism suggests that, in London's imagination, progressive ideas were subject to transfer and exchange rather than combination.

11. The relation between Lukács's literary criticism and his earlier political writings is complex. Shortly after its publication in 1923, *History and Class Consciousness* was denounced by the Fifth Congress of the Communist International. Most notably through the tirades of Laszlo Rudas and Abram Deborin, Lukács was accused of subjectivism and utopianism. In a text that remained secret until the 1990s, Lukács defended *History and Class Consciousness*, but by the mid-1920s he had altered his theoretical position. In 1928 he wrote a text that is known as the "Blum Theses," which advocated that the Hungarian Communist Party should take a social democratic turn. According to Löwy, the "Blum Theses" "are the culmination of Lukács's political development and the ideological foundation for his intellectual output after 1928" (201). For commentators such as Löwy, Lukács's literary criticism of the 1930s is a coded defense of Western democracy and an occasional and indirect critique of Stalinism. Yet in some respects Lukács's post-1928 literary criticism reiterates the ideas expressed in *History and Class Consciousness*. The model of history that he praises in the fiction of Balzac is one in which the bourgeoisie is able to take advantage of open-ended and undetermined circumstances. In

the course of such analyses, Lukács criticizes the determinism of naturalism in the same manner that he dismantles the determinism of social democracy in *History and Class Consciousness*.

12. In Matthew J. Morris's reading of *The Jungle*, Jurgis "must experience effects before he can understand causes" (58). It is difficult for Jurgis to appreciate the significance of these effects because he views them as causes that are ultimately shown to be false.

13. Scott Derrick states that *The Jungle* "contains an unconscious narrative of Sinclair's self-creation as an author" (85). The unconscious process of self-creation that Derrick discusses is predicated on an ambivalent attitude toward women, sexuality, and the body. Derrick states that the text expresses Sinclair's autobiographical wish to be free of the obligations of marriage, family, and home, which he regards as obstacles to his professional life as a writer. At the same time, notes Derrick, the naturalist tendencies of *The Jungle* invoke forces that are feminine in nature. Because, according to Derrick, "*The Jungle* massively and misogynistically defends against a feminine power that it creates itself" (94), Sinclair's novel illustrates "the fundamental incoherence of naturalism" (88). The incoherence addressed by Derrick also applies to the unstable conjunction of deterministic history and utopian space in the novel.

14. According to Tom Moylan, Bloch's analysis of religion highlights the "hypostatization of history" in his work (113). For Moylan, Bloch's theory of history accounts for his long-standing defense of Stalinism and is antithetical to the open-ended utopian spatiality that he elsewhere describes. Of course, in Bloch's own terms the hypostatization of history and the unrounded nature of utopian space are profoundly connected, because it is the unroundedness of spatiality that leads into the process of history. Nevertheless, Moylan is correct to locate the contradictory tendencies of Bloch's formulation of concrete utopia.

2. Hegemony, Culture, Space

1. As Townsend Ludington observes, Dos Passos had an "anarchistic spirit" and "favored the I.W.W. aim of building 'a new society in the shell of the old'" (244, 291). Elinor Langer frequently mentions Herbst's preference for anarchism over communism (116, 176, 227). Langer also states that Herbst's youthful experience of the syndicalist Wobblies inspired her radical activism for much of her life (38, 218, 242). For a discussion of the syndicalism of the Industrial Workers of the World, see Dubofsky 156–68.

2. There are two main distinctions between Lukács and Gramsci. Lukács theorized the dialectical relation of humans and distanced himself from the dialectic of nature. As Maurice A. Finocchiaro argues, Gramsci thought "that

such a dichotomy would be undialectical because man [sic] and nature would have been distinguished but not significantly related" (160). Gramsci links the dialectic of human subjects to the dialectic of nature by, in Martin Jay's terms, "assimilating the methods of the natural sciences to those of the cultural sciences" (159). In other words, Gramsci regards the natural sciences as expressions of human culture. The second distinction between Lukács and Gramsci concerns the issue of class. According to Ernesto Laclau and Chantal Mouffe, Lukács adhered to the principle of the working class as the revolutionary subject of history, but Gramsci posited the notion of the "articulation" of revolutionary alliances that cut across class lines (68). For Laclau and Mouffe, Gramsci's insistence on the working class as the hegemonic agent in revolutionary activity produces theoretical contradiction and incoherence (69).

3. For the connections between Gramsci and Luxemburg, see Boggs 212–20. Nicola Badaloni provides an interesting account of Gramsci's relation to Sorel on issues such as revolutionary tactics and the role of intellectuals (80–105).

4. Carl Levy's *Gramsci and the Anarchists* thoroughly discusses the role of anarchists in the Factory Council movement of 1919–20 (141–66).

5. As John Trombold argues, Dos Passos's transformation from radical sympathizer to conservative advocate occurred in 1937. Trombold states that the change in Dos Passos's outlook involved a rejection of European and modernist concerns and a revision of conceptions of history. In *U.S.A.*, Trombold argues, Dos Passos is a "novelist of the present,"but in later novels such as *Adventures of a Young Man* he is a "historian of the past." The "simultaneist" writing of *U.S.A.* is, for Trombold, associated with a revolutionary perspective on history that differs from the "historical continuity" of Dos Passos's post-1937 fiction ("From" 245, 239, 238). Dos Passos's interest in modernist simultaneity reflects a spatial imagination that encompasses the social terrain of the present and is not restricted to localized utopias. As Trombold suggests, the sense of historical rupture in *U.S.A.* can be identified with a revolutionary impulse. However, in Michael Clark's terms, Dos Passos "destructures history" in a manner that makes it difficult for him to embody the revolutionary impulse in a stable historical model (124).

6. References to *U.S.A.* will cite the one-volume edition in which *The 42nd Parallel, Nineteen Nineteen,* and *The Big Money* are separately paginated.

7. For an overview of Dos Passos's debt to Veblen in *U.S.A.*, see Diggins, "Dos Passos" 486–90.

8. "In treating reigning cultural ideas as the unconscious foundations of

social life," writes John Diggins, "Veblen was anticipating an issue in social theory that would later be discovered by Antonio Gramsci—the phenomenon of hegemony" (*Thorstein* 105). Diggins's comments indicate the congruence between Veblen's and Gramsci's theorization of the importance of dominant cultural meanings in social struggles.

9. In a very convincing article, Jon Smith argues that Dos Passos's "Anglo-Saxon self-image" underpins much of *U.S.A.* (289). According to Smith, Dos Passos's Anglo-Saxon pretensions result in racist and xenophobic representations. However, it is also true that Dos Passos associates Englishness with the hegemonic effects that he criticizes.

10. As Janet Galligani Casey observes, "Dos Passos' growing aversion to what he saw as the repressive tactics of the Communist Party [. . .] was accompanied by a philosophical conviction that orthodox Marxist philosophy could not accommodate the peculiar social landscape of the United States, a conviction that reveals the author's understanding of the irreducible complexity of American culture and its incapacity for elucidation via a simplistic class-conflict paradigm" (168). Dos Passos's representation of the Communist Party is therefore intertwined with his treatment of the complex landscape of cultural mediation. Whereas Gramsci's ideas about mediation bolster his communist commitments, Dos Passos's awareness of the power of cultural hegemony subverts his adherence to communist history.

11. According to Robert James Butler, "Dos Passos' fiction [. . .] treats movement ambivalently" (83). Butler makes this statement because he believes that American mobility "offers hope for the human race" (88). Butler's identification of American space with the human race is highly problematic, and his comments about Dos Passos's ambivalence are not borne out by the critique of compulsive movement in *U.S.A.* Yet Butler's suggestion that "movement in American literature is often aggressively non-teleological" is relevant to Dos Passos's trilogy (81). In *U.S.A.*, Dos Passos imagines transportation and mobility as components of the war of position between labor and capital. Like other forms of culture and ideology in *U.S.A.*, geographical movement is involved in the complex mediations of civil society that qualify the credibility of teleological history.

12. William Solomon argues that Dos Passos's "rhetorical awareness serves as the basis for his political intervention" (808). In his analysis of the section of *U.S.A.* entitled "The Body of an American," Solomon posits that Dos Passos subverts the "totalizing logic" of the trope of the Unknown Soldier (810). Solomon's observations indicate that linguistic issues are integral to Dos Passos's political critique. As an effect of this critique, argues Solomon, language

is "brutally dismembered" by Dos Passos and "there is no telling where a truly rigorous encounter with figural language may lead" (813). Solomon's comments are especially pertinent to the lack of historical direction or assurance in Dos Passos's attempts to envision political transformation in terms of linguistic renewal.

13. In his 1935 essay "The Writer as Technician," Dos Passos states that writers, as opposed to engineers, should constitute a mediating counterclass to that of publicity agents and financiers. Throughout this essay, the technician, or engineer, is simply a trope for the writer, and the use of this textual device transforms the technician into a merely decorative, if prominent, aspect of Dos Passos's thesis. Dos Passos's comments in this essay suggest that *U.S.A.*'s invocation of historical process as linguistic renewal reconfigures Veblen's model of historical development by replacing the revolutionary engineer with the middle class professional, specifically the professional writer.

14. As John Trombold notes, some of the popular songs that are quoted in the Newsreel sections "hit a defiant note that resounds defiantly among the jingoistic jingles" ("Popular" 291). However, radical lyrics are much less prevalent in the Newsreels than the "jingoistic jingles" that Trombold mentions. Also, the textual disjunction between these radical songs and the words of Sacco and Vanzetti exemplifies the absence of a unified national-popular language in the trilogy.

15. The role of the domestic sphere is intimately connected to the issue of Gramscian "feeling." Brett Levinson discusses Gramsci's concepts of knowing, understanding, and feeling in terms of Hegel's identification of these terms with, respectively, state, civil society, and family. The shift from feeling to knowing therefore entails a movement from "the subaltern family" to involvement in civil society and the state (72). Vicky and Rosamond undertake the journey noted by Levinson.

16. Herbst's interest in familial history also works against the possibility of the emergence of a strong theory of history in the Trexler trilogy. In Elizabeth Francis's terms, Herbst's "search for a usable past was an effort to recover the sources of and to give meaning to the experiences of the marginal and the dispossessed of the Depression, to embrace a more populist style of the vernacular and the folk with an unsentimental view of the effects of social and economic conditions on the lives of a wide array of people" (133). Francis's formulation captures the constellation of family history, folk culture, and political sensibility in Herbst's writing. Yet the radical dimension of Herbst's writing is so reliant on family history that it cannot seize upon a theory of the revolutionary future.

17. Anarchism negates existing capitalist society and appeals to utopian spatiality. However, it does not theorize the historical movement to the utopian future and derides all forms of organization that attempt to guide the process of history. Syndicalism is also a highly spatialized form of political activism because it theorizes the appropriation of the industrial space of the factory. Such activism is a form of historical process. Also, the Wobblies' program to unite workers in "one big union" represents a greater degree of organizational guidance than is evident in anarchism.

18. Vicky's experience resonates with that of Herbst. According to Elinor Langer, Herbst "wanted to be a woman and a Mensch in Rosa Luxemburg's terms" (91), and Luxemburg's relationship with Leo Jogiches highlights aspects of the intersection of love and politics that inform Vicky's predicament. As Elzbieta Ettinger describes, Luxemburg, unlike Jogiches, opposed the notion that participation in revolutionary politics should be conducted at the expense of a fulfilling personal life (xv).

19. Speaking of *Rope of Gold*, Julia C. Ehrhardt correctly observes that "the novel is not a failed attempt to imagine a successful female revolutionary hero[, . . .] because Herbst never intended to invent such a hero in the first place" (176). Through the breakdown of Vicky's relationship with Jonathan, Herbst indicates the difficulties that face women who seek to pursue successful personal and public lives. At the same time, Herbst affirms the politicizing function of domestic culture. Herbst's representation of the private sphere is therefore dualistic: the domestic realm generates the political sensibility that leads Vicky toward civil society and the state, but the maintenance of domestic culture in the wake of the move to the public sphere proves to be impossible. In Gramsci's language, the narrative goes from feeling to knowing but cannot return from knowing back to feeling.

3. The Divergence of Social Space

1. In an interview with Elisabeth Niebuhr, McCarthy states that even if her fiction "may have autobiographical elements in it that I'm conscious of, it has been conceived as a fiction, even a thing like *The Oasis*, that was supposed to have all these real people in it. The whole story is a complete fiction. Nothing of the kind ever happened; after all, it happens in the future" (8). The fictionality of *The Oasis* that McCarthy describes invites a theoretical analysis that differs from a perception of the novel as satirical autobiography.

2. McCarthy uses the economism of domesticity to expose the insubstantiality of Mac's theoretical opposition to Joe. Mac opposes Joe's hunting trip but realizes that the only sound basis of such an opposition would involve his

taking "the last step" toward animal rights and vegetarianism (89). Unwilling to take this step, Mac cannot find any convincing reason to distinguish himself from Joe.

3. Wendy Martin argues that in McCarthy's fiction "marriage and friendship are constructs which barely conceal the predatory nature of social life" (194). The conflict between Katy and Preston exemplifies the "Hobbesian power struggle" that Martin describes (194). Arendt claims that "the nature of household rule" is characterized by a greater degree of inequality than is evident in political rule (*Human* 27). In Katy and Preston's case, the equality of the public domain is absent and social struggle becomes a public spectacle of household characteristics.

4. Arendt claims that Dostoevsky's Grand Inquisitor brings terror because he applies compassion en masse to the social population. In "America the Beautiful," McCarthy also refers to the Grand Inquisitor, "who, desiring to make the Kingdom of God incarnate on earth, inaugurated the kingdom of the devil" (205). McCarthy makes this reference to illustrate the idea that mass consumerism might be designed to bring material benefit but actually creates homogeneity and meaninglessness. Since Arendt posits that the evils of mass society are linked to the pursuit of the social question, both writers' references to the Grand Inquisitor make essentially the same point.

5. As Margaret Canovan notes, Arendt's critique of the social question does not mean that she was hostile toward "authentic compassion" (170). As with so much of Arendt's discussion of the social, the problem involves the extension of a legitimate principle beyond the realm in which it is meaningful. For Canovan, Arendt only becomes critical of compassion "when it moves out of the sphere of direct, face-to-face personal relationships and becomes entangled with politics" (170).

6. Canovan explains why Arendt was critical of Marx's attempt to reduce politics to work: "Work is a matter of transforming material in order to make something: domination, violence and the sacrifice of the means to the end are inherent in the activity of fabrication. When this model is applied to politics, which is concerned with dealings between plural persons, it is other people who become the material to be dealt with violently and sacrificed to the end that is to be achieved" (73).

7. As Brightman argues, Arendt and McCarthy both abhorred the conformity and vulgarity that characterized midcentury American social life (*Between* viii). One of McCarthy's letters typifies the reasons why both writers were critical of mass society. Speaking of the political success of Richard Nixon, McCarthy is concerned that the "advertising techniques" and "re-

flexes" of "mass-conditioning" have extended from the social to the political sphere (*Between* 9, 10). As a result, the illusion of choice that is evident in consumer activity has eradicated the authentic differences of democratic politics.

8. The correspondence between Arendt and McCarthy shows evidence of these differing viewpoints. While McCarthy contrasts the "weird new civilization" and its "age of groupiness" with the beauty of Nabokov's *Pale Fire*, Arendt sees in Nabokov's novel the "vulgarity" that she dislikes in social discourse (Brightman, *Between* 133, 136). For Arendt, the "grotesque posturing and arrogant acrobatics" of novels such as *Pale Fire* and Günter Grass's *The Tin Drum* typify a despicable "genre of the displaced person" (Brightman, *Between* 140). Arendt's comments are consistent with her description of the novel as "the only entirely social art form" (*Human* 39). This difference of opinion suggests that McCarthy, more so than Arendt, regarded fiction as a counterweight to the social realm that they both criticized.

9. Goodman articulates his anarchist principles in the essays collected in *Drawing the Line*. Numerous aspects of these political essays are also expressed in *The Empire City*. However, there is not an absolute equivalence between these essays and the novel. In "Revolution, Sociolatry, and War," Goodman demands that a "natural society" be founded (29). Such views are consistent with the ideas of nineteenth-century anarchist writers, such as Peter Kropotkin, who believed that the only natural human community would be one that was nonhierarchical and egalitarian. In *The Empire City*, Goodman is diffident about the viability and desirability of a human society based on the authority of nature. Because of this difference between political theory and fictional practice, it is preferable to speak of the novel in terms of critical space rather than the politics of space.

10. In order to distinguish the different volumes of Lefebvre's *Critique*, I will refer in the citations to the first volume as "I" and the second volume as "II."

11. As Rob Shields notes, Lefebvre is known in France as "the father of the dialectic" (109). Shields also observes that Lefebvre's dialectic was influenced by Nietzsche's theory of "overcoming" (72). Discussing Nietzsche's theory, Shields identifies "the importance of reversibility and instability in everyday life" and claims that "outcomes were never guaranteed" (72). By incorporating these aspects of Nietzsche's theory into his own ideas, Lefebvre imagines the dialectic as an open-ended process that has no predetermined temporal direction. As Michael E. Gardiner suggests, Lefebvre is "not prone to either nostalgic ruminations about a lost 'golden age' or abstract utopian predictions about a perfect future society" (77). Lefebvre's interest in the dialectics of social space displaces concerns with temporal movements from the past

and into the future. For his articulation of the transition from a historical to a spatial dialectic, see Lefebvre, *Survival* 17–19.

12. The question of alienation raises the issue of Goodman's ideas about human subjectivity. Donald Morton convincingly argues that the model of subjectivity in Goodman's writing is neither essentialist nor wholly an effect of linguistic and cultural constructions. Morton's comments specifically refer to Goodman's representation of sexual identity, but they are also applicable to the representation of subjectivity in *The Empire City*. For Morton, Goodman's model of subjectivity is based on "the fragility of a knowledge" ("Cultural" 230), a knowledge of actual social circumstances that is distinct from inherent selfhood. Social circumstances mean that this subject of knowledge can be alienated.

13. In "Utopian Thinking," Goodman advocates "the conflictual community" (22), which he describes as a community that is continually subject to dialectical transformation. Noting that Goodman was interested in the "community in passage" (62), Lewis Fried emphasizes the processual nature of this dialectical idea. George Woodcock states that Goodman's anarchism is linked to his dialectical ideas about community. For Woodcock, Goodman lacked both "the despairing inertia of the purist anarchist" and "the idealistic futility of those who [. . .] see the fulfillment of anarchist expectations as a distant point on a far horizon" (34). Rather, Goodman's anarchism was characterized by "the realistic awareness that in the foreseeable future the best we can expect is a vigorously pluralist society" (20). In Taylor Stoehr's terms, Goodman was a "practical anarchist" (87).

14. Mark Poster argues that, for Lefebvre's theory of everyday life, "it is [. . .] the human in its totality that is at issue" (747). Lefebvre's language, Poster claims, uses the "excessive terms" of the "truly free individual" (747). However, as Highmore notes, Lefebvre "struggl[es] against th[e] jargon of authenticity," and he uses the Marxist conception of the "total man" as a "heuristic" that refers to no more than "a pure potentiality for humankind" (125, 127). Shields reminds us that Lefebvre is known as "a humanistic Marxist" (73), but his humanism never rests with any fixed or essentialist notions. Lefebvre's denial of humanist essentialism is a function of his open-ended spatial dialectics and unwillingness to project into the future. As he states, he is more interested in "transitional man" (sic) than "total man" (I 65).

15. Several critics link Lefebvre's critique of state power to an anarchist sensibility (Gardiner 77; Highmore 119; Poster 744). However, such observations should be considered in relation to Lefebvre's critique of the anarchist opposition to work.

16. Everett C. Frost states that Goodman disliked being described as a "utopian thinker" (129). Also, in "Utopian Thinking," Goodman is highly critical of technological and other forms of utopianism. Even in *Communitas*, the book Goodman wrote with his brother, Perceval Goodman, the "Three Community Paradigms" that the authors propose are presented in circumspect and highly qualified terms (117).

17. Goodman is a social regionalist. Donald Morton observes that the reflexive narrative qualities of *The Empire City* portray the "situated" contexts of "historically determined [. . .] political contestations" ("Crisis" 412). Through the reflexivity that Morton discusses, Goodman highlights social experiences of space rather than empirical or physical regional geography.

18. Droyt and Lefty are the two sons of Laura and Mynheer.

4. Realizing Abstract Space

1. *The Production of Space* and *The Urban Revolution* were originally published, respectively, in 1974 and 1970. Despite differences in analytic range between the two texts, they articulate similar perspectives on the production of urban and abstract space. In this chapter I discuss the two texts as alternative perspectives on these shared concerns.

2. Contra Soja, Derek Gregory regards *Urban* and *Production* as histories of space in the tradition of "mainstream Marxism" (359). Gregory's comments reinforce the strong distinction he proposes between Althusser and Lefebvre. For Gregory, Lefebvre articulates the Hegelian characteristics of humanism and historicism that Althusser rejects. Mark Gottdiener agrees with this view and suggests that Lefebvre's humanism and historicism have returned Marxism to "a Gramscian world" (154). Such observations reiterate the close connection between Gramsci and Lefebvre, but it is important to note that Lefebvre, unlike Gramsci, proclaims a definitive replacement of historical with spatial dialectics.

3. In the discussion of Pynchon, all references to Lefebvre will cite *The Production of Space*.

4. As Rob Shields notes, the use of "representational spaces" in the English translation of *Production* is inaccurate. Lefebvre's terminology is more properly translated as "[s]paces of representation" (161).

5. Soja describes Los Angeles as "a confusing collage of signs which advertise what are little more than imaginary communities and outlandish representations of reality." Underneath this "semiotic blanket," he writes, "there remains an economic order, an instrumental nodal structure, an essentially exploitative spatial division of labor" (*Postmodern* 245, 246). In *The Crying of*

Lot 49, Oedipa's focus on the semiotic blanket of Tristero prevents her from observing the social and economic structure that Soja describes. Interestingly, Soja notes the common etymological root of "semiotics and spatiality" (*Postmodern* 246n). Pynchon's novel suggests that the semiotic blanket serves to mask and stand in for spatiality.

6. In *Postmodern Cartographies*, Brian Jarvis argues, "Oedipa's inability to get her bearings in the disorientating hyperspace of the late capitalist city is a function of its dispiriting opacity, the invisibility of the forces that mould it" (63). However, Oedipa's limitations are primarily due to the "semiotic fetishism" that Jarvis elsewhere describes (61).

7. Jon Simons relates Oedipa's failed revelation to Fredric Jameson's theory of cognitive mapping. For Simons, Jameson's desire to map social totality from the perspective of "the individual's location in social reality" is equivalent to Oedipa's failed wish for revelation (209). However, Jameson's program for cognitive mapping is to some extent antithetical to Oedipa's semiotic and historical interests. Pynchon's novel does not strive to articulate the absolute and nonideological social totality that Simons attributes to Jameson. Rather, *The Crying of Lot 49* portrays a realm of social space that exemplifies the "excluded middles" that Oedipa fears and Simons advocates. In the novel, social space is identified with neither the "transcendent meaning" that Oedipa desires nor simply "the earth" (181).

8. Ellipses in quotations from *Gravity's Rainbow* are, unless bracketed, from Pynchon's text.

9. Speaking generally about Pynchon's fiction, Stefan Mattessich observes a conjunction of signs and visuality that he links to Lefebvre's theories (4).

10. As Andy Merrifield argues, Lefebvre's notion of abstract space is akin to Marx's theory of abstract labor. Abstract labor is labor turned into exchange value. According to Merrifield, "This standard becomes the common denominator for all things as commodity relations colonize everywhere and everybody" (175). In Lefebvre's theory, abstract space also colonizes and becomes the general standard for social space. Like money, writes Merrifield, abstract space "has a very real *social existence*" and should not be regarded as "a mental abstraction" (176).

11. The strongest account of the extension of the v-2 rocketry program into the technological domain of postwar American society is of course made by Dale Carter.

12. "Contrary to popular opinion," writes Soja, "Los Angeles is a tightly planned and plotted urban environment" (*Postmodern* 238). Citing Foucault, Soja also describes Los Angeles as a "carceral city" that is regulated by control

and surveillance (*Thirdspace* 235). As part of his analysis of the carceral city, Soja refers to the freeway system as a locus of "Orwellian" surveillance that was "designed with national defense in mind" (*Thirdspace* 210; *Postmetropolis* 135). Pynchon's representation of the abstract space of the city's freeway system shares Soja's concerns. As the outcome of rocketry technology and its contribution to the formation of abstract space, the freeway system is linked to the defense industry. The freeways are also a site of planned control and surveillance. In "Journey into the Mind of Watts," Pynchon states that the freeway makes young African American men vulnerable to police harassment: "Catching you mobile widens the man's horizons; gives him more things he can get you on" (151).

13. For example, Jeffery S. Baker views the Counterforce as a critique of the "politically oriented" members of the counterculture in the 1960s (107), and Patrick McHugh suggests that the "full-fledged messianic delusion" of the Counterforce illustrates the "limits" of "cultural politics" (12).

14. The question of totality once again raises the concerns of Jameson's "Cognitive Mapping." According to Steven Best, *Gravity's Rainbow* undertakes a Jamesonian cognitive mapping of the post–World War II transition to multinational capitalism. However, the role of spatiality in Pynchon's novel is more fundamental than Best suggests. For Best, Pynchon "uses creative paranoia to map real historical forces and to catalogue a myriad of discourses, codes, and sources of power in modern capitalist societies" (74). Pynchon "maps" the issues noted by Best in terms of the dialectics of social space. Also, the social space of the novel constitutes neither a totality nor the absolute "unmappability" noted by José Liste Noya (513). Rather, Pynchon represents a movement of abstract and lived space that is fissured by discontinuities.

15. According to David Harvey, "Lefebvre is resolutely antagonistic to the traditional utopianisms of spatial form precisely because of their closed authoritarianism. [. . .] The effect, unfortunately, is to leave the actual spaces of any alternative frustratingly undefined" (*Spaces* 182). The same is also true for Pynchon.

16. Unless otherwise stated, all subsequent references in this chapter to Lefebvre will cite *The Urban Revolution*.

17. The issue of postindustrial society is of course highly contentious. As Soja remarks, postindustrial sociology often exaggerates the decline of industrial production and "reduce[s] the significance of spatial specificities and the geographical" (*Postmetropolis* 166). In Lefebvre's case, a postindustrial orientation is essential to his prioritization of the significance of urban space.

18. Shields notes that Lefebvre "was always inspired by New York" (145). He also refers to Lefebvre's participation in the colloquium on "The Institutions of the Post-Industrial Society" at New York's Museum of Modern Art in 1972 as a key moment in the development of his ideas about urban space. It is therefore not surprising that there are numerous points of connection between Gaddis's representation of New York and Lefebvre's urban theory.

19. Susan Strehle reads *JR* in terms of the modernist distinction between authentic subjective time and a debased, spatialized, public time. She claims that the novel highlights "a character's confinement in public time" and argues that the "circular and repetitive" movements of the characters are due to their entrapment in spatialized time (121, 127). It is a compelling argument, but the public spatiality within which the characters are trapped is primarily that of the urban configuration of business interests.

20. The fusion of physical and conceptual space that is evident in this example is typical of *JR*'s orientation toward urban form. As Christopher J. Knight argues, the organization of conceptual space has significant effects in *JR*: "[I]t is the belief that society's components can be bracketed, so that its ethical and religious beliefs are assigned to one space, its culture and arts another space, and its laws of business a third, that makes it possible, in the absence of a larger, more encompassing telos, for the more aggressive of these components to infiltrate the others" (86). It is, however, important to note that the spatial array described by Knight exists in a dialectical relation with physical space.

21. As John Johnston notes, *JR* "relentlessly demonstrates that it is not production or intelligible purpose but the ceaseless movement and proliferation of useless information and objects that define our world" (163). The flows of information associated with *JR* are inseparable from the colonization of urban space by business practices.

22. The homogenizing effects of these technologies are addressed by Patrick O'Donnell and Joseph Tabbi. O'Donnell notes that Frigicom "promises to homogenize culture to the extent that 'military and artistic barriers' can be severed" (16). O'Donnell's comments indicate that Frigicom is another example of the concomitant transformation of physical and conceptual or social space in the novel. In this example, the homogenized silence produced by Frigicom is equivalent to the eradication of the conceptual space of art. Referring to an allusion to Thoreau's *Walden* in Gaddis's evocation of Teletravel, Tabbi suggests that this technology is associated with homogenized meaninglessness and having "nothing to communicate" (150).

23. Lefebvre's emphasis on culture exemplifies the marginalization of eco-

nomic concerns with which many commentators take issue. See Katznelson 101–02 and Smith 92.

24. According to Lefebvre, "The centralized management of 'things' and of 'culture' tries to avoid this intermediary tier, the city." In this statement, Lefebvre indicates that culture and the urban centers of decision making work together to impose the global level of urban planning on the intermediary level of urban space. Similarly, he claims that culture serves an "integrative" social function that works in tandem with urban "segregation" ("Right" 128, 144).

25. Lefebvre's writings on urban form shed light on his ideas about utopia. In "Right to the City," his distaste for urban planners leads him to attack all forms of utopia based on "positivism." Any plans for the transformation of social space must not, according to Lefebvre, be considered in terms of "their utopian aspect." Yet he does advocate a "radical metamorphosis" of urban form. Lefebvre's adherence to spatial transformation is derived from his critique of social totality. For Lefebvre, social space is "incomplete" and contains "holes and chasms" and "places of the possible". The utopianism that Lefebvre espouses is characterized by a dialectical transformation of the discontinuities that actually exist in social space: "Utopia controlled by dialectical reason serves as a safeguard against supposedly scientific fictions and visions gone astray." Such a project would, for Lefebvre, "assert that the maximum of utopianism could unite with the optimum of realism" ("Right" 151, 155, 156, 157).

26. Knight states that Gaddis articulates an "almost sotto voce" version of Bloch's anticipatory utopianism (2). However, as Gregory Comnes suggests, "[i]n a decentered world of globalized commodity fetishism there is no dialectic at work, no status-based, use-value revolutionary aesthetic possible in a world where there is only contractual exchange value" (87). In Johnston's terms, Gaddis provides a "demonstration" rather than a "compensation" or "redemption" (170).

5. Territoriality and the Lost Dimension

1. John S. Howard urges us not to read Deleuze and Guattari's "pluralism" as a version of dialectics (115). For discussions of Deleuze's infamous critiques of Hegelian dialectics, see Hardt 32–37 and Brusseau 22–28.

2. According to Douglas Kellner, Virilio "has no theory of justice and no politics to counter, reconstruct, reappropriate or transform technology, as well as no counter-forces that can oppose technology" ("Virilio" 120). Kellner's reference to "counter-forces" highlights the absence of dialectics in Vir-

ilio's writing. Virilio describes himself as "an anarcho-Christian" (Armitage, "From Modernism" 30). For a summary of Deleuze and Guattari's relation to anarchism, see Patton 4.

3. Just as Deleuze and Guattari state that the notion of "becoming-woman" has a privileged role in the movement of deterritorialization (275), so too Didion associates the line of flight with female experience. While several feminist critics have insisted that Deleuze and Guattari's idea of becoming-woman marginalizes women, other commentators, such as Elizabeth Grosz, Verena Andermatt Conley, and Dorothea Olkowski, argue that there are "fruitful" connections between feminism and Deleuze and Guattari's theory (Grosz 197). Lines of flight have varied results in Didion's fiction, but they are sometimes the means by which female characters escape restricted and segmented circumstances.

4. According to Stephen Jarvis, the other narratives to which Didion refers are probably Graham Greene's *A Burnt-Out Case*, Joseph Conrad's *Victory*, and Rudyard Kipling's *Plain Tales from the Hills*. As Jarvis states, "[T]he literary references do not quite fit or add up to convey a convenient and unified meaning" (96).

5. In the language of Alan Nadel, *Democracy* is "about the erosion of our ability to believe in our personal and national allegories" (96). As Nadel discusses, the United States used the policy of containment as a means of realizing the national allegory of democracy in the Cold War era. Nadel states that George F. Kennan's 1947 foreign policy statement, "The Sources of Soviet Conduct," portrays the Soviet Union as "a source of essential fluids" that must be dammed and contained (98). Stating that the containment policy became "a narrative of expansion, of spreading democracy" (101), Nadel describes the "unimpeded sense of direction and goal" that characterizes state power in *Democracy*. However, the expansive striations of political authority in Didion's novel seek both to contain and to deploy the smooth flow of the war machine.

6. Relating Deleuze and Guattari's concept of imperceptibility to that of becoming-woman, Jerry Aline Flieger comments that imperceptibility is "not a function of invisibility or lack of importance; it is a function of a recomposition, a radical change in consistency, where the connecting 'thread' is not one of subjective identity" (46).

7. Slavoj Zizek notes two conflicting trends in Deleuze's writing. For Zizek, Deleuze's treatment of the "productive Becoming" of the "body without organs" in the books he wrote with Guattari is simplistic and uninteresting (21). Conversely, Zizek applauds the discussion of the "immaterial becoming" of

the "sense-event" and "the desubstantialization of affects" that is evident in Deleuze's *The Logic of Sense*. In Zizek's account, sense-events are "organs without body" that are opposed to the Becoming-flows of *Capitalism and Schizophrenia* (30). However, *A Thousand Plateaus* combines the trends noted by Zizek. For Deleuze and Guattari, the haecceities of haptic perception are desubjectified sense-events that constitute and are constituted by the smooth flow of the line of flight. In *Democracy*, Inez's haptic perceptions similarly effect and are effected by her smooth mobility.

8. See *Politics* 13, 29; *Pure* 108; *War* 73, 80.

9. "News is dynamite, information explodes like a bomb" (*Art* 24), argues Virilio. In support of his view that the media are by definition an executive limb of the military, Virilio argues that in founding the "communications complex" of the industrial press, Napoleon extended the "mediatization," which meant "being stripped of one's IMMEDIATE RIGHTS" (*Art* 6), of his defeated enemies to the French populus.

10. Virilio emphasizes how the "chemical defoliation" of Vietnam was conducted so as "to empty the screen of parasitic vegetation" and thus improve image production (*War* 82).

11. Philip Nel is one of the few critics to argue that DeLillo's critique of cyberspace is not qualified by a religious appeal (742–43).

12. Virilio advocates the idea of the "milieu" or "event landscape" to designate the configuration of human activity and materiality that he seeks to renew, and he thinks that land art is a limited form of such renewal because it does not emphasize living human spaces (*Politics* 109, 110). Also, for Virilio, nose art pin-up images reinforce rather than undermine the "perceptual logistics" of the war machine (*War* 23). Just as the landscape was reified as target by the imaging systems of World War II bombers, so too, argues Virilio, were women's bodies objectified by the exaggerated images that adorned the bombers' cockpits. See also Green 582–84.

Bibliography

Arendt, Hannah. *Between Past and Future*. New York: Penguin, 1977.

———. *The Human Condition*. Chicago: University of Chicago Press, 1958.

———. "Labor, Work, Action." *The Portable Hannah Arendt*. Ed. Peter Baehr. New York: Penguin, 2000. 167–81.

———. *On Revolution*. New York: Viking, 1965.

Armitage, John. "From Modernism to Hypermodernism and Beyond: An Interview with Paul Virilio." Armitage, *Paul Virilio* 25–55.

———, ed. *Paul Virilio: From Modernism to Hypermodernism and Beyond*. London: Sage, 2000.

Auerbach, Jonathan. *Male Call: Becoming Jack London*. Durham: Duke University Press, 1996.

Badaloni, Nicola. "Gramsci and the Problem of the Revolution." *Gramsci and Marxist Theory*. Ed. Chantal Mouffe. London: Routledge & Kegan Paul, 1979. 80–109.

Badiou, Alain. *Deleuze: The Clamor of Being*. Trans. Louise Burchill. Minneapolis: University of Minnesota Press, 2000.

Baker, Jeffrey S. "A Democratic Pynchon: Counterculture, Counterforce and Participatory Democracy." *Pynchon Notes* 32–33 (1993): 99–131.

Becker, George, ed. *Documents of Modern Literary Realism*. Princeton: Princeton University Press, 1963.

———. "Introduction. Modern Realism as a Literary Movement." Becker, *Documents* 3–38.

Begley, Adam. "The Art of Fiction CXXXV: Don DeLillo." *Paris Review* 128 (1993): 274–306.

———. "Don DeLillo: *Americana*, *Mao II*, and *Underworld*." *Southwest Review* 82 (1997): 478–505.

Bellamy, Edward. *Looking Backward, 2000–1887*. 1888. New York: Penguin, 1986.

Benhabib, Seyla. *The Reluctant Modernism of Hannah Arendt*. Thousand Oaks: Sage, 1996.

Benton, Graham. "Riding the Interface: An Anarchist Reading of *Gravity's Rainbow*." *Pynchon Notes* 42–43 (1998): 152–66.

Berressem, Hanjo. *Pynchon's Poetics: Interfacing Theory and Text*. Urbana: University of Illinois Press, 1993.

Best, Steven. "Creative Paranoia: A Postmodern Aesthetic of Cognitive Mapping in *Gravity's Rainbow*." *Centennial Review* 36.1 (1992): 59–87.

Bloch, Ernst. *The Principle of Hope*. Trans. Neville Plaice, Stephen Plaice, and Paul Knight. 3 vols. Cambridge: MIT Press, 1986.

Bloodworth, William A. *Upton Sinclair*. Boston: Twayne, 1977.

Bogard, William. "Smoothing Machines and the Constitution of Society." *Cultural Studies* 14.2 (2000): 269–94.

Boggs, Carl. *The Two Revolutions: Antonio Gramsci and the Dilemmas of Western Marxism*. Boston: South End, 1984.

Bosteels, Bruno. "From Text to Territory: Félix Guattari's Cartographies of the Unconscious." Kaufman and Heller 145–74.

Brightman, Carol, ed. *Between Friends: The Correspondence of Hannah Arendt and Mary McCarthy, 1949–1975*. San Diego: Harcourt Brace, 1995.

———. *Writing Dangerously: Mary McCarthy and Her World*. New York: Clarkson Potter, 1992.

Briscoe, Erica. "*The Iron Heel*: How Not to Write a Popular Novel." *Jack London Journal* 5 (1998): 5–38.

Browder, Laura. *Rousing the Nation: Radical Culture in Depression America*. Amherst: University of Massachusetts Press, 1998.

Brown, Bill. "The Dark Wood of Postmodernity (Space, Faith, Allegory)." *PMLA* 120.3 (2005): 734–50.

Brusseau, James. *Isolated Experiences: Gilles Deleuze and the Solitudes of Reversed Platonism*. Albany: SUNY Press, 1998.

Buchanan, Ian, ed. *A Deleuzian Century?* Durham: Duke University Press, 1999.

———. "Lefebvre and the Space of Everyday Life." *Southern Review* 27.2 (1994): 127–37.

Butler, Robert James. "The American Quests for Pure Movement in Dos Passos' *U.S.A.*" *Twentieth Century Literature* 30.1 (1984): 80–99.

Canovan, Margaret. *Hannah Arendt: A Reinterpretation of Her Political Thought*. Cambridge: Cambridge University Press, 1992.

Carter, Dale. *The Final Frontier: The Rise and Fall of the American Rocket State*. London: Verso, 1988.

Casey, Janet Galligani. *Dos Passos and the Ideology of the Feminine.* Cambridge: Cambridge University Press, 1998.

Clark, Michael. *Dos Passos's Early Fiction, 1912–1938.* Selingsgrove: Susquehanna University Press, 1987.

Comnes, Gregory. *The Ethics of Indeterminacy in the Novels of William Gaddis.* Gainesville: University Press of Florida, 1994.

Conder, John J. *Naturalism in American Fiction: The Classic Phase.* Lexington: University Press of Kentucky, 1984.

Cowley, Malcolm. "A Natural History of American Naturalism." Becker, *Documents* 429–51.

Crang, Mike, and Nigel Thrift, eds. *Thinking Space.* London: Routledge, 2000.

Daniel, Jamie Owen, and Tom Moylan, eds. *Not Yet: Reconsidering Ernst Bloch.* London: Verso, 1997.

Debray, Régis. *Media Manifestos: On the Technological Transmission of Cultural Forms.* Trans. Eric Rauth. London: Verso, 1996.

DeLanda, Manuel. "Immanence and Transcendence in the Genesis of Form." Buchanan, *Deleuzian* 119–34.

Deleuze, Gilles, and Félix Guattari. *A Thousand Plateaus: Capitalism and Schizophrenia.* Trans. Brian Massumi. Minneapolis: University of Minnesota Press, 1987.

DeLillo, Don. *Underworld.* New York: Scribner, 1997.

Denning, Michael. *The Cultural Front: The Laboring of American Culture in the Twentieth Century.* New York: Verso, 1997.

Derrick, Scott. "What a Beating Feels Like: Authorship, Dissolution, and Masculinity in Sinclair's *The Jungle.*" *Studies in American Fiction* 23.1 (1995): 85–100.

Didion, Joan. *A Book of Common Prayer.* 1977. New York: Vintage, 1995.

———. *Democracy.* 1984. New York: Vintage, 1995.

———. *The Last Thing He Wanted.* 1996. New York: Vintage, 1997.

Diggins, John. "Dos Passos and Veblen's Villains." *Antioch Review* 23 (1963): 485–500.

Diggins, John Patrick. *Thorstein Veblen. Theorist of the Leisure Class.* Princeton: Princeton University Press, 1999.

Doel, Marcus. "Un-glunking Geography: Spatial Science after Dr. Seuss and Deleuze." Crang and Thrift 117–35.

Dos Passos, John. *U.S.A.* 1938. Boston: Houghton Mifflin, 1974.

Dubofsky, Melvin. *We Shall Be All: A History of the Industrial Workers of the World.* Chicago: Quadrangle, 1969.

Ehrhardt, Julia C. *Writers of Conviction: The Personal Politics of Zona Gale,*

Dorothy Canfield Fisher, Rose Wilder Lane, and Josephine Herbst. Columbia: University of Missouri Press, 2004.

Elden, Stuart. *Mapping the Present: Heidegger, Foucault and the Project of a Spatial History.* London: Continuum, 2001.

Ettinger, Elzbieta. "Introduction." *Comrade and Lover: Rosa Luxemburg's Letters to Leo Jogiches.* Ed. and trans. Elzbieta Ettinger. Cambridge: MIT Press, 1979. xiii–xxxiv.

Finocchiaro, Maurice A. *Gramsci and the History of Dialectical Thought.* Cambridge: Cambridge University Press, 1988.

Flieger, Jerry Aline. "Becoming-Woman: Deleuze, Schreber and Molecular Identification." *Deleuze and Feminist Theory.* Ed. Ian Buchanan and Claire Colebrook. Edinburgh: Edinburgh University Press, 2000. 38–63.

Foley, Barbara. *Radical Representations: Politics and Form in U.S. Proletarian Fiction, 1929–1941.* Durham: Duke University Press, 1993.

Folsom, Michael Brewster. "Upton Sinclair's Escape from *The Jungle*: The Narrative Strategy and Suppressed Conclusion of America's First Proletarian Novel." *Prospects* 4 (1979): 237–66.

Foner, Philip S. *Jack London: American Rebel.* New York: Citadel, 1964.

Foucault, Michel. "Nietzsche, Genealogy, History." *Language, Counter-Memory, Practice: Selected Essays and Interviews by Michel Foucault.* Ed. Donald F. Bouchard. Ithaca: Cornell University Press, 1977. 139–64.

———. "Of Other Spaces." Trans. Jay Miskowiec. *Diacritics* 16 (1986): 22–27.

———. "Questions on Geography." *Power/Knowledge: Selected Interviews and Other Writings, 1972–1977.* Ed. Colin Gordon. New York: Pantheon, 1980. 63–77.

Francese, Joseph. *Narrating Postmodern Time and Space.* Albany: SUNY Press, 1997.

Francis, Elizabeth. *The Secret Treachery of Words: Feminism and Modernism in America.* Minneapolis: University of Minnesota Press, 2002.

Frank, Joseph. *The Widening Gyre: Crisis and Mastery in Modern Literature.* New Brunswick: Rutgers University Press, 1963.

Fried, Lewis. "The Kingdom of *The Empire City*: Paul Goodman's Regional Labor." *Parisi* 57–79.

Frost, Everett C. " "The News for Now and Here: Paul Goodman as Utopian Prophet." *Parisi* 118–135.

Gaddis, William. *JR.* 1975. New York: Penguin, 1993.

Gardiner, Michael E. *Critiques of Everyday Life.* London: Routledge, 2000.

Geoghegan, Vincent. *Utopianism and Marxism.* London: Methuen, 1987.

Glass, Loren. "Nobody's Renown: Plagiarism and Publicity in the Career of Jack London." *American Literature* 71.3 (1999): 529–49.

Goodman, Paul. *The Empire City*. 1959. New York: Vintage, 1977.

———. "Revolution, Sociolatry, and War." *Drawing the Line: The Political Essays of Paul Goodman*. Ed. Taylor Stoehr. New York: Free Life, 1977. 25–35.

———. "Utopian Thinking." *Utopian Essays and Practical Proposals*. New York: Vintage, 1962. 3–22.

Goodman, Perceval, and Paul Goodman. *Communitas: Ways of Livelihood and Means of Life*. New York: Vintage, 1960.

Gottdiener, M. *The Social Production of Urban Space*. Austin: University of Texas Press, 1985.

Gramsci, Antonio. *The Antonio Gramsci Reader: Selected Writings 1916–1935*. Ed. David Forgacs. New York: NYU Press, 2000.

Green, Jeremy. "Disaster Footage: Spectacles of Violence in DeLillo's Fiction." *Modern Fiction Studies* 45 (1999): 571–99.

Gregory, Derek. *Geographical Imaginations*. Oxford: Blackwell, 1994.

Grosz, Elizabeth. "A Thousand Tiny Sexes: Feminism and Rhizomatics." *Gilles Deleuze and the Theater of Philosophy*. Ed. Constantin V. Boundas and Dorothea Olkowski. New York: Routledge, 1994. 187–210.

Hamill, John. "Confronting the Monolith: Authority and the Cold War in *Gravity's Rainbow*." *Journal of American Studies* 33.3 (1999): 417–36.

Hardt, Michael. *Gilles Deleuze: An Apprenticeship in Philosophy*. Minneapolis: University of Minnesota Press, 1993.

Harvey, David. *Spaces of Hope*. Berkeley: University of California Press, 2000.

Herbst, Josephine. *The Executioner Waits*. 1934. New York: Warner, 1985.

———. *Pity Is Not Enough*. 1933. New York: Warner, 1985.

———. *Rope of Gold*. 1939. Old Westbury NY: Feminist Press, 1984.

Highmore, Ben. *Everyday Life and Cultural Theory: An Introduction*. London: Routledge, 2002.

Homberger, Eric. *American Writers and Radical Politics, 1900–39: Equivocal Commitments*. Basingstoke, UK: Macmillan, 1986.

Hornung, Alfred. "Literary Conventions and the Political Unconscious in Upton Sinclair's Work." *Upton Sinclair: Literature and Social Reform*. Ed. Dieter Herms. Frankfurt: Peter Lang, 1990. 24–38.

———. "The Political Uses of Popular Fiction in the Muckraking Movement." *Revue Francaise d'Etudes Americaines* 8.17 (1983): 333–48.

Howard, John S. "Subjectivity and Space: Deleuze and Guattari's BwO in the New World Order." Kaufman and Heller 112–26.

Howard, June. *Form and History in American Literary Naturalism*. Chapel Hill: University of North Carolina Press, 1985.

Hudson, Wayne. *The Marxist Philosophy of Ernst Bloch*. New York: St. Martin's, 1982.

Jameson, Fredric. "The End of Temporality." *Critical Inquiry* 29.4 (2003): 695–718.

———. "Marxism and Dualism in Deleuze." Buchanan, *Deleuzian* 13–36.

———. *Marxism and Form: Twentieth-Century Dialectical Theories of Literature*. Princeton: Princeton University Press, 1971.

Jarvis, Brian. *Postmodern Cartographies: The Geographical Imagination in Contemporary American Culture*. New York: St. Martin's, 1998.

Jarvis, Stephen. "Didion's *Democracy*: 'Dated in a Deconstructing Universe.' " *Angelaki* 5.3 (2000): 93–104.

Jay, Martin. *Marxism and Totality: The Adventures of a Concept from Lukács to Habermas*. Berkeley: University of California Press, 1984.

Johnston, John. "*JR* and the Flux of Capital." *Revue Francaise d'Etudes Americaines* 15.45 (1990): 161–71.

Kaplan, Harold. *Power and Order: Henry Adams and the Naturalist Tradition in American Fiction*. Chicago: University of Chicago Press, 1981.

Katznelson, Ira. *Marxism and the City*. Oxford: Clarendon, 1993.

Kaufman, Eleanor, and Kevin Jon Heller, eds. *Deleuze and Guattari: New Mappings in Politics, Philosophy and Culture*. Ed. Minneapolis: University of Minnesota Press, 1998.

Kellner, Douglas. *Critical Theory, Marxism, and Modernity*. Baltimore: Johns Hopkins University Press, 1989.

———. "Virilio, War and Technology: Some Critical Reflections." Armitage, *Paul Virilio* 103–25.

Kershaw, Alex. *Jack London: A Life*. New York: St. Martin's, 1997.

Kestner, Joseph A. *The Spatiality of the Novel*. Detroit: Wayne State University Press, 1978.

Kiernan, Frances. *Seeing Mary Plain: A Life of Mary McCarthy*. New York: Norton, 2000.

Kim, Yung Min. "A 'Patriarchal Grass House' of His Own: Jack London's *Martin Eden* and the Imperial Frontier." *American Literary Realism* 34.1 (2001): 1–17.

Knight, Christopher J. *Hints and Guesses: William Gaddis's Fiction of Longing*. Madison: University of Wisconsin Press, 1997.

Kuehl, John, and Steven Moore. "An Interview with William Gaddis." *Review of Contemporary Fiction* 2.2 (1982): 4–6.

Laclau, Ernesto, and Chantal Mouffe. *Hegemony and Socialist Strategy: Towards a Radical Democratic Politics*. London: Verso, 1985.

Langer, Elinor. *Josephine Herbst*. Boston: Northeastern University Press, 1994.

Lefebvre, Henri. *Critique of Everyday Life, Volume 1: Introduction*. Trans. John Moore. London: Verso, 1991.

———. *Critique of Everyday Life, Volume 2: Foundations for a Sociology of the Everyday*. Trans. John Moore. London: Verso, 2002.

———. "The Everyday and Everydayness." *Yale French Studies* 73 (1987): 7–11.

———. *The Production of Space*. Trans. Donald Nicholson-Smith. Oxford: Blackwell, 1991.

———. "Right to the City." Trans. Eleonore Kofman and Elizabeth Lebas. *Writings on Cities*. By Henri Lefebvre. Ed. Eleonore Kofman and Elizabeth Lebas. Oxford: Blackwell, 1996. 61–181.

———. *The Survival of Capitalism: Reproduction of the Relations of Production*. Trans. Frank Bryant. New York: St. Martin's, 1976.

———. *The Urban Revolution*. Trans. Robert Bononno. Minneapolis: University of Minnesota Press, 2003.

Lehan, Richard. "American Literary Naturalism: The French Connection." *Nineteenth-Century Fiction* 38.4 (1984): 529–57.

Levitas, Ruth. "Educated Hope: Ernst Bloch on Abstract and Concrete Utopia." Daniel and Moylan 65–79.

Levinson, Brett. "Feeling, the Subaltern, and the Organic Intellectual." *Angelaki* 6.1 (2001): 65–74.

Levy, Carl. *Gramsci and the Anarchists*. Oxford: Berg, 1999.

London, Jack. "The Dream of Debs." *The Bodley Head Jack London*. Ed. Arthur Calder-Marshall. London: Bodley Head, 1963. 225–46.

———. "Goliah." *Fantastic Tales*. By Jack London. Ed. Dale L. Walker. Lincoln: University of Nebraska Press, 1988. 87–108.

———. *The Iron Heel*. New York: Regent, 1907.

———. *Martin Eden*. 1909. New York: Penguin, 1967.

———. *The Valley of the Moon*. 1913. Berkeley. University of California Press, 1999.

Löwy, Michael. *Georg Lukács: From Romanticism to Bolshevism*. Trans. Patrick Camiller. London: NLB, 1979.

Ludington, Townsend. *John Dos Passos: A Twentieth Century Odyssey*. New York: Dutton, 1980.

Lukács, Georg. *Essays on Realism*. Ed. Rodney Livingstone. Trans. David Fernbach. Cambridge: MIT Press, 1980.

———. *The Historical Novel*. Trans. Hannah and Stanley Mitchell. New York: Penguin, 1969.

———. *History and Class Consciousness: Studies in Marxist Dialectics*. Trans. Rodney Livingstone. Cambridge: MIT Press, 1971.

———. Realism in the Balance." *Aesthetics and Politics*. Trans. ed. Ronald Taylor. London: Verso, 1980. 28–59.

———. *Studies in European Realism*. New York: Grosset & Dunlap, 1964.

Luke, Tim, and Gearóid Ó Tuathail. "Thinking Geopolitical Space: The Spatiality of War, Speed and Vision in the Work of Paul Virilio." Crang and Thrift 36–79.

Malmgren, Carl Darryl. *Fictional Space in the Modernist and Postmodernist American Novel*. Lewisburg: Bucknell University Press, 1985.

Marsh, Kelly A. " 'All My Habits of Mind': Performance and Identity in the Novels of Mary McCarthy." *Studies in the Novel* 34.3 (2002): 303–19.

Martin, Wendy. "The Satire and Moral Vision of Mary McCarthy." *Comic Relief: Humor in Contemporary American Literature*. Ed. Sarah Blacher Cohen. Urbana: University of Illinois Press, 1978. 187–206.

Massumi, Brian. *Parables for the Virtual: Movement, Affect, Sensation*. Durham: Duke University Press, 2002.

Materese, Susan M. *American Foreign Policy and the Utopian Imagination*. Amherst: University of Massachusetts Press, 2001.

Mattessich, Stefan. *Lines of Flight: Discursive Time and Countercultural Desire in the Work of Thomas Pynchon*. Durham: Duke University Press, 2002.

McCarthy, Mary. "America the Beautiful." *Commentary* 4.3 (1947): 201–07.

———. *The Oasis*. New York: Random House, 1949.

McHugh, Patrick. "Cultural Politics, Postmodernism, and White Guys: Affect in *Gravity's Rainbow*." *College Literature* 28.2 (2001): 1–28.

McLuhan, Marshall. *Understanding Media: The Extensions of Man*. Cambridge: MIT Press, 1994.

McQuire, Scott. "Blinded by the (Speed of) Light." Armitage, *Paul Virilio* 143–59.

Merrifield, Andy. "Henri Lefebvre: A Socialist in Space." Crang and Thrift 167–82.

Morris, Matthew J. "The Two Lives of Jurgis Rudkus." *American Literary Realism* 29.2 (1997): 50–67.

Morton, Donald. "The Crisis of Narrative in the Postnarratological Era: Paul Goodman's *The Empire City* as (Post)Modern Intervention." *New Literary History* 24.2 (1993): 407–24.

———. "The Cultural Politics of (Sexual) Knowledge: On the Margins with Goodman." *Social Text* 8–9 (1990): 227–41.

Moylan, Tom. "Bloch against Bloch: The Theological Reception of *Das Prinzip Hoffnung* and the Liberation of the Utopian Function." Daniel and Moylan 96–121.

Nadel, Alan. "Failed Cultural Narratives: America in the Postwar Era and the Story of Democracy." *boundary 2* 19.1 (1992): 95–120.

Nel, Philip. " 'A Small Incisive Shock': Modern Forms, Postmodern Politics, and the Role of the Avant-Garde in *Underworld*." *Modern Fiction Studies* 45 (1999): 724–52.

Niebuhr, Elisabeth. "The Art of Fiction XXVII: Mary McCarthy—An Interview." *Conversations with Mary McCarthy*. Ed. Carol Gelderman. Jackson: University Press of Mississippi, 1991. 3–29.

Noya, José Liste. "Mapping the 'Unmappable': Inhabiting the Fantastic Interface of *Gravity's Rainbow*." *Studies in the Novel* 29.4 (1997): 512–37.

O'Donnell, Patrick. "His Master's Voice: On William Gaddis's *JR*." *Postmodern Culture* 1.2 (1991). 5 May 2003 <*http://williamgaddis.org/jr/jrarticlemastersvoiceodonnell.shtml*>.

Parisi, Peter, ed. *Artist of the Actual: Essays on Paul Goodman*. Metuchen: Scarecrow Press, 1986.

Parrish, Timothy L. "From Hoover's FBI to Eisenstein's *Unterwelt*: DeLillo Directs the Postmodern Novel." *Modern Fiction Studies* 45 (1999): 696–723.

Patton, Paul. *Deleuze and the Political*. London: Routledge, 2000.

Peyser, Thomas. *Utopia and Cosmopolis: Globalization in the Era of American Literary Realism*. Durham: Duke University Press, 1998.

Pfaelzer, Jean. *The Utopian Novel in America, 1886–1896: The Politics of Form*. Pittsburgh: Pittsburgh University Press, 1984.

Pitkin, Hanna Fenichel. *The Attack of the Blob: Hannah Arendt's Concept of the Social*. Chicago: University of Chicago Press, 1998.

Pizer, Donald. *The Theory and Practice of American Literary Naturalism: Selected Essays and Reviews*. Carbondale: Southern Illinois University Press, 1993.

Plekhanov, George V. *Fundamental Problems of Marxism*. New York: International, 1969.

Portelli, Alessandro. "Jack London's Missing Revolution: Notes on *The Iron Heel*." *Science-Fiction Studies* 9 (1982): 180–94.

Poster, Mark. "Everyday (Virtual) Life." *New Literary History* 33.4 (2002): 743–60.

Pynchon, Thomas. *The Crying of Lot 49*. New York: Harper & Row, 1966.

————. *Gravity's Rainbow*. New York: Penguin, 1973.

————. "Journey into the Mind of Watts." *Man against Poverty: World War III.* Ed. Arthur I. Blaustein and Roger R. Woock. New York: Random House, 1968. 146–58.

Rabinowitz, Paula. *Labor and Desire: Women's Revolutionary Fiction in Depression America*. Chapel Hill: University of North Carolina Press, 1991.

Reesman, Jeanne Campbell. "Jack London's New Woman in a New World: Saxon Brown Roberts' Journey into the Valley of the Moon." *American Literary Realism* 24.2 (1992): 40–54.

————. "Prospects for the Study of Jack London." *Resources for American Literary Study* 25.2 (1999): 133–58.

Roemer, Kenneth M. *The Obsolete Necessity: America in Utopian Writings, 1888–1900*. Kent OH: Kent State University Press, 1976.

Ross, Kristin. *The Emergence of Social Space: Rimbaud and the Paris Commune*. Minneapolis: University of Minnesota Press, 1988.

Sachar, Arnold. "Paul Goodman." *The 60s without Apology*. Ed. Sohnya Sayres et al. Minneapolis: University of Minnesota Press, 1984. 292–94.

Seltzer, Mark. *Bodies and Machines*. New York: Routledge, 1992.

Shields, Rob. *Lefebvre, Love and Struggle: Spatial Dialectics*. London: Routledge, 1999.

Shulman, Robert. *The Power of Political Art: The 1930s Literary Left Reconsidered*. Chapel Hill: University of North Carolina Press, 2000.

Simons, Jon. "Postmodern Paranoia? Pynchon and Jameson." *Paragraph* 23.2 (2000): 207–21.

Sinclair, Upton. *Boston*. 1928. 2 vols. Clair Shores: Scholarly, 1970.

————. *King Coal*. 1917. Pasadena: Upton Sinclair, 1930.

————. *Oil!* 1927. Berkeley: University of California Press, 1997.

————. *The Jungle*. 1906. Urbana: University of Illinois Press, 1988.

Smith, Jon. "John Dos Passos, Anglo-Saxon." *Modern Fiction Studies* 44.2 (1998): 282–305.

Smith, Neil. *Uneven Development: Nature, Capital and the Production of Space*. Oxford: Blackwell, 1984.

Soja, Edward W. *Postmetropolis: Critical Studies of Cities and Regions*. Oxford: Blackwell, 2000.

————. *Postmodern Geographies: The Reassertion of Space in Critical Social Theory*. London: Verso, 1989.

————. *Thirdspace: Journeys to Los Angeles and Other Real-and-Imagined Places*. Oxford: Blackwell, 1996.

Solomon, William. "Politics and Rhetoric in the Novel in the 1930s." *American Literature* 68.4 (1996): 799–818.

Stoehr, Taylor. "Paul Goodman as an Advance-Guard Writer." *Kenyon Review* 25.1 (2003): 82–96.

Strehle, Susan. "Disclosing Time: William Gaddis' *JR*." *In Recognition of William Gaddis*. Ed. John Kuehl and Steven Moore. Syracuse: Syracuse University Press, 1984. 119–34.

Tabbi, Joseph. "The Cybernetic Metaphor in William Gaddis's *JR*." ANQ 2.4 (1989): 147–51.

Trombold, John. "From the Future to the Past: The Disillusionment of John Dos Passos." *Studies in American Fiction* 26.2 (1998): 237–56.

———. "Popular Songs as Revolutionary Culture in John Dos Passos' *U.S.A.* and Other Early Works." *Journal of Modern Literature* 19.2 (1995): 289–316.

Tumir, Vaska. "The City, the Labyrinth and the Terror Beyond: Delineating a Site of the Possible in *Gravity's Rainbow*." *Pynchon Notes* 42–43 (1998): 134–51.

Veblen, Thorstein. *The Theory of the Leisure Class: An Economic Study of Institutions*. New York: Modern Library, 1934.

Virilio, Paul. *The Art of the Motor*. Trans. Julie Rose. Minneapolis: University of Minnesota Press, 1995.

———. *The Lost Dimension*. Trans. Daniel Moshenberg. New York: Semiotext(e), 1991.

———. *Open Sky*. Trans. Julie Rose. London: Verso, 1997.

———. *Politics of the Very Worst: An Interview by Philippe Petit*. Trans. Michael Cavaliere. Ed. Sylvère Lotringer. New York: Semiotext(e), 1999.

———. *Popular Defense and Ecological Strategies*. Trans. Mark Polizzotti. New York: Semiotext(e), 1990.

———. *The Virilio Reader*. Ed. James Der Derian. Oxford, UK: Blackwell, 1998.

———. *The Vision Machine*. Trans. Julie Rose. Bloomington: Indiana University Press, 1994.

———. *War and Cinema: The Logistics of Perception*. Trans. Patrick Camiller. London: Verso, 1989.

Virilio, Paul, and Sylvère Lotringer. *Pure War*. Trans. Mark Polizzotti. New York: Semiotext(e), 1983.

Walcutt, Charles Child. *American Literary Naturalism: A Divided Stream*. Minneapolis: University of Minnesota Press, 1956.

Wald, Alan. "The 1930s Left in U.S. Literature Reconsidered." *Radical Revisions: Rereading 1930s Culture*. Ed. Bill Mullen and Sherry Linkon. Urbana: University of Illinois Press, 1996. 13–28.

———. *The New York Intellectuals: The Rise and Decline of the Anti-Stalinist Left from the 1930s to the 1980s*. Chapel Hill: University of North Carolina Press, 1987.

Wegner, Philip E. *Imaginary Communities: Utopia, the Nation, and the Spatial Histories of Modernity*. Berkeley: University of California Press, 2002.

Weisenburger, Steven. "Hysteron Proteron in *Gravity's Rainbow*." *Texas Studies in Literature and Language* 34.1 (1992): 87–105.

Wolcott, James. "Blasts from the Past." *New Criterion* 16.4 (1997): 65–70.

Woodcock, George. "The Anarchist as Conservative." *Parisi* 15–35.

Zayani, Mohamed. *Reading the Symptom: Frank Norris, Theodore Dreiser, and the Dynamics of Capitalism*. New York: Peter Lang, 1999.

Zipes, Jack. "Introduction: Toward a Realization of Anticipatory Illumination." *The Utopian Function of Art and Literature: Selected Essays*. By Ernst Bloch. Trans. Jack Zipes and Frank Mecklenburg. Cambridge: MIT Press, 1988. xi–xliii.

Zizek, Slavoj. *Organs without Bodies: Deleuze and Consequences*. New York: Routledge, 2004.

Index

abstract space (in Lefebvre), 139–78; as "absolute space," 156–57; as conceived space, 141, 142, 148, 154; definition of, 6, 223; dialectic of, with lived space, 141, 142–43, 147–48, 154–55, 156–57, 160; geometric "formants" of, 148; as perceived space, 142, 149, 150; phallic and visual "formants" of, 149, 150–51; and postwar urbanism, 150–51, 160–62, 166–67, 173–74, 224
—(in other authors): in Deleuze and Guattari, 182; in Gaddis, 6, 141, 160–62, 166–71, 177–78, 223–24; in Marx, 243n10; in Pynchon, 6, 141–43, 147–60, 177, 223–24, 244n12, 244n14
Accumulation of Capital, The (Luxemburg), 21–22
Adventures of a Young Man (Dos Passos), 235n5
Althusser, Louis, 242n2
"Americanism and Fordism" (Gramsci), 62, 79
American literary naturalism. *See* naturalism
"America the Beautiful" (McCarthy), 239n4
anarchism: Bloch on, 48, 54–55, 56, 57; in Deleuze and Guattari, 180, 182, 218; Gramsci on, 61; importance of, 10–11, 218; Lefebvre on, 127, 241n15; Lukács on, 22, 57; utopian space of, 177, 238n17, 241n13; in Virilio, 180, 218, 246n2
—(in spatial fiction): in Dos Passos, 59, 67–68, 75–76, 80–81, 234n1; in Goodman, 11, 117, 127, 130, 240n9, 241n13;

in Herbst, 87–88, 89, 234n11; in London, 23; in McCarthy, 106, 109–10, 117; in Pynchon, 11, 140, 157–58, 177; in Sinclair, 48, 51, 54–58
Appeal to Reason, The, 40, 95
Arendt, Hannah: and Lefebvre, 117, 137; on Marxism, 104–05, 110–11, 239n6; and McCarthy, 5, 101–16, 222, 239nn3–4, 239n7, 240n8; on "the social," 103–08, 109, 110, 112–13, 222, 239n5
—Works: *Between Past and Future*, 104; *Human Condition, The*, 103–05, 109, 112, 115, 239n3, 240n8; *On Revolution*, 104, 110, 114; *Origins of Totalitarianism, The*, 104; "Society and Culture," 106–07
Art of the Motor, The (Virilio), 205, 209, 248n9
Atlas Shrugged (Rand), 8
Auerbach, Jonathan, 233n9

Badaloni, Nicola, 235n3
Badiou, Alain, 180
Baker, Jeffery S., 244n13
Balzac, Honoré de, 19, 233n11
Baudelaire, Charles, 123
Bauhaus, 150
Becker, George, 15
Begley, Adam, 215
Bell, Daniel, 115
Bellamy, Edward: *Looking Backward*, 3–4, 25, 230n4
Bellow, Saul, 14
Benhabib, Seyla, 107
Benjamin, Walter, 8

—Works: *Cosmopolis*, 226. See also *Underworld*

28; "Mexican, The," 27; *Sea-Wolf, The,*
17–18; "South of the Slot," 27; *Val-*
ley of the Moon, The, 28, 34–37, 58,
233n10; *White Fang,* 17–18. See also
Iron Heel, The; Martin Eden
Looking Backward (Bellamy), 3–4, 25,
230n4
Lost Dimension, The (Virilio), 201–02,
203, 207, 208
Löwy, Michael, 231n3, 233n11
Ludington, Townsend, 234n1
Lukács, Georg: on anarchism, 22, 57;
compared with Gramsci, 60, 234n2;
compared with Lefebvre, 101; on
Plekhanov and Kautsky, 16, 231n3;
political development of, 233n11; on
revolutionary subjectivity, 21–22, 33–
34, 39, 49–50; on Rosa Luxemburg,
21–22, 23; on social democracy, 16–
17, 44–45, 233n11
Lukács, Georg (and spatial fiction):
compared with Sinclair, 4, 13–14, 44–
45, 51–53, 57; contrasted with Sinclair, 16–17, 39–41, 49–50, 58, 220; on
naturalism, 16–17, 19–20, 39–40, 49–
50, 52, 233n11
—Works: "Blum Theses," 233n11; *His-*
tory and Class Consciousness, 14, 16,
20, 21–22, 33, 53, 231n3, 233n11; *His-*
tory of the Evolution of Modern Drama,
19; *Soul and Form,* 19
Luke, Tim, 201
Luxemburg, Rosa, 61, 93, 238n18; *Ac-*
cumulation of Capital, The, 21–22;
Lukács's critique of, 21–22, 23

Macdonald, Dwight, 103
Mailer, Norman, 14
Malmgren, Carl Darryl, 230n5
Marsh, Kelly A., 102
Martin Eden (London), 28–34; critical space in, 28–29, gender in, 35,
233n10; idealized space in, 28–32,
232n8; socialist critique in, 32–34,
232n9
Marx, Karl: Arendt on, 111, 239n6; and
determinism, 15–16; and Lefebvre,
118–19, 126, 243n10; utopian spatiality of, 3, 229n3
—Works: *Civil War in France, The,*
229n3; *German Ideology, The,* 16

—, and Friedrich Engels: *Communist*
Manifesto, The, 64
Marxism: and literary naturalism, 15–
17; McCarthy's critique of, 5, 101,
102–12; and spatiality, 2–3, 8, 219,
226, 229n3. *See also* Arendt, Han-
nah; Bloch, Ernst; Communist Party;
Gramsci, Antonio; Lefebvre, Henri;
Lukács, Georg
Massumi, Brian, 3
Materese, Susan M., 230n4
Mattessich, Stefan, 243n9
McCarthy, Mary, 101–16; compared
with Arendt, 101–02, 103–05, 106–
09, 110, 112–14, 222, 239n4, 239n7;
compared with Goodman, 5–6, 100–
101, 116–17, 222–23; contrasted with
Arendt, 114–16, 240n8
—Works: "America the Beautiful,"
239n4. *See also Oasis, The*
McHugh, Patrick, 244n13
McKinley, William, 230n4
McLuhan, Marshall, 200
McQuire, Scott, 217
Melville, Herman: "Billy Budd," 110
Merrifield, Andy, 243n10
"Mexican, The" (London), 27
Michaels, Walter Benn, 14
Morris, Matthew J., 234n12
Morris, William, 25
Morton, Donald, 241n12, 242n17
Mouffe, Chantal, 235n2
Moylan, Tom, 234n14

Nabokov, Vladimir: *Pale Fire,* 240n8
Nadel, Alan, 191, 247n5
Napoleon, 248n9
Narrating Postmodern Time and Space
(Francese), 230n5
naturalism, 13–58; critical space in, 3–
5, 14, 17, 57–58; and gender, 35, 47,
234n13; Lukács's critique of, 16–17,
19–20, 39–40, 233n11; in Marx, 15–16;
socialist, 3–4, 13–14, 16–39, 42–45, 47–
53, 56–58; theories of, 14–15; utopian,
3–4, 13–14, 16–19, 24–37, 47–58, 59–
60, 220–21. *See also* determinism; historical determinism
Negri, Antonio, and Michael Hardt:
Empire, 226
Nel, Philip, 248n11

Lightning Source UK Ltd.
Milton Keynes UK
UKOW020747190112

185642UK00002B/32/P